The Aı

PATRICK CHALMERS was born in Fife, Scotland in 1966, spending most of his first two decades in Moray, further North. He studied engineering at Bath University and journalism at London's City University before working as a freelance reporter in Brussels. There he joined Reuters, in 1994, staying 11 years with the company. During that time he took postings to London, Kuala Lumpur and back, and reporting assignments elsewhere. *Fraudcast News* is his first book.

(Photo: Martin Soeby / martinsoeby.com)

Fraudcast News

How Bad Journalism Supports Our Bogus Democracies

Patrick Chalmers

Author's blog:

http://fraudcastnews.wordpress.com/

Twitter: @PatrickChalmers

To my wife, Natacha

Table of Contents

Preface

Writing about democracy is a crazy exercise – something no sensible person would dare to attempt. Great minds have etched their names into history exploring its complexities since the Ancient Greeks invented the word, if not the concept. How could there be anything more to add, particularly from someone whose primary expertise is not political science? Somehow, under the pressure of professional and mental necessity, I'm certain there is.

Mass, global communications and cheap air travel have opened our horizons to other people, places and cultures. The exotic has become familiar. These developments have had profound impacts on our politics and governance. They affect our societies from local to global levels in rich and poor countries alike, making them unavoidable for journalists. At the same time, journalism faces profound challenges, not least from its failing credibility with audiences.

I grew alive to these issues at Reuters while also realising my employer was not much interested in pursuing them. Once I'd got that, my only choice was to leave and look for alternatives elsewhere. The result, which took far longer than I imagined, is *Fraudcast News*. It summarises contemporary governance failures and how journalists must do a far better job of bringing them to public light.

These are complicated issues but not impossible ones. I wavered between using academic and laid-back styles to get them across. I settled on a personal approach, using the story of my own political and professional path to make the points. The result weaves together my efforts to do the journalism I'd always dreamed of with my slowly awakening political consciousness. Its examples range across many subjects from around the world. I covered the European Union, financial markets, UK news, Southeast Asia and global stories on trade, the environment and development. Each helped me see the embedded governance problems of modern political systems and journalists' persistent failure to acknowledge or address them.

That makes *Fraudcast News* a sobriety check for anyone planning to take on personal loans to do a media studies course. Despite doing one myself in the early 1990s, I'm pretty sure I wouldn't today. The pressure of debt and perpetually higher tuition fees, along with the ever-shrinking supply of real journalism jobs, makes that a risky strategy. Far better that aspiring journalists live more cheaply and learn their skills directly, by trial and error and from peers, using ever-cheaper technologies and free-to-use self-broadcast channels. That approach, while a compromise, cuts out the ill-paid apprenticeships so often touted as the sole route in.

The book is also for existing journalists, those frustrated by their work and the gap between what they dreamed of doing and the reality. That was me at Reuters, where I juggled the pressures of holding down a secure job with writing the financial-market-pleasing stories my editors always demanded. I don't regret trading that soul-sapping compromise for the uncertain promise of alternatives.

Fraudcast News is also for media consumers, the few activists agitating for change and the many others disgusted at the poor quality of our political processes. It summarises our systems' failings, and the journalism that describes them, and suggests alternatives to be built from the ground up. It is deliberately optimistic, served up against the diet of gossip, fear and loathing we get daily from more conventional media. Its message is that there are other ways, for our politics and our journalism, ones people can adapt to wherever they live.

It is easier to be hopeful about chances of change today than when I began this project in mid 2005. Governance failures, bar the glaring ones surrounding the second Iraq invasion, were less obvious then than now. The global financial crisis made clear our lack of influence over governments versus the immense power of finance. World leaders' pitiful attempts at finding a fair response to global climate change, laid bare in Copenhagen in 2009, saw corporate interests overwhelm ordinary people's. Both made our governments' accountability deficits clearer than ever. The same goes for journalism's failures, not least in Britain with its phone-hacking scandals and the Leveson inquiry. At the same time, budding liberation movements have electrified North Africa and the Arab world more widely. They inspired the global Occupy movement and raised a flag for radically better governance. Our task is to bring these strands together and to take them on in search of workable alternatives.

The US media writer and commentator Dan Gillmor, whose variable book-pricing model inspired my publishing approach for *Fraudcast News*, talks of our evolving roles as media consumers and producers. This exciting trend holds rich promise for radically improving the quality of our governance and its treatment by reporters.

That won't happen overnight or without sustained mental and physical effort. This book is aimed at speeding people's journeys on that path.

London, January 2012

Acknowledgements

This book exists thanks to many people, only some of whom I mention here. Those I can directly acknowledge include my father and mother, Iain and Fiona Chalmers. The loving home they provided through their long marriage was the best springboard from which to head off into journalism. Knowledge of its existence allowed me to be braver. I am eternally grateful to them both.

Fraudcast News took far longer than I thought, even allowing for various life episodes that slowed its progress. That I could keep going was thanks to the patient forbearance of my wife, Natacha Yellachich, and my daughter Maya. Natacha's sharp intelligence, and wise advice on rooting the entire project within a mindful whole, made a profound difference to the quality of the book's execution and its conclusions.

My lifelong friend Peter Hill was also an inspiration. His wide-ranging curiosity from an early age opened my eyes to the joys of learning for fun. He taught me to go beyond what was required to complete a task to look instead for what intrigued.

Within Reuters I had many colleagues who helped my progress and taught me journalism. Among them were Simon Alterman, Terry Williams and Jeremy Gaunt in Brussels, Steve Hays and David Holmes in London and Brian Williams on assignment in Kyoto. There were also the reporters, sub-editors, photographers and camera operators I worked with, many of whom remain friends.

Of those who helped me formulate and write the book none did more than my ex-Reuters colleague Daniel Simpson. His passion for dissecting journalism, astute brain and exacting logic all made my work more thorough, better-argued and coherent than it would otherwise have been.

The staff and speakers at Z Media 2005 helped speed the re-tuning of my political antennae, opening my mind to the inescapable necessities of radical political reform. That process continued more practically in my adopted home in southwest France, where alternative thinking comes naturally to a population of locals and incomers lodged in the Pyrenean foothills. My friends in the *Collectif Chiapas de l'Ariege,* who support the Zapatista rebels by supplying the area with indigenous Mexican coffee, all helped me understand the universal nature of our political problems.

I would also thank Robert Young for his guidance to the Greeks and Peter Maguire and Bernhard Warner for help with geeks.

Paddy Coulter and Peter O'Donnell read early part-drafts of the book, offering well-observed critiques and enthusiastic encouragement to keep going. I was then lucky to have family and friends read complete versions and offer feedback. They included my father, Matt Crooks, Richard Dwyer, Greg Welby, Anthony Hallgarten, Julian Fitzgerald and Lucy Allen. Joe Diomede, author of *Cycles of a Traveler,* combed-through for sense, spellings and typos. Sue Pleming, another ex-Reuters colleague, checked it out for its arguments and overall balance and fairness. For all the help I got, those errors that undoubtedly remain are mine alone.

In addition to those I name are countless others on whose original thinking and struggles this work rests. Some I cite in the endnotes. The many others are thinkers and activists down the ages, their efforts and sacrifices underpin all the ever-fragile freedoms we enjoy today.

Introduction

I'd been a journalist nearly 20 years when I stepped from Copenhagen's Tårnby station into the early morning sleet of mid-December 2009. I had only the vaguest of plans for the day ahead. Would I be a reporter or protester during a march intended to force an entry into global climate change talks a couple of miles away? What part should I play in a planned people's assembly to discuss the deadlocked process? I couldn't decide, the police sirens and nervous chatter from a crowd of several hundred people around me not helping matters. I'd have to see how things developed.

My journey to Denmark had taken me across half a continent with a busload of French civil disobedience activists. For the last week, we'd slept on bare floors in abandoned office buildings. I wanted to explore alternative types of journalism and politics having fallen completely out of love with conventional forms of both. There'd already been mass, often arbitrary arrests and the use of tear gas and water canon against protesters, some of them fellow passengers. Pictures of violent clashes between police and activists filled news bulletins and splashed newspaper front pages.

My hesitation came from having chucked away my old reporting codes without yet having worked out what to put in their place. Gone were the certainties of Copenhagen's equivalent meeting 12 years earlier in Kyoto. Then I'd been inside the negotiations hall, a Reuters press badge swinging from my neck and mobile phone pressed to my ear. My work had been to scurry about harvesting quotes from the powerful and calling in stories that flashed onto financial trading screens and out to the world's media. I'd had no doubts then about my work or the legitimacy of the political process I was covering. In conventional terms, I'd done a good job, scooping hundreds of fellow

15

reporters to break news of the framework climate deal to the world, just the thing to keep my editors happy.

Not this time though. Now I despaired of climate change politics and their evident hijack by the money politics and vested interests of Washington and other major world capitals. A US Senate veto threat had loomed over events in Kyoto and was back in place for Copenhagen. Its effect was to give huge power over a globally critical question to a handful of industry-beholden US politicians, some of them in office thanks to just a few hundred thousand votes.

For all the complexity of climate change, our failure to do anything about it stems from this much simpler question of political legitimacy. The people empowered to negotiate solutions do not represent the vast numbers most threatened by the predicted effects of climate change. Polluters hold sway over the polluted, delaying any workable deal. The US position is only the most glaring example of many, made all the more obvious by Washington's pivotal influence over talks.

That same legitimacy problem – the huge gap between what our leaders decide in our names and what people want – applies across all governments on the most important issues. Even the most accountable ones, none of them among the world's most influential countries, fall way short of answering their citizens' wishes in today's globalised economy. That leaves us prey to economic policies geared to perpetual growth, to murderous foreign interventions, to pitiful efforts to resolve poor-country debt and the ruinous effects of corporate-dominated globalisation. Such questions raise fundamental problems for journalists. On what grounds should we transmit the views of the powerful in news stories, essentially what we did at Reuters, if they lack all accountability to the majority of ordinary people, not to mention credibility? To whom should journalists be accountable?

I'd tried to tackle that question while still at Reuters. As one of a handful of global news agencies, the organisation wields enormous, if largely unseen influence. Its network of reporting bureaus feeds out video footage and text stories to financial trading screens, TV stations, newspapers and other media around the world. While still an employee I'd suggested various ways to address these political accountability questions but failed to get any traction with editors. So I'd grabbed the chance of a redundancy pay-off and set out to find alternatives myself.

All this ran through my head as I readied to march in Copenhagen, as did a sense of fear. The very real threat of police violence and prolonged arrest overshadowed the morning. I'd thought a lot about it, weighing the legitimacy of Danish police protecting negotiators' security with all force required versus the arguments of protesters who said standard politics had failed. I personally support non-violent civil disobedience – breaking the law with the clear intent of forcing policy change in the face of discredited conventional means. It sounded great in the abstract while being frightening in the actual. It was also totally at odds with my previous journalistic training on objectivity. I was about to test out both.

The gulf between official climate negotiators and protesters had been evident from chants and banners on the previous weekend's demonstrations. None had captured it better than "System change, not climate change". Climate change issues strike at the heart of our economic model, which is why our governance structures have failed to tackle it. The problems go far deeper than too much of the wrong type of gas in the air, challenging fundamental ideas about growth and the chronic boom-and-bust effects of our debt-based money systems. Two decades of talks had got next to nowhere while the predicted and observed effects of inaction got worse. The case for civil disobedience was never more compelling.

My reporter's instincts had me questioning those around me about what was happening and what people planned to do. I spoke to an Englishwoman called Heather Hunt, a 63-year-old veteran of the Greenham Common Women's Peace Camp of the 1980s and 1990s in Britain. Her thoughts on how to disarm police aggression were to come back to me during the day. She gave an immediate master class, striking up a conversation with a policeman who might have been her son. Behind an opening question on what the day's weather held, she was British after all, lay calculated purpose. Not missing a beat, she followed up by telling the officer of her intention to protest peacefully and her right to the same, all somehow with gentle, playful motherliness.

For Heather, climate change was already underway, quite possibly unstoppably. She favoured creating grassroots, local groups to cope with its effects while being open to contacts with other people from around the world. "We are going to have to be generous, to take care of climate refugees, we are going to have to make an awful lot of local movements yet keep these links going with the outside," she said.

Heather's ideas sounded cheaper, more coherent and practical than anything I'd heard in years of following official talks. That seemed the least that we in the world's richer countries could do, not least because we are largely to blame for the problem after two centuries of burning fossil fuels. The favoured remedies in talks, including carbon emissions trading, were a mad tangle of impractical, expensive and difficult-to-enforce complexity that paid out huge dividends to the worst polluters.

As we started to march, I could tell we were in for something other than the largely joyful procession of a hundred thousand people I'd joined a couple of days before. Even that had been a first for me, demonstrating for my political convictions rather than just reporting on others doing the same. Today's "Reclaim the Power" event was to be a deliberate act of peaceful confrontation, widely flagged as such in advance. Our unlikely aim was to enter the Bella Centre conference venue for a people's assembly with those inside.

The day's planning, as I'd witnessed the night before in our "squat" accommodation, drew on the collected experiences of some seasoned protesters. I was to join a group of nine or so people from our bus, whose job it would be to stay together, forming a chain at the back left of the march. We would face outwards as we walked, our arms joined to prevent the whole being split apart by police along the way. Keeping a hold of my reporter's role, I'd promised to phone in details to the alternative *Indymedia* news centre during the day.

With Heather in mind, I tried hard to make contact with the police walking alongside. One of the officers, Alan he said he was called, seemed friendly. "We believe in what you're doing, we think it's praiseworthy," he said. I learnt later he'd let slip that admiration, energetically beating a seated woman protester with his truncheon.

Amid all the talk was my sense of rising tensions. I could feel thumping pulses through the arms of those in front of me and behind. Maybe it was just my own.

"It's not us who are the criminals, it's those inside the Bella Centre," shouted a woman directing our progress via the demo truck's sound system. She was Stine Gry Jonassen, a Danish spokesperson from the global network Climate Justice Action. Later that day Stine would be arrested and imprisoned for several weeks on charges of organizing and instigating acts of violence and vandalism.[1]

Too soon, for me, we passed under an elevated metro line, bang in front of one of the summit entrances. I had been here the previous Saturday along with a cheerful, dancing throng demanding climate justice. The vibe was different today with a couple of thousand of us at most, probably not even that. Stine urged us to stick together, to keep our arms chained around the periphery of the group.

I tried to reassure myself with the get-out-of-jail-free card I had in my wallet, an NUJ press card I could wave at police if needed. I decided not to use it. My neighbours Nicole, a retired flight attendant, and Estelle, a state-employed psychologist, had no such talismans. When they decided to pull out of the gathering crush, I couldn't blame them.

A stalemate ensued as several lines of people, arms linked, stood facing police. A big push forward came suddenly to my right and with it, the first injuries. People passed back through the crowd to the rear, eyes streaming from pepper spray or with minor cuts to their heads. Chains broke to let them through to rhythmic chants of: "This is what democracy looks like!"

The injuries brought home to me where the day's lines lay. On one side were demonstrators whose long-declared intention had been to enter the talks using peaceful means. On the other, state power 2009 style. I asked myself if I knew what I was doing and what the implications of my choice might be for my professional credibility, whatever that meant. Images from the film *Gandhi* flashed into my mind, the scene where lines of Indian demonstrators advance deliberately on a line of British colonial forces, each one being beaten back in turn.

Was this what I was looking for? Did it have anything to do with examining democracy or journalism? Somehow the answer was a startlingly simple "yes". I thought of the late American writer George Plimpton, a wonderful talent whose speciality was to attempt at a professional level the sports about which he wrote. That meant enduring the fear and risk of physical injury from sparring with professional boxers, of playing quarter back in a pre-season game for the Detroit Lions and pitching in a pro-baseball game.

I took off my glasses.

Having made peace with the decision, I was quickly called to honour it. Surges to the right and then to the left found me suddenly in the front rank. To one side was Thierry, until this moment a stranger. To my left was a friend from the bus and further on was Ronan, one of our drivers, his eyes already streaming. "That I should have tears running down my face is because of the gas but also because I'm sad," he told the policeman in front of him. "But you are my brother, you are my friend, I love you," he said in heavily French-accented English.

I couldn't help trying the same myself, my journalistic qualms now gone. In front of me was a policewoman, all fired up, shoving us back and shouting. Behind her stood a second line of police, batons cocked and looking unquestionably ready for action. I was inside their truncheon arcs, my arms locked into my neighbours' ones, physically defenceless. I breathed deliberately, holding a surprising calm and recalling Heather's words about these people being the same human beings as all of us.

All of a sudden I was asking the police in front what their kids would think of their behaviour, and their parents. A woman officer replied that they'd be proud, to which I couldn't help firing back: "Proud of what? Of defending talks that are going nowhere?" We didn't have time to dwell on the intricacies of the thing.

There was a call to move left, to stop police seizing the sound system with their inching advance. The human chains defending it were too few and too weak. More truncheons fell just yards away from me, people dropped to the ground and a woman screamed. I was still in the front rank and things weren't looking too funny. Keep breathing, I told myself. More pushing, from behind and in front, and suddenly I was taking truncheon blows to both arms. I shouted at my assailant, a small, dark-haired man, yelling at him to stop, to calm down. I was cushioned by cold weather clothing and, to their credit I suppose, the police were hitting only arms and hands rather than heads.

The chain broke and before I knew it I was hit with a cold jet of liquid right across both eyes. Shit! Pepper spray. I jammed them closed but couldn't do it for long. People were shouting and screaming all around me and I was standing among them with my eyes clamped shut. It didn't seem like a good idea. So I opened them, an equally bad one as they stung like hell. Time to test that activist support network I'd grown used to in recent days. I called out "first aid" or "help", I can't remember which, and hands quickly took mine. I was led, temporarily blinded, out of the contact zone. Someone asked me what happened – pepper spray – he explained I'd need to open my eyes for him to pour liquid in. "Your eyes will hurt for a couple of hours but this will help," he said. He was right on both counts.

I felt moments of panic, nausea, suffocation almost, though they quickly passed. I drew strength from the volunteer's calm. Sat on a roadside barrier, I could tell a peak had passed for me and, I sensed, also for the day's action. We were blocked in, police lines ahead and behind, on a stretch of road outside the conference centre. My eyes burned yet I was keenly aware that things might have been much worse. The prospect of arrest seemed irrelevant and unthreatening given our numbers.

The planned assembly took place on the ground between police lines, though I was too washed out to take part, or even to listen. Instead, I scribbled furiously in my notebook with memories still fresh, guessing we'd made our point.

World leaders had yet to hit Copenhagen, their arrival certain to whip the media into a climax I would previously have been part of. Yet I knew my summit was already nearing its end. I was ready to go home.

Before long, police opened their lines, directing us back towards town by a different route. We'd given it a go. They'd kept us out. It was time to withdraw. We'd escaped adding to the 2000 people arrested during the two-week summit, by far the majority of whom were released without charge. Curious children waved hesitantly as we passed, people leant from apartment windows taking pictures while office workers stood gawking, their jobs ignored in the gathering gloom of a northern winter afternoon.

I was partly elated, partly frustrated by the day. It was clear that what we'd faced was a polite scuffle in the wider scheme of things – intense as it had all seemed to me at the time. Other people, journalists included, face far worse around the world each day struggling for social and political justice. Many suffer beatings, detention or summary murder for their troubles. For all those who stand up, countless more suffer in silence, too frightened, resigned or plain busy with daily survival to think of asserting their political rights.

Physical dramas apart, I'd certainly gained new insights into politics and journalism. For one, I'd got a sense of the courage it takes for people to act on political beliefs in the face of injustice, knowing their efforts bear real personal risk and little hope of immediate success. Such acts are part of a noble canon stretching back through human history the world over. While it includes obvious giants across different times and continents, the majority are never known. Their collective courage and sacrifice, and occasional victories, brought the freer parts of our world the liberties they enjoy today.

I'd witnessed protests and arrests before, principally political dissidents in Malaysia being arbitrarily swept up by police. While impressed by the protesters' spirit and passion, I lacked then what I'd now gained on Copenhagen's streets half a world away. It had taken my direct physical involvement in a protest to appreciate their courage. The connection between them and us was direct – both showed people's hopeful and determined response in the face of conventional political impotence – a clear sign of democratic failure. If people feel bound to take to the streets to make their voices heard, something fundamental isn't working in their governance systems.

Democratic failure, and its relationship with journalism, first occurred to me far more prosaically as an issue in Brussels, back in the mid 1990s. European leaders had tossed out a proposal by their environment ministers for an EU carbon tax to limit pollution from burning fossil fuels. What struck me then more than the policy arguments, or even the underlying issue, was the hierarchy of power in play and what that said about democracy. Environment ministers had spent months haggling over the proposal, their minions even longer. They were lobbied all the while by business and environmental groups. My involvement was to report each twist and turn, though my main function seemed to be lolling bleary eyed through the night on press centre sofas, waiting for news.

The debate ended with EU leaders' summary rejection of the proposal. The decision took place behind closed doors and with only the scantest of detail released to the outside world. That that should be the climax of political decision-making among 15 representative democracies seemed scandalous. The whole affair was a colossal waste of time, appearing all the worse to me given I disagreed with the result. It also reeked of secret, unaccountable government.

No news for savvier politics watchers and activists but to me, back then, it certainly was. It made me reflect on broader questions of political legitimacy and what I thought was journalism's role in examining and explaining that. The process lead me eventually to Copenhagen.

Journalism's great boast is that it speaks truth to power, something rarely achieved in practice. In cases of democratic failure, a commonplace for political issues stretching from local to global levels of governance, what matters more is that journalism speaks truth about power. Those EU leaders opened hairline cracks in my very conventional understanding of democracy and journalism, and how they are practised. They widened only slowly at first, before splitting apart completely to pitch me towards more radical interpretations of both.

What follows is an account of that evolution, my attempt at explaining this step change in my understanding. I began as an eager-but-untutored journalist wannabe, politically guileless to boot. Along the way I became an experienced reporter with an allergy to using the term "democracy" without accompanying health warnings. I went from unquestioning acceptance of democracy as "a good thing" to becoming aware of representative democracy's fundamental flaws and their global, political consequences.

For all the rhetoric on democracy from our political leaders and elite classes generally, the realities are starkly different. Representative democracy, basically the chance to vote for a handful of candidates as our leaders every few years, is a farce. It gives we the people an illusion of influence but no real power. Money, acting via private channels, corporations and financial markets, crowds out the political power vacuum in our absence.

Nowhere has that been more obvious than in the rolling financial crisis of 2007 and since. The financial deregulation begun in earnest under Ronald Reagan and Margaret Thatcher in the 1980s grew all the more furious through subsequent administrations "right" and "left" in both Washington and Westminster. Those two centres matter more than any others for their virtual stranglehold on global finance. The cumulative effects of deregulation and near-abandonment of political checks and oversight gave progressively freer rein to markets. Only a few of the banks behind the epic crash and grab of 2007 went bust. The others, including some of the biggest gamblers, got massive state bailouts at our collective expense. Nothing in the official responses so far has mended the underlying regulatory problems that caused the crisis or sorted the failures of governance that let them take place. That makes continuing, rolling crises more likely to become the norm, not the exception, unless these problems are resolved.

The sums of money involved are so huge as to put financial deregulation above the many other critical political questions facing the world. Incredibly, it trumps the looming effects of climate change, the interminable US "war on terror" and warped national spending priorities at a time of widening inequality between the rich few and the poor many. The extent of democratic failure we face is colossal. The answer is not to advocate some more-or-less benign dictatorship or bloody revolution but to fight for something closer to real democracy, which means government in the hands of the people. This is not something exotic, utopian or unobtainable – versions of it already exist around the world in the form of direct, deliberative and participatory democratic initiatives. None yet exists at a national level but there are myriad examples on smaller scales or for one-off policy questions. It is in these that we have a hope of finding real revolutions in governance.[2]

What place for journalism in all this? My experience of the conventional version, bar a few rare exceptions, is of routine blindness to the failures of our democracies and their bias towards narrow interests. The prime reason is that journalism is beholden to the people who own or fund it, making it prey to the exact same problems of capture as our governance models. It explains news organisations' fidelity to conflicted-and-contradictory ideas about economic growth and the supremacy of what we lazily and inaccurately call "free" markets.

If journalism is to have any societal value, any chance of helping its audiences to determine how they are governed, it requires a radical revamp. We need to revolutionise our journalism so as to revolutionise our democracies.

These are absurdly ambitious goals, the work of human lifetimes. They are part of a story dating back thousands of years, beyond the time of the Ancient Greeks who gave us a name, and practical models, for power in the hands of the people.

This account describes my own, tiny part in that process. It concludes with proposals for a cheap, practical approach to building pro-democracy journalism from the ground up, from where people live. It has a work-in-progress example from southwest France, a variation of others springing up around the world. As these individual nodes take root, their reporters' story horizons will travel out along lines of governance and accountability. On the way, they will find journalistic collaborators, leading to more ambitious journalism projects tackling common issues.

These relationships contain the makings of embryonic global reporting networks, whose work could straddle all the layers of politics that make up our modern governance structures.

The challenge is to get people started. This book lays out the groundwork.

Chapter 1

A foot in journalism's door

It was that rare thing, the spark for a lifetime's obsession, found where I least expected it – the university careers office. Standing out from piles of applications for dull-looking jobs was one for a Reuters traineeship. The form, complete with mock news story exercises, was my chance to persuade the renowned world news organisation to hire a novice engineer and French speaker. Sadly, they didn't see it that way.

As one among hundreds of hopefuls for a handful of places, I didn't even get an interview. It was 1988, the Soviet bloc was teetering and editors wanted people who spoke Russian or something similar. That, at least, was what they said when I called to ask: "Why the brush off?" Yet the seed was sown. Against all the odds, my careers office visit had resolved that trickiest of questions: "What should I do with my life?" My unequivocal answer was journalism.

The trouble was I knew nothing of journalism's realities or how to get a job in it. I'd eagerly trawled the news for years but never thought of writing it. I'd no idea it would take so long to turn my new-found dream into reality.

Besides the practical barriers I faced were subtler questions concerning journalism's relationship with political questions and the nature of my own, personal politics. Both would prove far tougher to pin down. My motivations for doing journalism were pretty basic, some sense of promoting social justice and helping people who were treated unfairly by their societies. I lacked the personal, political landscape for any deeper perspective. Journalism's most immediately compelling draw was the lure of seemingly important work performed in exotic parts of the world.

Such shallow ambitions didn't matter for now. My first challenge was to get some sort of toe-hold in the business, with little clue about where to start. I fluked a commissioned newspaper article within weeks of the Reuters rejection but got nothing more in print for months. That first piece came thanks to a *Bath Evening Chronicle* journalist at my final-year design engineering show. When I told him no way would I be an engineer, and that I was set on journalism, he asked me to write explaining why. I harped on about engineers' undeservedly poor status and why new graduates like me were avoiding the profession. The simpler truth, which I left out, was that engineering bored me and I fancied something racier.

The *Chronicle* wasn't hiring though, at least not me, nor were the dozens of other papers I wrote to in search of a reporter's job or traineeship. The least I learnt from the fat pile of rejections was bloody-mindedness. Journalism has always been popular, despite the species being on a par with estate agents and such like in public affections. My graduation year was no different. With the Internet not yet available as an outlet, the ways into any sort of journalism were obscure, those into paid journalism even more so.

There were plenty of other jobs though – this being the crest of an inflationary boom in Britain. Banks, accountants, management consultants and other blue chip FTSE 100 firms were snapping up graduates, their promises of stellar careers seeming all the more plausible after free booze and food. I was beguiled enough to apply for a merchant banking job, realising my mistake only when asked at interview why I wanted to go into the City. My answer? Actually, I don't. It was easy to be flippant. We students were lucky to be leaving with modest debts versus today's equivalents, most having had maintenance grants and free tuition. I'd spent my three years with the cushion of a sponsorship from the chemical company ICI, meaning I graduated in the black. I needed money from somewhere though while plotting a route into journalism, so took an examiner's job at the

European Patent Office in The Hague. It matched my degree and languages while also paying a fat salary. I didn't expect to stay long.

Deferring the start for a couple of months, I left on a freelancing-come-holiday trip to Southern Africa. I dreamed up and researched various stabs at photo-illustrated feature articles – on gold mining, about a children's orphanage in Soweto and Zimbabwean safaris. I sold none. It was no real surprise as I'd little idea what I was doing. I went through what I thought were the motions of being a news reporter, hitch hiking from the Zimbabwe border to Johannesburg and back. On the way I talked to white and black South Africans of all persuasions, getting a taste of the national politics with apartheid still in place. I remember speaking to a black gardener at the *Voortrekker* monument in Pretoria, asking him what he thought of the giant tribute to the Afrikaans pioneers who now ran the country. "It's their history" was the sum of his gracious reply. I felt embarrassed for asking and embarrassed at my general haplessness. Some journalist.

With no outlet for my efforts or any real grasp of the politics involved, I was destined to failure. That basic-but-critical first barrier remained: no job in journalism. Were I a new graduate doing something like that trip today, carrying a smart phone or a cheap video camera with editing software on a laptop, I could bypass the job's formal entry barriers. I'd just stick my reports on a blog, a video channel or social media. It's easier to publish today than ever before, an unquestionable boon for our global conversations. It doesn't mean what gets produced is automatically any good.

Journalism demands practical story-telling skills and those take training. Electronics technologies and the Internet explosion are nothing if what gets made lacks context or coherence. For that, reporters must learn how to structure stories, to check facts and give fair and accurate accounts of events as best they can. Their efforts are wasted otherwise, their potential audiences inaccessible or quickly turned off.

Those are just the practicalities of journalism, skills I knew I lacked even then and needed to learn. I hadn't yet clocked my lack of political depth or how that would influence the sort of journalism I would end up doing.

As a recent engineering graduate, with little but science and maths training since 16, my politics at the time were wholly mainstream. I was sympathetic to the SDP/Liberal Democrat alliance but only up to a point. It had not been enough to stop me voting for the Conservative MP Chris Patten in the 1987 general election, my first as a voter. What swung me to Patten was his party's support for private over public ownership, a policy greased by discounted share offerings to voters. I was too green, and greedy, to see how selling national assets to private interests would damage society and increase inequality.

As far as I was concerned, governments *were* accountable to their people. If ever they weren't we voters could turf them out at the next election. To the limited extent I'd thought at all about democracy I considered it unquestionably a good thing. My idea of the link between democracy and journalism was similarly simplistic – journalists wrote stories that highlighted an issue, influencing public opinion and politicians and prompting political change.

Back from South Africa, I moved to the Netherlands. I managed just four months at the Patent Office, being scared witless by the idea of a life inside the gilded cage of a European civil servant.

My journalistic aim improved a little with my escape route, a London job doing public relations for the trade exhibitions arm of Reed International, now Reed Elsevier. The logic was sort of sound, weaving my existing knowledge of engineering into a job with some form of writing and contact with journalists. I soon found out that PR's exchanges with journalism usually work the other way around – journalists migrate to better-paid public relations jobs towards the ends of their careers rather than the reverse. Oh well.

My job was to increase the media coverage for Reed's industrial trade shows, to write news releases and articles promoting the events so as to drive up visitor and exhibitor numbers. Though it didn't land me directly in journalism, it was good preparation for most mainstream versions. I got to write stories, albeit framed to promote what we were selling. It was the sort of corporate puffery, more or less subtly done, that should make journalists rightly wary of PR people. There is a legitimate case for some PR, a business or interest group's overt communication to news media or offer of associated expertise in comment. Far more insidious and problematic, for journalism and the information it brings us, is the unacknowledged and often unimagined penetration of news by corporate and financial interests and their agendas.

Mine was pretty entry-level stuff, the journalists I phoned could hardly have complained about getting the wool pulled over their eyes. Some were still arrogant and dismissive, treating what they saw as a lesser media species as some sort of toxic invasion of their hallowed editorial ground. While there's sometimes truth in that there is also hypocrisy, naivety even, given the stacks of PR material sold as news in most journalists' output. That is to say nothing of the inherent bias of most media publications towards those in power, including the business establishment buying adverts from them.

For the moment it was my turn to soak up the toxic-trash treatment. It didn't bother me much and was more training in journalistic doggedness in a masochistic sort of way. Years later, on the other end of PR calls, I had no illusions about the press/PR relationship. I could politely decline or accept its sugary offerings without having to slag off its messengers.

What encouraged me at Reed was that my work would often appear verbatim in a mass of trade magazines, as would the occasional articles I was commissioned to write. Among my earliest was a piece for *Plastics and Rubber Today*, which sounds much more exciting than the reality. I was excited enough just to see my name in print.

For all that, it was pretty obvious the magazines were not too demanding in what they used. Short staffed, with space to fill between their bread-and-butter-earning adverts, they were eager for any material they could get. What was generally true then for the trade and business press has become the case for daily newspapers, radio and TV, with all that means for the dumbing down of people's understanding of politics and government.

The trend is well captured in *Flat Earth News*, a book by British journalist Nick Davies. It charts how great chunks of material written either by PR companies or national news agencies such as the Press Association get slotted directly into newspapers. His analysis of stories in the UK's four main broadsheet newspapers and the mid-market *Daily Mail* should be drummed into the head of all newspaper readers. It showed 60% of the stories were based either on PR material or news agency stories received by them all. Another fifth contained clear elements of news agency or PR material, while the source of 8% could not be clearly determined. That left only 12% of stories as original ones written by the respective newspapers' own reporters.

The book's researchers concluded that meaningful, independent work was the exception in day-to-day British journalism. That implied the almost wholesale abandonment by journalists of standard disciplines of news judgement, fact-checking, balance, criticism, source interrogation and so on. The main driver, grown ever stronger over a generation, is media owners' slashing of both staff numbers and editorial budgets and the closure of freelance reporting networks.

The resulting stories, hidden under newspaper bylines such as "staff reporter", overtly or covertly pump the agendas of whoever pays the bills for PR and communications work. Those with most cash get most play, crowding out perspectives from people with neither the budget nor the inclination for self promotion. The vast bulk of PR goes towards commercial profit, not political or social justice. As for improving public accountability, good governance or democracy, its effects are typically the reverse.

Not everything we get from our media is worthless – some of its content is excellent, with genuine impact that provokes real change. Work by the same Nick Davies is a fine example. His dogged investigation into phone hacking by *News of the World* journalists over years planted a series of print bombs under Rupert Murdoch's News Corporation. Some of the other news washing over us daily provides useful facts about day-to-day events. We must be alert, though, as relevant facts are often buried low down in stories or presented in ways that skew their context or undermine their significance. What little there is is under threat, constantly eroded by staffing and budget pressures that open the gates to more PR material.

My first experience of the tension between business interests and editorial came while I was still at Reed. One of our trade shows began disastrously, with poor attendance and a leaking roof at the Birmingham National Exhibition Centre. The show's daily newspaper, produced by a trade magazine partner onsite as an advertising vehicle, did a respectable reporting job for the next day's edition. It needn't have bothered: the issue went straight to pulp as soon as the exhibition director read its front-page splash. So much for news being about what happens, as I'd naively imagined.

That's not to say I met no good journalists or journalism while at Reed, I certainly did. I was even tempted when a reporting job offer finally came along. I declined though, wary of getting stuck in specialist trade media. My heart was still set on the foreign and political news I'd imagined when first applying to Reuters. The news agency's global network of correspondents, in Beirut or Baghdad not Birmingham, was where I wanted to work. My reading of choice wasn't *Metal Bulletin* or *Engineering News* but Robert Fisk's *Pity the Nation*, on the 1982 Lebanon war, or compilations of John Pilger's hard-hitting dispatches in the book *Heroes*. Even Ben Elton's *Stark*, a climate-change comedy novel dotted with witless human and animal characters, was closer to what I wanted to do. While some sort of political awareness was emerging to inform my journalistic ambitions, any practical expression of it in the form of paid work still eluded me.

All I managed at the time was to land a page-lead letter in *The Independent* newspaper, criticising the US invasion of Panama. I'd heard the news on the radio before going into work and bridled at the hypocrisy. President George H Bush had recently lectured his Russian counterpart Mikhail Gorbachev about not interfering with countries in his own backyard. Now here he was doing exactly that himself. I was savvy enough to understand newspaper deadlines so I wrote a letter once I got to work and faxed it through for publication. Though the letter was more instinctive than thought-through, at least it showed I was waking up to political contradictions.

I'd recently been to El Salvador for a couple of weeks. Despite travelling with a friend from the country, I'd struggled with the politics of its ongoing civil war. The fight between a tiny, rich elite and the mass of poor was misleadingly wrapped up in tales of communist insurgents and the Cold War. I knew little, and understood even less, of US meddling in Central and South America or the corporate interests driving that agenda. I'd read and heard stories of state-sanctioned murder and torture and could certainly sense the unmistakable fear among ordinary people I met there. What I lacked was an idea of the extent and intent of all the killings, torture and intimidation or their trans-continental context. It would have helped to have had better news coverage of events there.

It was around then that Edward Herman and Noam Chomsky published *Manufacturing Consent*, an enduring analysis of US media's terminally skewed reporting. Had I had a copy I'd have understood El Salvador better. I would also have grasped why there were so few foreign news stories with the necessary background and context to make the place more comprehensible. It was years later that I came across the book and absorbed its broad thesis about Western media. Its authors describe how money and establishment power influence what news is fit to print in major representative democracies. The problem is most acute in places such as my native Britain and the United States, where wide freedoms to speak and to publish are effectively neutered by both commercial and state-funded media. The effects of media ownership, income streams and story sourcing combine to obscure governments' fundamental lack of accountability to their electorates. The result is news stories that are chronically biased towards what powerful people say and do, or what they want.

The book also explained my experience of the exhibition daily getting pulped – the censoring effects of media ownership and advertising income sources together. Back at the time I'd filed it in the mental box labelled "things that just don't seem right".

All the while at Reed I had my eyes on Reuters. Two years after my first try, it was time for another go, which failed once again. The rejection letter this time prompted me to take a day off work and head for their London offices and a talk with George Short, who oversaw recruitment. George was out, training staff, which pricked my indignant bubble. His friendly advice on the telephone later was simply that I keep trying. Around the same time my first effort at getting on London City University's journalism graduate course also fell flat, convincing me of an urgent need to change tack.

It was clear I'd got all I could from Reed, some basic writing practice and an insight into business and trade press. So I quit, first to organise the press and publicity for a mass, charity bike ride being run by a friend. When my money ran out, I tried my hand at freelance work.

I got some commissioned articles for a *Daily Telegraph* supplement on exhibitions, a step up the ladder of sorts though really only a broadsheet version of the trade press I knew already. I also got interviews for traineeships with the Brighton *Evening Argus* and *The Sunday Times*. I got both by doing front-page mock-ups of the papers with lead stories about them having hired me. While I'd at last prised open some doors to editors' offices, I promptly blew it with the interviews, combining poor preparation and forethought with a general lack of savvy about newspaper journalism.

The chance of an *Argus* job evaporated with the editor's first question. My attempt at a light-hearted reply to why I wanted to move to Brighton – because my girlfriend lived there – fell flat on its metaphorical face. I learnt later the editor was particularly hostile towards candidates he thought would roll up for the training only to head for London at the first chance of brighter journalistic baubles. Why wouldn't he be? His ambitions for the post were local and long term while mine were the opposite. Had I bluffed the mismatch more effectively in the interview maybe I'd have got the job.

My real mistake was to accept the standard guidance to journalist wannabes, which is to try to get into the business via local newspapers. I could have done with a warning from the author and journalist George Monbiot about counter-educational career paths. These are the ones that teach you to do what you don't want to do by being what you don't want to be. It's a big hazard for young journalists, who pitch for local newspaper jobs when they want to write about something totally different. Once stuck on that employment formula, they risk repeating it. The result is that they become specialists in what Monbiot calls the moronic recycling of what rich and powerful people deem to be news. Onwards I went towards that goal.[3]

I failed again with the *Sunday Times* interview, though I did wangle a week's unpaid work experience as consolation. Walking into its Wapping headquarters in East London, I remembered the controversy surrounding the place. The owner Rupert Murdoch had moved his operations there a few years earlier in a huge dust up with the print unions, a fight he'd won with government help. I pushed its complexities from my mind, the tangle of an abusive owner versus entrenched union practices, as I went through the gates. Those concerns I had were lost in my eagerness for a job in journalism.

Some job it proved to be. My week involved helping the property correspondent stand up a story about a non-existent revival in UK house prices. I called dozens of estate agents for quotes, some of which made it into what was an absurd puff piece. The best thing I took away was a first-hand glimpse of how truly pitiful the *Sunday Times* had become. The newspaper was by then long past its heyday under Harold Evans, the editor whose *Insight* team of investigators broke stories that got in the faces of government and business. One was the outing of KGB spy Kim Philby as a major intelligence wheel. Another story series championed compensation for several hundred children suffering birth defects from the drug thalidomide.

Insight's exploits are often held up as a gold standard for investigative reporting, one Evans made clear was possible only with money. It is increasingly rare. Recent US innovations such as *ProPublica* have tried to redress the balance but it's nothing like enough nor is it easily scaleable. *ProPublica* bills itself as a force for positive change and reform yet it sticks to single issues, keeping clear of the more fundamental crises in US public accountability and governance quality generally. Britain's Centre for Investigative Journalism is another rare bright spot that supports journalists and others working to improve public integrity and to defend the public interest.

The most promising combination of old and new investigative journalism had pretty much bitten the dust by the end of 2011. The whistleblowers' website Wikileaks, launched in 2006, put out a series of documents on Iraq, Afghanistan and corruption in Kenya. They included gun-sight video footage of US troops shooting to death several civilians and two Reuters staff in Iraq, which it released in 2010. It coordinated with five conventional newspapers to publish a trove of US diplomatic cables later the same year, though those relationships later broke apart. Publication of the cables prompted a fierce backlash against Wikileaks from governments and businesses, including the throttling of its donations channels by the payments companies Visa, Mastercard and Paypal.

Whatever the future of Wikileaks and its multi-award-winning, editor-in-chief Julian Assange, the site has blazed a trail for anonymous whistle blowing that exposes wrongdoing. For all Assange's personal prickliness – which can be towards friends as well as foes – his organisation's techniques have great promise for journalism that holds governments and businesses to account. Offering whistleblowers a secure route to release information, via servers that are able to evade the suffocating effects of British libel laws, would be a huge service to journalism and the public.

The only investigative journalism I was doing in 1991 was looking for a job. It brought me to Nick Cater, a caffeinated freelance jack-of-all-media-trades I'd first met while punting the charity bike ride. He did me two big favours – looking over my latest application to City University and getting me some paid work. It was a relief, after all my thwarted efforts, to get some solid, practical advice.

His advice helped me get a City University place at the second time of asking. I just missed a *Guardian* bursary, again making do with the bridesmaid's prize of a couple of weeks' work experience. Things were at last starting to move, even if I was still out of my depth when it came to anything politically substantial. My main work at the paper was to design and execute a poll of historians' views on Margaret Thatcher's place among British prime ministers, written up by the political columnist Hugo Young. More journalistically satisfying was a paid commission to write a feature on kids' environmental awareness and education. It ran to a full page with an accompanying photograph.

Waiting for the City course to start, I got work with the International Broadcasting Trust, an educational and media charity. It was in the throes of launching the Third World and Environment Broadcasting Project, a coalition of development, environment and human rights charities working for better media cover of their target issues. It woke me up to the difficulties of getting foreign news and current affairs on to British TV screens, or any screens in fact. The implications for foreign journalism were clear, it wouldn't last long without an outlet. The result would be a hole in people's knowledge of what happened abroad and far less chance that they would understand how their own governments' policies affected the world's poorest countries. It coincided with pressure being applied to Oxfam for its campaign for sanctions against apartheid South Africa. A complaint by the pro-apartheid International Freedom Foundation prompted Oxfam's censure by the Charity Commissioners. I found the decision shocking, a galling contrast to the covert lobbying on behalf of a government such as South Africa's. Both highlighted the difficulties faced in getting a wide airing for social justice issues.

Starting at City felt like a major breakthrough, at last a chance to learn the basics of a vocation I'd hit on three years earlier. Debates on the merits of university journalism training, particularly at undergraduate level, were already well underway. Traditionalists argued that the best training was on the job. That was fine enough in principle but there were few genuine journalism jobs going and fewer that paid more than a pittance if at all. Things are worse today with many more journalism courses available, increasingly costly ones at that, and still fewer real jobs to go around.[4]

Yet practical journalism training is critical, something I acknowledged by going to City. A couple of decades later the case for buying formal training is unclear. The plummeting costs of technology and the Internet's knowledge-pooling potential mean there could be lower-cost training options available for far more people. Low-cost, local workshops in the rudiments of journalism could let people report from where they live. Their work might be paid, in their own time, or both. Spreading the skills base more widely would take journalism beyond the hands of a richer few working for profit-driven outlets, with all that means for the elitism of views presented.

For myself in the early 1990s, I figured I'd recoup the money via future work. There's no doubt I learnt the practical skills for conventional journalism jobs with big commercial media. Set against that is the question of whether the training, and the pressure of having spent several thousand pounds on rent and fees, pushed me into the wrong sorts of jobs. It would take me years to figure I was off track, nowhere near my original ambition to write about social and political justice. The same equation today carries far heftier tuition fees and loans, from undergraduate level onwards. I'm no longer sure it's worth it.

That's easy to say now. Back then it was a sweet release to report and write news and feature articles and get quality feedback. Lectures on defamation and the structure of UK government were important bonuses, filling voids in my engineer's shaky knowledge of both. Learning to sub-edit – the checking of other people's work for content, grammar and journalistic style – was also useful. The most potent reporting tool I learnt came from daily shorthand classes, which took the few of us who hung in there up to speeds of 100 words per minute. The skill has been invaluable, not least years later for the reporting record it gave me when I was sued for libel. Voice recordings, while often providing vital back up, are never as immediately wieldy for reporting and not always to hand.

The year at City also woke me up to media racism. It was evident in newspaper coverage of Winston Silcott, a black man wrongly convicted of murdering police constable Keith Blakelock during a north London riot in 1987. Silcott and his two co-defendants had their murder convictions thrown out in November 1991, while I was at City, after forensic tests showed police had concocted their confessions.

It was hard to dig that story from the grudging coverage in newspapers such as the *Daily Mail* and the *Sun*. They were more intent on harking back to the original murder during the Broadwater Farm riots, illustrating their articles with a shocking picture of PC Blakelock's police jacket, its multiple stab wounds highlighted with yellow tape. The mob killing was unquestionably horrific but it was not the story four years later after what had been a clear miscarriage of justice. Silcott was back in the news because he'd been framed by police, the appeal judge having gone as far as expressing his profound regrets for the criminal justice system's failures. Follow-up coverage might have examined how or why police had perjured themselves or asked who'd done the put-up job. That wasn't good enough for newspapers that refused to backtrack from having branded Silcott the "machete monster" and the "face of evil" at the time of his original conviction.

My involvement was tangential – I decided to dissect the media coverage for one of my City assignments. I phoned the newspapers who'd run the Silcott-as-Beelzebub-line, asking them how they could justify that approach given he'd just been acquitted. I did a decent reporting job, getting named quotes from several tabloid journalists and comment writers, some of whom even conceded their coverage had been unfair. But I lacked the confidence, maturity even, to nail the resulting article as pungently as it deserved and demanded, or to highlight the underlying racism. Something along the lines of "Newspapers concede Silcott coverage unfair" or more tabloid-like: "It's a fair cop – our Silcott shots were cheap" would have caught it better. Journalists are notoriously reluctant to apologise or to criticise either themselves or the industry. Though I failed to get the piece commercially published, as we students were always encouraged to do, I was slowly developing a more politically critical eye for the media.

Being at City also helped with work placements, some of them paid. My first involved three weeks at the Elgin office of the Aberdeen *Press & Journal* in northeast Scotland, where I'm from. There I met Alastair Bisset, a generous tutor steeped in his local news patch, where he'd also grown up. He saved my embarrassment early on by quietly re-writing my first story. It was an attempted jokey take on a reader's lost rough collie, the breed made famous by the *Lassie* films. You can guess where I was headed with that one.

I shadowed one of the staff journalists on court reporting, a skill requiring accurate notes of proceedings without use of audio recorders. It's tricky. Wrongly spelling a defendant's name, or misstating their age, address or occupation is a professional hazard. It can land the wrong person in the crime pages and a reporter and their newspaper in court for libel. It is less of a risk now only because of the near-wholesale collapse in UK court reporting, with cash-starved newsrooms having neither the time nor the editorial inclination to do it.[5]

Being unpaid at the *P&J* left me free to do what stories I could in my time there, though without touching the wheels of local council politics or governance, which was Bisset's beat. I was happiest with a piece I did on a local shelter for women facing domestic violence. The volunteers were initially wary of the interest, particularly from a male reporter, but eventually agreed to talk. It was the right time of year to be highlighting the centre's work, with post-Christmas blues and family debt raising domestic tensions. Aside from the mix of subjects, the best part of the placement was doing basic news stories that got published. It would never have suited me longer-term at the time – I was nowhere near settling.

A second placement, in the spring of 1992, involved copy-editing for European masters students at the Danish School of Media Journalism in Århus. Part of their course involved publishing the magazine *Euroviews*, tagged that year as "Europe – coming together or falling apart?" Its content stretched from the gathering war in Yugoslavia to the disappearance of lesser-spoken European languages. The work was a thoughtful counterpoint to the generally ill-informed rants about Europe I was used to reading in British media. What I didn't realise was how soon I'd be tackling those issues myself.

As my City training drew to a close it was time for my third and final attempt to get on the Reuters graduate programme. The straight-out rejection didn't hurt so badly this time, not least because I had another option. My last work placement at City took me to the English desk of Agence France Presse in Paris for what turned out to be two months of glorified speed translation. AFP is the French-language equivalent of Reuters though without the latter's focus on financial and business news for global market traders. AFP's stories go to francophone media worldwide for use as they are or to be woven into TV and radio bulletins or newspapers. Their stories gave other media a French perspective on world news and an alternative to the likes of Reuters, which made AFP popular with newspaper clients in Asia.

AFP and Reuters are among a handful of world news agencies that include the US-based Associated Press, Spain's EFE, Japan's Kyodo and China's Xinhua. They amount to a few, narrow pinch points funnelling the bulk of what becomes foreign news to the world's seven billion people. What those agencies choose to cover, or ignore, is hugely significant, as are the perspectives they use to frame their stories. Their prodigious output determines the bulk of what people learn about the rest of the world from wherever it is that they live, whether they know it or not. Agency news generally comes to us via more familiar national media, delivered old-style or via the Internet. Google News, personal blogs, Twitter and Facebook may have nibbled at the agencies' former stranglehold on breaking news but none shows signs of becoming consistent news providers for sustained periods. That makes agencies hugely important influences over what we know of global issues and what we don't know. That in turn determines what we can or can't do in order to tackle them.

For all the attractions of a paid summer job in the majestic French capital, AFP was no place for a non-native French speaker set on a global journalism career. Though a Scottish friend of mine did get a general reporting job by passing via the AFP sports desk, that option seemed too way off track for me. The best thing I took away from that summer was a colleague's advice to head for Brussels, the European capital and a plentiful source of freelance journalism work.

So four years on from university, with a couple of hundred pounds to my name, I boarded an overnight bus-ferry from London, arriving on the Brussels streets before dawn. While I had no work to go to, I figured that as a middle-class graduate, with long-suffering parents who'd take me in if all else failed, I had little to lose. And of course I didn't, even if the early months were a bit stressful as I got sorted out.

My first commissions, fitted in between renovation work I did for a friend in return for rent, were for a specialist financial publication called the *EC Times*. No surprises there, there's tonnes of that sort of journalism because people see the business case to pay for it. Making the financial case for socially and politically progressive journalism is far harder, hence my difficulties in trying to find or do such work. Little did I know that banking and finance interests would be the main funders of my journalism for the next 13 years, with all that implied for the stories I got to write.

The good thing about my first Brussels string, journalist-jargon for a regular writing commission, was that the work agenda was totally clear. The subscriber-led *EC Times's* existence relied on it giving readers the digested detail of European finance laws. It was hardly Pulitzer Prize journalism and no great service to the cause of social justice either. I felt in no position to be picky as I had no money. In reality, I was delighted to have work that gave me a toe-hold in Brussels and journalism. Little matter that I knew nothing about European finance law or finance itself. All I did know I'd gleaned from flirting with a job in investment banking a few years back and by developing a generalist's knowledge of business and money. I had an equally patchy grasp of how European institutions worked.

Luckily ignorance is no professional death sentence for journalists. Deft juggling of facts plus some quotes from the right officials masks the essential shallowness of most content. Usually, it's all that's needed, a journalistic version of official events. Far trickier is to get paid for the sort of journalism I'd dreamt of doing from the start, something that would have involved digging out what officials didn't want published. I made do by telling myself the work would keep me fed while I built up the necessary file of published articles for future jobs with bigger media outlets. Banging the drum on social or political justice issues would have to wait.

This sense of suspended animation, the idea my next job would get me closer to this ill-defined ideal, kept me captive for years. It is a classic mistake I would repeat several times before even realising I was making it, let alone appreciate its effects or how to do something different. It kept me from looking more deeply into the fundamentals of journalism or how to go about doing a more meaningful version of it.

Back then, conventional media options had all my attention. The *EC Times* and its like were my entry tickets to the machine, which promised press accreditation and access to other practical advantages. They included the chance to hobnob with the established press corps, to make friends and contacts and to look for future work. It was an intoxicating environment, for all the reputation of Brussels as being boring. It was also the start of getting used to asking questions of public figures in public, not that various visiting heads of state, government ministers or their designated mouthpieces would then answer them.

Over the months I picked up more, specialised commissions, on a variety of environmental topics, mainly for trade publications put out by the *Agra Europe* group. I also got a piece in the Brussels weekly news and events magazine, *The Bulletin*, the most fun thing I worked on in all that time. It involved finding and interviewing Plastic Bertrand, a

Belgian pop star whose fame had lasted about as long as it took his frenetic "*Ça plane pour moi*" to climb and fall European pop charts. He was a charming and reflective interviewee. It was only years later that I learned it wasn't even him who'd sung his signature song.

A valuable part of the experience was learning to navigate the European policy-making maze. That meant getting past the spokespeople and their pre-cooked answers to officials who weren't supposed to talk to the media. Once I'd begun to find my way, in July 1993, I got a full-time post at the twice-weekly *European Report*. That lifted the pressure of looking for new commissions only to replace it with a constant push to fill pages. I switched from writing about what I could get paid for to covering specific subject areas as part of a reporting team. What was a step up the professional ladder, and some payback for several years' effort trying to get into the business, took me no closer to my original goal in journalism.

If that even crossed my mind I quickly dismissed it in the excitement of my apparent progress. It was enough to be learning the practical mechanics of journalism even as I ignored the fact of my stunted understanding of power and politics. I wasn't complaining. Less than a year after my punt on Brussels, I'd taken a big step towards a regular staff job. It pushed me deeper into single issues, allowing me to build up my contacts and specialist knowledge. Of them all, the most challenging was global trade, just as the Uruguay Round of international talks reached its climax.

Trade rules had yet to take their place among the chief bogeymen of global justice campaigners. The movement was still years from exploding into public consciousness with mass protests in Seattle. That made trade a perplexing topic. Barely schooled in the political wheels of Brussels, I now had another layer of obscure political governance mechanisms and terminology with which to grapple. I took no notes during my first one-on-one briefing with Peter Guilford, a former *Times* journalist turned spokesman for the then European Trade Commissioner Leon Brittan. He affably spieled out the Commission's thoughts on the state of play in talks while I nodded away pretending to know what he was on about.

Though trade made little sense to me at first, I'd no reason to worry that ignorance might damage my professional prospects. I'd learnt already it was easy enough to match the media herd's cover, to stick close to the briefing points pumped out by the main parties. I would weight their prominence in stories according to the relative power of each one. The result was proforma stories reporting the A said, B said of well-matched negotiators from Europe and the United States. They gave little sense of the broader stakes in talks.

I saw it as logical rather than biased to start with the more powerful parties' positions given they were most likely to determine the outcome. It didn't occur to me the extent to which that biased my stories towards those same parties' agendas or worked against my own ambitions to do journalism that promoted social and political justice. I didn't ignore the less powerful parties or their arguments, they just didn't get so much reporting attention or play.

My approach, a pretty standard one among my peers, had the inevitable effect of skewing stories to the agenda of those in power. To have done otherwise, something I couldn't even conceive of at the time, would have required me to think independently of the mass of media and to put myself out on an ideological limb. Unlike many news organisations, with more constraining editors, I could have probably got away with that at *European Report*. Its francophone publishing culture included a more sceptical perspective towards the claimed benefits of "free" trade.

Jean-Pierre Delorme, one of my editors, kept asking me to dig deeper into the trade story, to say something more than what we were getting from the day-to-day material. His request kept playing on my mind without me ever being able to nail what it was that he was after. My politics at the time, my understanding of incumbent power and the realities of international talks, were not yet up to that approach. I tended to reflect the powerful status quo rather than question it with more balanced stories.

That left me nowhere near explaining the reality of talks or anticipating how their eventual outcome would hurt the world's poor for years to come. I failed to understand how the undoubted benefits of trade were parcelled out in private to favour a few major powers at the expense of the many, weaker ones.

I was alert enough to know I wasn't doing a very good reporting job on talks without knowing what a good job would be. That niggle lay behind my question to a packed Brussels news conference featuring the talks' major parties – the European Community and the United States. It pitched Leon Brittan against his counterpart Mickey Kantor just as negotiations neared their conclusion. Among the men's responsibilities were rules on trade in audiovisual products, principally films and TV series. France was particularly wary of cheap US productions being dumped cheaply on European screens, their costs already covered by domestic revenues. Without regulation, they feared Europe's linguistically fragmented markets would be swamped by cheap US imports. It was a sensitive issue, with major implications for the economics of European productions and what people got to watch on their screens.

I caught Guilford's eye as he scanned the room for raised hands as the conference began, noting names as he went. The result was that among detailed questions on the esoterica of talks there was a rather more basic one – from me. I asked what recent films the two negotiators had seen at the cinema, a cheeky effort to learn something about the supposed defenders of European and US culture themselves. Kantor, a natural showman, fired back through audience laughter that he'd recently seen *Jurassic Park,* twice, and *In the Line of Fire.* Brittan spluttered, clearly not having been to the cinema in ages. He eventually mumbled something about having heard much talk of *Germinal* during a recent trip to Paris. Though it was fun to watch him squirm, my question failed to bring any light to the reality of talks, nothing less than a global corporate stitch up taking place right under our noses.

No one else in that rare news conference got anywhere nearer that truth. None of the questioners appeared to have much more sense of what was at stake, or who the winners and losers would be. I certainly didn't.

A few weeks later, in December 1993, the talks concluded in Geneva, headquarters of world trade regulation. Few of the Brussels-based media made the trip, leaving us prey to the European Commission's press machine in the hours after the deal was done. I remember my ears pricking up at a reporter's question on how poor countries would do from the eventual compromise and whether it was fair. Guilford brushed it off with the notorious line of a "rising tide lifting all boats", the idea everyone would benefit from growth generated by the deal.

That proforma claim was a variation of "trickle-down" economics, the idea US and British governments were using to justify lowering taxes on the rich. It soon rang hollow for the world's poorest countries, not least the African ones. For me, I realised only gradually that what the governments and businesses of wealthier countries cynically called "free" trade was nothing of the sort. The deal their officials secured left trade decidedly unfree, hugely weighting the benefits in their industries' favour. European and US subsidies for industrialised farming were among the most glaring examples. Their farmers' dumped their surpluses on poor countries' markets, trashing local food production chains and helping obliterate what benefits might have "trickled down" from the new trade deal.

That outcome wouldn't have worried the main negotiators. Kantor went on to join the Washington law firm Mayer Brown, whose clients included multinationals who most certainly did benefit from his negotiating efforts. Among them was Monsanto, the monopolistic seeds and pesticides giant whose practices epitomise the logical outcome of "free" trade. Brittan also did well, his subsequent jobs including that of vice-chairman at the Swiss investment bank UBS, the world's second largest manager of private wealth assets. The men's credentials, not to mention the lack of accountability in their political appointments, never occurred to me as issues back then. I don't remember it registering much among my peers either. Yet those men and their retinues carried enormous real power, wielded generally in closed-door negotiations from which a few details leaked sporadically to the public via a barely trade-literate news media.

The unfairness and unaccountability of trade rules had yet to gain the wider currency it achieved only a handful of years later. Even so, there should have been plenty to criticise with the knowledge available at that time, not least the farm subsidies. These were particularly damaging to poor countries, blocking their access to one of the few sectors they might have exploited and exposing them to subsidised surpluses dumped on their markets. The effect literally starved their farmers off the land, driving them into the slums bordering major cities. At the same time, the same subsidies did little to help smaller farmers in the rich countries, ones in whose names the handouts had been misleadingly justified by negotiators.

I could have done with knowing more eloquent defenders of the world's majority poor, people such as Martin Khor of the Third World Network in Malaysia or Lori Wallach of Global Trade Watch in Washington. Such credible critics of rich country governments' arguments are easy to weave into stories. More was the pity for my efforts to cover what was, and remains, a complex global story. My time for trade stories was constrained by the others I had to do, a familiar problem for all journalists. Time pressures have got steadily worse due to ever-shrinking editorial budgets and staffing. The result is what BBC business journalist Waseem Zakir dubbed "churnalism". Fewer reporters producing more stories means their cover becomes increasingly reactive, relying on copy sourced from press releases or news conferences with little additional reporting. It all sounds horribly familiar. While churnalism may not matter much for niche publications such as *European Report*, its effects are far worse with bigger news outlets, exactly the ones I was still aiming to join.

On global stories such as trade, concentrations of journalists in news centres such as Brussels or Washington bias the overall news coverage towards the institutional views that predominate in those places. They grandstand official government sources and the views of those lobby groups with the money and staff to feed their views into negotiators and the massed media. Majority world perspectives get buried at the bottom of stories if they get written up at all. It is rare to read mainstream news that leads with those views. As for those of people caught up in the consequences of trade decisions taken thousands of miles away without their knowledge or consent, you can forget it.

This is a particular problem for the global issues dealt with by the Kantors and Brittans of this world. The power dynamic has certainly shifted since 1993, not least with China and India's surging growth and better coordination between poorer countries and their allies. Western journalism, still the dominant voice of global media, has generally failed to reflect that change. "Free" trade arguments are forever tripping off political leaders' lips to be fog horned on by unquestioning journalists. While that concept may no longer gull poorer countries into new rounds of talks, it does help smother calls for a wholesale revamp of global trade governance. Fair trade rules, along with the cancellation of historically abusive loans to the same countries, could bring huge benefits directly to the world's poorest people.

If trade were a purely national or even local story, a newspaper in the territory affected might seize on the case for reform. It would bank on some of its audience getting on board with its efforts, while also buying the paper, making its advertisers happy. Such a campaign might highlight how today's main economic powers secured their wealth only by using the same trade protections they now deny others. Yet that's not what happens.

Trade is a global story with no major media voice bearing witness to the coherence of would-be reformers' arguments. At the same time, there is an abundance of media quoting the many politicians and well-funded business interest groups who campaign and coordinate their actions under the specious banner of "free" trade. The latter include a cabal of multinational corporations who totally understand the benefits of quietly acting in concert and speaking with one voice. Their arguments populate the pages of Anglophone business bibles such as the *Wall Street Journal*, the *Economist* and *Financial Times*. The business agenda dominates the discourse, not just on trade but on all aspects of global capitalism.

As barely an understudy to that conventional media chorus, I remained too much in awe to spot the holes in those arguments. I was more intent on personal promotion than political coherence. If I had any reservations about those publications, they failed to dent my enthusiasm for getting a job with them or their like. I thought I could graduate on to stories of social and political worth once I got established. Wrong-headed as that would ultimately prove to be, it was finally set to pay off in the shape of a big brand media job. On my fourth attempt, via a side door far from the London entrance, I finally got into Reuters. In a field this time of just three rather than hundreds, I was hired as its European environment and transport correspondent, starting on April Fool's day 1994.

Was someone trying to tell me something?

Chapter 2

Europhile turned foul

Newsrooms are intimidating places for the uninitiated, a category that certainly included me in my first months at Reuters. Despite being six years on from the first inklings of a journalism career and having worked hard to learn the basics of reporting, I was overawed by my new surroundings. Helping that feeling was Nick Doughty, the then Reuters NATO correspondent, who sat facing me on our shared desk. It wasn't his fault.

Nick was generous in his welcome and encouragement of a new colleague. The problem was my job as European environment and transport correspondent. For all my excitement at having landed it, the position seemed impossibly prosaic beside what he was covering. Nick would be calling through news flashes about NATO air strikes on Serb forces somewhere in Bosnia as I shuffled off to conferences on European aviation law. On my second day in the job, going to just such an event, I remember thinking about Reuters staff reporting from conflicts all around the world as I fought off the effects of some sort of gastric bug I'd picked up. During serial visits to the bathroom, interspersed with haphazard attention towards conference proceedings, I reflected on my sorry start.

Looking back I realise the comparison of roles was absurd. The pyrotechnics of falling bombs will always be more spectacular and dramatic, not to mention fatal for the people underneath. Yet the political issues I was assigned to cover are as critical in the long term, if not more so. Nick's job was to plug himself into the briefing network of NATO diplomats and spokespeople in Brussels, a sure-fire route to reproducing the priorities and perspectives of established power, not to mention the lies. We are too easily dazzled and distracted by media spectacle, my young journalist self being as prone as any. The result is we fail to dig more deeply into underlying questions of who wields power, on whose account and in whose interests.

Job envy apart, I was thrilled to have joined the organisation that first got me set on journalism. I was in, after all this time, who cared what I was doing? It wasn't the glamorous foreign correspondent's post I'd dreamed of – unearthing difficult truths in pursuit of social justice – but I felt I'd made a big step forward. My assigned beats were much the same as those I'd done before but the way I wrote them up and where they went most certainly weren't. Reuters's clients then, before the Internet took off, stretched across the world's media, financial screen traders, embassies and the boardrooms of international businesses. I felt I'd climbed the journalistic food chain, assuming that would carry me nearer the sort of journalism I'd originally imagined. It took me years to discover that isn't how things work.

The biggest change from before was the never-ending deadlines. News agencies push out stories as soon as possible after they happen, near instantaneously if they can. At its most extreme, that requires reporters to condense the most urgent ones into 80-character "snaps" conveying the essence of an event or news development. Their main targets are traders who buy or sell market positions on the news. This skill, a precursor to tweets, was totally alien to me. It was all the more intimidating because our output was timed against that of competing news wires. It was no use being fast with the news but wrong. A skilful "snapper" would accurately record an event or remark, distil it into 80 characters for dictation to a colleague and immediate transmission to clients. I'd had a taste of this always-on pressure during my brief summer stint at AFP. It introduced me to the addictive thrill of playing a part in breaking news as it emerged piecemeal in real time.

That pressure was mostly absent from my assigned "beats", neither of which threw up much of instant interest to financial market traders or media clients. My main exposure to it came from other reporting duties and when working weekends. It came home to me with a clunk during my first weekend duty shift, a few months after joining Reuters. I missed the importance of a news release announcing the Austrian currency's entry into the European Exchange Rate Mechanism, which I should have snapped to news screens even on a weekend. It prompted a grumpy reprimand come Monday morning from our editors in London.

Learning new ways of working while trying not to miss anything that happened on my beats made for a busy schedule. As one of the specialist European reporters I was urged to "empty my notebook" for a briefing service Reuters sold to its Brussels-focused clients. It left little time to think more deeply about the job. I was still bowled over by the idea being part of an organisation whose reporters had witnessed 150 years of history, drafting first-person accounts of events from around the world.

I gradually mastered the skills I needed to get on, marvelling at the resources at my fingertips versus those I'd had while scrabbling a living as a freelance reporter. Less than two years before, I'd typed my first Brussels stories in computer shops on machines rented by the hour, handing them over on floppy disks before the days of email. Now I could access Reuters archives straight from my desktop, trawling for background material to use as needed in stories. It seemed a massive advance from working alone.

All that combined with a regular salary, friendly, able colleagues and the sheer kudos of Reuters made for a heady mix. I wonder what my 28-year-old equivalent would make of the same offering today. The choice of a salaried job versus continued freelancing would certainly be different. My imaginary, modern self would be far better off than the real, past one in some ways. There would be cheaper technology and more source material directly available. That would make remote, independent working more technically feasible though it might not help the chances of making a living. For all that, the clincher on the deal would be the same as ever. It would depend on whether my modern equivalent understood how financial security and the twinkly allure of a big brand media job come with a hefty cost. The price is lost independence over editorial thinking and story selection.

These are the serious downsides of the job I'd grabbed with both hands. They are ones my real self, back in 1994, didn't get. Had someone suggested these to me, I'd probably have dismissed the person as being somehow jealous or politically paranoid. To me, the only apparent downside of joining Reuters seemed to be in my comparing what I got to cover versus what my new colleagues around the globe were doing. I would have to live out for myself the constraining effects of media ownership, audience and ideology before I would be ready to hear such arguments.

Before even imagining such subtleties, I had to improve my base knowledge of politics, something left stunted by my science-focused education. It improved gradually as I bathed in the daily detail of a major hub in Europe's network of political power. My beats, for all that I now appreciate their broader importance, were always niche ones, more so given I had to shovel out as much detail as possible. Clients of our specialist service wanted every twist and turn of the Brussels policy-making machine, the latest draft of a proposal or chance remarks by officials responsible for turning it into law. That meant tracking the daily workings of the European Commission, the EU's civil service arm, and regular meetings of European government ministers and officials within the Council of Ministers. We tended to cover the European Parliament more as an after-thought, a hard-nosed editorial call reflecting the lack of real power in the most nominally democratic part of the EU's undemocratic whole.

Accountability questions didn't bother me much when I joined Reuters, they weren't in my remit and I was too wrapped up in learning the new job in any case. I did my work with little thought to the legitimacy either of the European Commission or the Council of Ministers. They were extensions of national governments I regarded as representatives of their citizens' wishes. Our news focus invariably picked up conflicts between these different EU bodies, between the Commission and member states or between different blocs of member states. Little matter that those differences were usually variations on the theme of increased European integration. There was plenty of noise from all those official sources to keep me distracted from closer scrutiny of the underlying realities. That entailed skating over what was at stake in the integration process, which was nothing less than a tectonic shift in power. Alternative or dissenting voices, those of the vast, under-represented majority who had to live with all these decisions, were rare. They were generally limited to the few who managed to make themselves heard in the European capital. They got little play on our news file.

I'd begun at Reuters during the last months in office of Commission President Jacques Delors. His tenure oversaw the start of the single market and single currency projects that whipped up such anti-Brussels thinking among my fellow Britons. Reuters was its classic self in reflecting the debate, playing up the institutional positions for what were decidedly elite-friendly projects. We relied heavily on official sources, information and briefings for our stories. That came at a price, not understood by me at the time, which was lost independence and perspective with respect to the views of wider society, which is to say ordinary people. Had Reuters reporters elsewhere picked those up, had their editors been alive to the need for such balance, our Brussels team could have been excused its institutional bias. But they didn't.

What my then colleagues and editors would have called the absence of a position on European matters was of course a position. We unquestioningly accepted as legitimate the European institutions, the member state governments and their complex plans for enlarging and deepening the European political land grab. It was never expressed as such, or certainly never explicitly, rather it was wrapped in the idea that our job was to relay what was said and done by those in power. We might dab in a few contrarian views from within the establishment but rarely the many from outside. That attitude explains why, as Europeans have become more hostile to the EU over the years, media cover has not generally reflected the shift. The problem affects not just Reuters but all major media in their different ways. It means the EU's declining political accountability to its citizens becomes ever more chronically under-examined.

None of that is to say news organisations should impose their editors' or owners' views on their audiences, far from it. They do already. By fixing editorial attention and reporting resources on the powerful, on the decision-makers, news media such as Reuters skew debate towards those people's opinions and agendas. In this case, it was closer European integration.

The approach would be perfectly justifiable if those decision makers were properly accountable to the people in whose name they were acting. European institutions are, after all, the creations of governments chosen in elections by their citizens. That line of argument is critically undermined by the reality, which is the near-total lack of influence ordinary people enjoy over EU decision-making structures.

My personal politics at the time didn't help me spot what we supposed citizen watchdogs in the media were missing. I'd shed my mildly Conservative leanings for Labour ones in the 1992 British general election, which Labour had lost. I was naturally antagonistic to the "Up Yours Delors" constituency so skilfully championed by the mass tabloid *Sun*. The newspaper's deft populism was undeniable, never better than with its two-fingered salute and front-page headline taunting the Commission president in 1990. Delors had sold Europe to Britain's Labour as a route to stronger social and employment protections, or at least a guarantor of existing ones. That inflamed Margaret Thatcher and her echo chamber the *Sun*. All reason enough on its own for me to sympathise with the French socialist Delors and his agenda.

As a Scot, I had another reason, which was my idea that closer European integration would be a counter to London's power within the United Kingdom, wrong-headed though that would prove to be. Both positions, coupled with a semi-insider's arrogance, left me blind to the EU's lack of democracy and prone to ignore the so-called eurosceptics. Given the style and tone of their criticisms, often laced with ugly baiting of all things foreign, I easily dismissed what they said as the rantings of little Englanders. All the more so given their odes to the joys of democracy usually applied only to failings in Brussels, rarely to Westminster's or those of other European capitals.

Such twisted logic left me with a big political blind spot while in Brussels. Instead of seeing the lack of political accountability in Europe's inner workings, I ended up plain confused. To this day what public debate there is about Europe usually stalls on much the same question, certainly in British circles. Arguments split into pro or anti-EU camps based on little knowledge of its workings and no subtler examination of who most benefits from European sovereignty pooling. That suits the beneficiaries just fine.

It is a big mistake for anyone who believes a government's policies should follow the will of its people. Europe's political structures as constituted today are a paradise for special interest groups, the richer they are the better they fare. Those same structures are virtually impenetrable to the ordinary citizen and near impervious to their influence. Dwelling on that detail, however painful it may be, is a critical first step in doing something about the problem.

My time in Brussels coincided with the Maastricht Treaty's ratification in 1993, which laid the ground for a single European currency and closer cooperation among EU member states on foreign policy and justice and home affairs matters. It swallowed big chunks of national capitals' decision-making powers, the effects of which have rumbled through to the serial euro crises following the 2007 global financial meltdown.

Though I'd no deep sense of what was at stake to start with, I soon began to develop one. Once the first fog of work and wonder at my new job dispersed, some mental space opened up for more critical political and journalistic faculties to take root.

As transport correspondent I reported on occasional talks between Swiss and European officials about patching up relations after Swiss citizens rejected joining the European Economic Area (EEA). They'd narrowly baulked at allowing more EU heavy lorries to crawl through their narrow Alpine passes, belching pollution into the still mountain air. I got their thinking but was surprised the issue had persuaded them to pass up the chance of closer EU ties. It seemed to me such an obvious choice. Steeped in their culture of direct democracy, Swiss voters clearly understood the issue better than I, the then europhile. Whether to join the EEA went far deeper than having more, heavier lorries on their roads. It would have swept away a slab of their rights to decide how they were governed – and they hadn't bought it. Lucky for them they got the chance to decide.

One of the early questions to emerge for me concerned the hierarchies of power, why it was that one policy priority would trump another and who got to decide. It came up when the EU's environmental priorities crashed into its trade obligations, with the latter prevailing. It was no big deal but again, it set me thinking. What happened was that European Commission officials simply ignored EU environment ministers' instructions to prepare a ban on imports of fur from animals caught in leg-hold traps. They said a ban risked provoking retaliatory suits under World Trade Organisation rules by the countries targeted. I was sympathetic to arguments for a ban, a topic I'd followed during months of ministerial debate enlivened by protester groups carrying around a huge, inflatable beaver. Yet I also favoured rules-based global trade. What shocked me in how things turned out was the way EU bureaucrats went over the heads of elected ministers, ditching their proposal on the grounds it would provoke a WTO suit. While that approach may have been legally and tactically astute it also reeked of unaccountable power. What sort of system allowed officials to trump the instructions of elected ministers, I wondered?

These incidents, along with the decision by European heads of government to bin their environment ministers' carbon tax proposal, unsettled my enthusiasm for integration. I lacked an overall perspective on the EU's public accountability deficit but was starting to sympathise with critics' concerns about the mechanics of its operations.

It was another niche subject that finally broke the EU's spell on me, and then only years after I'd left Brussels. It concerned EU institutions' approach to regulating genetically modified (GM) food and crops. I'd written about the environment for a couple of years before coming across GM issues myself in 1996, so I already knew something of its accompanying controversies. One concerned the mighty stink kicked up by Oxford scientists' attempts to kill caterpillars with a virus engineered to express a scorpion toxin. That story played in my mind the day I met US biotechnology lobbyists at a media event in Brussels, when they pumped up their industry as a new saviour to the world's starving poor. The boast irritated me at once. It was absurdly unrealistic, plain cynical even, but also patronising that they thought us stupid enough to swallow it. I knew enough about hunger issues myself to understand people usually starve due to poverty rather than lack of available food. Whatever noble thoughts biotech firms might have had about feeding the world, I knew they weren't the ones driving their business models.

I wrote a lot on GM over the years but found nothing to convince me its potential benefits in field-scale crops outweighed its many possible perils. I accepted that cases may emerge in future where the balance of risk favoured cultivation but none was apparent then. EU regulators were being called to respond on two fronts, with member states applying to cultivate GM crops and looming maize exports from the United States demanding approval. It was controversial from the start, more so for the smouldering row over an EU ban on hormone-treated US beef and European consumers' shaky trust in food regulators after their inept handling of mad cow disease.

My time in Brussels was taken up trying to fathom and explain the near-impenetrable EU rules for determining decisions on GM issues. I fell into an ever-present trap for reporters, EU ones maybe more than most, which is to get buried in detail while missing the broader political picture. Hindsight makes obvious the most pertinent point: that GM crops and animal fodder spread inexorably on to European markets despite wide popular opposition and unease. EU citizens, despite putting the brakes on most full-scale cultivation of GM crops, proved powerless in the face of a few determined multinationals and their supporters in European governments and the EU executive. The result was a vast-scale, uncontrolled experiment that no one could claim to be monitoring, let alone predict its outcomes.

By the time I left Brussels, in September 1997, EU authorities were tied in knots over their policies and procedural rules for crop approvals, imports and labelling. I would have done my job better by sticking to democratic first principles, to have thought, and wrote, from the perspective of ordinary citizens whose views were reached in a process of informed debate. That was what happened with Britain's GM Nation consultation in 2003, one of the few processes worldwide to engage the public in debate. It showed that the more people learned about GM technologies, the more intense became their concerns. It found widespread mistrust of both government and multi-nationals. Typical of our cynical governors, as I was starting to realise by covering the subject myself, those people's views were then ignored.[6]

These various stories changed my view of Brussels and sparked a broader evolution in my journalism and politics, changing them from the conventional mainstream to something more radical. I'd begun with the idea our political structures, while not perfect, were at least responsive to their constituents' political demands as expressed in elections. Today I see them as so unresponsive to popular concerns, so beholden to special interests, as to require wholesale reform. Of them all, EU structures are probably the worst of a very bad lot.

The crowning example from Europe, played out after I left Brussels, spanned the eight years leading up to the Lisbon Treaty's entry into force. The text was rammed into law thanks to the barefaced chicanery of political leaders in European member states. Their manoeuvring was just the opposite of all the grand talk that launched the reform process in 2001. They pledged then, with no apparent irony, to bring EU institutions closer to the people of Europe.[7] They said they accepted citizens' wishes that the EU steer clear of issues more suited to nationally or regionally elected representatives. They acknowledged that some people saw EU lawmaking as threatening their identities. "More importantly, however, [citizens] feel that deals are all too often cut out of their sight and they want better democratic scrutiny," the leaders observed.

Subsequent events were to prove the utter cynicism of those words. For Europe's political elite, the idea of citizens having a say was fine for rhetoric, propaganda even, but never for reality. Their behaviour was a classic example of why we must always scrutinise politicians for what they do not what they say. For journalists on deadline, producing their instant drafts of history for top-of-the-hour news bulletins, such wariness is an all-but-impossible luxury. The job demands that they shove the story out first and ask questions later, by which time their shovelling has already set the news agenda. That is certainly the Reuters way, all the more strikingly so with every rung up the global power ranking of whoever's doing the talking. The only way to avoid that problem as a journalist is to bypass the glamour and razzamatazz of major, set-piece political events. It's not an option if you work for the likes of Reuters – you either bang the drum or leave the orchestra.

Whatever the journalistic benefits of getting close to power – in putting questions to leaders directly or to their staff as and when you can – they come at a high price. Getting and staying close usually means a reporter's knowing or unknowing co-option into someone else's agenda. Better to leave politicians to the 24/7 TV news channels, to their official press services or blogs even, and use the reporting time and resources more productively to dig out things people don't know. At the very least, that should involve alternative perspectives or analyses of the issues leaders are claiming to address. That turns their events into opportunities to push on different story angles, not just to reproduce the ones handed down from on high like some sort of official news foghorn. The main challenge is to avoid being gulled by grand rhetoric while defending against the charge of being cynical.

This tension between official make believe and political reality is no grand secret, as journalists readily admit in private. Their grumbling about the guff they are obliged to churn out doesn't stop them churning it out just the same, their jobs depend on it after all. The way to avoid it is to quit the media herd to do something other than journalism that presents the public face of power. That alternative could be to explore power's accountability to ordinary people and the gap between what the powerful say and do. It is a project for the long haul, which needs to start with journalists scrutinizing their own politics and their understanding of governance.

It is a challenging path to follow, attracting inevitable taunts from peers of being polemical, cynical or biased. Such accusations are to be both expected and endured. In the cynic stakes, it is the political elites that reign supreme. Among them are the likes of former French president Valéry Giscard d'Estaing, who chaired the group that produced the draft EU constitution. When French voters spat it out, in May 2005, his response was classic of those same elites. "It is not France that has said no. It is 55 percent of the French people," he said.[8]

Three days later a majority of Dutch voters added their "*nee*" to the French "*non*", prompting EU leaders to cancel the other votes for fear of irreparably damaging their plans for concentrating powers. Their proposal disappeared for a few months before re-emerging as pretty much the same thing, served up as the draft Lisbon Treaty. Giscard d'Estaing was unembarrassed, saying the new version was "very, very near" to the old one in "all the key elements". All the earlier elements remained, he said, albeit "hidden and disguised in some way".[9]

Europe's politicians were cuter this time around, ruling out more public votes to prevent people getting their answers wrong again. Everywhere that is except Ireland, where a Supreme Court decision mandated that voters be consulted on any significant change to the European treaties.[10]

When they duly rejected the text, in June 2008, their decision was ignored and they were asked to vote again the following year. Political sleight of hand, the fear of a full-blown financial crisis and a business- and media-led blitz for the "yes" camp reversed the outcome second time around.[11] Treaty fans heralded the result as a great day for Ireland and a greater one for "Europe". No one could credibly say the same for democracy or, for that matter, for journalism.

Momentous changes to EU governance rules were bludgeoned through with only Ireland's voters getting a chance to raise questions and pass judgement on the answers they got. They were then ignored. On a large range of issues the new Treaty made EU laws and institutions constitutionally separate from, and superior to, those of member state governments. The absence of popular influence on the process should shock anyone who believes democracy somehow relates to "we the people".

Among the shocked were the EUDemocrats, a parliamentary alliance considered beyond the pale by the EU's major political groups by virtue of its criticisms of Europe's ever-deepening integration. It described the reforms as a constitutional "revolution by stealth" that stripped EU members of their character as true sovereign states.[12]

EU fans might cry "foul" at that, pointing to the Lisbon Treaty article allowing citizens to raise a million or more signatures to petition the European Commission to act on any chosen issue. It is a fig leaf, not just because the rule is unwieldy and uncertain in its application. Given the woeful democratic credentials of the EU's three main institutions, no foliage imaginable would be big enough. Step forward the European Parliament, the Commission and the Council of Ministers.

Starting with Parliament, which has the greatest claim to represent ordinary citizens' interests in Europe, it has always had a fundamental flaw in its structure. The relationship between citizens and their EU representatives is nothing like the one, albeit horribly idealised, that ties them to national deputies. The distance between people and their MEPs, geographically, numerically and conceptually even, is immense.

Czech President Václav Klaus, despite being a fan of liberalised markets and the lost public accountability they imply, proved a telling critic of Parliament in a 2009 speech. He said the assembly's lack of a government and opposition meant there was only ever one option on the table, that of ever deeper European integration.[13]

"Here, only one single alternative is being promoted and those who dare thinking about a different option are labelled as enemies of the

European integration," Klaus said. He likened Europe's arrangements to those of the former Communist bloc, where no alternative political systems were permitted and no parliamentary opposition. His speech caused a "large number of MEPs" to walk out.[14]

What MEPs found so offensive is a mystery, their President Hans-Gert Pöttering's later remarks being neither reassuring nor logical. He told Klaus previous parliaments would not have let him give such a speech. Why not? What was the big deal? Klaus had said nothing revolutionary yet was treated with theatrical disdain. Such is the lot of anyone who dares criticise the European project as defined by our political elites. Anyone daring to criticise the EU should expect the same. It goes with the territory.

Nigel Farage, leader of the UK Independence Party, is the sort of person I would have bypassed during my Brussels reporting days, for all the mistaken reasons already described. That attitude would have meant me missing his lampooning of Lisbon and Parliament's failure to do its supposed job as guardian of EU democracy. A classic was one delivered in May 2009 to conclude the Parliament's five-year mandate.

"The defining moment for me in this house was we had the French say no, we had the Dutch say no and then we had the Irish say no and this parliament has wilfully carried on ignoring the wishes of the people. You just don't get it do you? No means no," he said.

"What kind of a parliament is this? If you believed in democracy you would not just bulldoze aside those three referendum results," he said. The abuse routinely hurled his way was proof that Treaty supporters had lost the argument, he added.[15]

I don't agree with UKIP's broader political agenda, which includes lower taxation, privatisation, market deregulation and other policies broadly identified with laissez-faire capitalism. Britain's experience of privatisation and deregulation are easy proof those positions are directly at odds with Farage's professed affection for democracy. Just ask a British railways passenger or a privatised utilities customer. Ignoring that glaring paradox, what remained was that UKIP's leader was one of the rare elected politicians to speak forcefully on behalf of democracy when it came to Lisbon. He could of course afford such radical talk, coming from a party with no prospect of power.

Why was it we heard no such concerns from politicians in the major political parties? What happened to the European Parliament's liberal parties, grouped together within the Alliance of Liberals and Democrats for Europe? Why is it their fine talk of democratic accountability and direct democracy stayed at home while deputies boarded their planes for Brussels?[16]

Political strategists talk solemnly of expediency, the need for politicians to maintain party discipline by speaking with one voice, to keep their powder dry for bigger battles. For us, the public, there is no bigger political battle than subjecting our governors to the full force of real accountability. For journalists, embedded with their official sources, such structural deficiencies get ignored in routine cover. Fundamental debate about the poverty of our political structures is left to the likes of Farage. Colorful as he may be, the former metals trader is no knight in shining armour for the public accountability of government.

Politicians' reticence is hardly surprising – if people understood the arguments better they would never get away with the status quo. Having democratic accountability in Europe while also ratifying the Lisbon Treaty was always logically and practically impossible. Any politician or journalist pretending otherwise was either ignorant of EU structures, deluding themselves or just plain lying. As a recovering euro-enthusiast myself, I'd allow them to plead delusion.

Holding two conflicting ideas simultaneously – such as believing Lisbon wouldn't damage public accountability while pledging allegiance to more democracy in the EU – creates mental tension psychologists call cognitive dissonance. There's something that jars but we're not sure what. That was what emerged with the work I was doing at Reuters. I knew it was off track but didn't get why. Our tendency as humans is to try to ease dissonance by changing our attitudes, actions or beliefs. Those who must resist change, like politicians or journalists whose jobs depend on them maintaining necessary fictions, keep dissonance at bay by robustly defending their positions. They blame someone or something else for any problems or plain deny there's anything wrong.

It's all too painfully familiar. The unease that eventually drove me out of Reuters was barely perceptible during the three and a half years I spent with them in Brussels and totally absent at the start. It emerged as my confidence grew, along with my development of some political and professional nous. At first, I shrugged off questions about the journalistic effectiveness of the work I was doing. The constant hope, soothing my version of dissonance, was of the next posting bringing me nearer my journalistic ideal. Then I'd be free to do more of what I still see as journalism's main purpose, to serve the broad interests of society and do something more to tackle social justice issues.

For all that, if someone had accused me then of having failed in my reporting on Europe, of not being impartial or objective, I would have jumped down their throats. I would have pointed to all the training I'd had, the multiple sources I consulted, how I balanced opposing views in copy, what a decent, honest person I was. Whatever force powered that imagined response and my genuinely held convictions of the time, it wouldn't have made me any less wrong. From what I could tell, I was in good company among my fellow journalists. Those people I dismissed at the time as "eurosceptics" would have seen my error while I remained blind. I see it better now.

It took me five years' work in Brussels and years more reporting inside and outside of Reuters to reach my current views about the European Union. In essence, I think its structures are so rotten as to require either root-and-branch reform or removal. That position crystallised only once I'd dug deeper into the fundamental tenets of both democracy and journalism, which led smack into the EU's shortcomings.

Having doubts about EU accountability is one thing, arguing for root-and-branch reform or the project's abandonment, is quite another. It takes persistence of inquiry to understand the problem and what feels like courage, foolhardiness perhaps, to then stand up and talk about it.

Such EU opposition is not the easy option, not least because fellow critics include those who deliberately stoke people's fear of foreigners to whip up anti-Brussels sentiment. Anyone wanting to overhaul Europe's democratic credentials must address the hate-based scaremongering of anti-immigrant parties who claim the same political territory. Fear is a powerful emotion, a totally human and legitimate one, particularly when coupled with the anger that accompanies political impotence and economic weakness. Calling someone racist for being frightened and angry is both condescending and self-defeating, most of all when no account is taken of that person's underlying circumstances. Any EU critic, to be effective and credible, must acknowledge people's fear and anger. That most certainly doesn't mean accepting anyone's hostility towards foreigners or leaving hate-based arguments unchallenged. It is a delicate balance to strike, particularly for journalists, in what is generally a highly charged debate. What is sure is that critics will suffer all manner of hostility. That might be in attacks on themselves, on the quality or nature of the publications that carry their criticisms or in "free"-market-inspired charges of being "protectionist". All are part of the territory.

My own perspective of Europe, transformed in 20 years, is that of a Briton who has worked not only in Brussels but also in several other European capitals and in Asia. For me, equating support or criticism of the European Union with a love or hatred of foreigners is patently absurd. Equally, criticism of the existing structures of European integration doesn't mean I reject the idea of political cooperation across national borders or think it has no possible merits. The ease of moving to live in southwest France rather than my native Scotland is only the most obvious personal advantage I enjoy from the European project. For all that, none of the EU's benefits justifies its political costs, which are most obvious in the hardwired structures that all but exclude popular influence.

This is not some 007-style conspiracy but evidence from a clear-eyed look at EU institutions and where powers landed under Lisbon. The main reason we hear so little about this further loss of influence is because those most closely implicated either planned it that way or just don't accept it as a problem. One argument MEPs gave for their support of the reforms was that they would get more powers of scrutiny, a position ex-deputy Jens-Peter Bonde describes as understandable if misguided.[17]

Marginal gains in influence for a few hundred well-paid, well-expensed MEPs are not enough for what was lost by the bloc's 500 million ordinary voters. Lisbon all but choked off their voices from the policy making process.

The EU's two other main branches are even less likely champions of popular will. Certainly European Commissioners, who head the institutional trio's least accountable member, are not about to yield anything back to citizens. Together they hold that most basic of political powers, the right to propose new laws. Under Lisbon, these unelected officials now draft nearly every new text, in many more policy areas than before.

These are no heroes of democracy, prone to shouting "Power to the people!" across Brussels rooftops. Nor is the Commission to be dismissed as some boring hive of civil servants, whatever appearances might suggest. EU leaders appoint the Commission president in just the sort of back-room deal that typifies the bloc's illegitimacy. MEPs' scrutiny of this hugely important appointment is a sop to public accountability, they being able only to accept or reject the candidate. Mister President, and it has always been a mister so far, then parcels out jobs to other commissioners, accompanied by more of the usual horse trading between capitals. The choices colour all that follows during each Commission's five-year term. In the last couple of decades, that has meant an inexorable drift towards the interests of business and finance, to deregulation and privatisation and the integration of business executives into policy-making processes. While Europe's heads of state and government at least face occasional elections, the

Commission's unelected president sits pretty for five years or more as gatekeeper-in-chief to the EU legislative pipeline.

Not only do Commissioners hold a near monopoly on proposing EU legislation, they can even adopt laws themselves using new treaty powers to legislate by decree.

"If this is a good system for Europe – why not also use it in the member states?" says Bonde, with obvious irony. "Then we should forbid our national MPs to initiate and decide the laws. Instead, they should only send recommendations to the heads of civil service department at the various ministries, who should then meet behind closed doors and decide whether the advice of the elected representatives is good or not."[18]

The scale of the shift in power to Brussels is stunning, with 85% of all EU laws adopted by national and European civil servants in some 300 closed-door working groups under the Council of Ministers in Brussels. They consider drafts drawn up and implemented by some 3,000 other secret working groups attached to the Commission.[19] This epidemic of committees was a problem during the 1990s that got worse under Lisbon. Greater transparency in the process would help, for ordinary citizens and for journalists, with guaranteed access to the decisions taken and the documents supporting them. Even if such concessions were allowed, committees' membership rosters, their rules of operation and lack of accountability would remain.

These groups' decisions are mostly rubber stamped without debate during regular meetings of the Council of Ministers. Though outside public scrutiny, they don't exist in a vacuum. Much of what they do is directly influenced by the industries and businesses affected by their decisions. It was out of this labyrinth, for example, that rules for GM crop approvals emerged in the late 1990s. The approvals went ahead despite hostile public opinion, helped along by a Commission structure and staff steeped in biotech industry thinking.[20]

The EU's third arm, the Council of Ministers, represents national governments. Its make up varies according to the matters at hand.

Farm ministers form the farm council, transport ministers the transport council, and so on in a six-monthly cycle. Council and Parliament share the task of scrutinising EU legislation, with Council in the senior role.

Ministers from the 27 EU member states all come from elected governments and as such face a degree of accountability to their voters. That counts for little when it comes to Brussels deal-making and its trade offs across multiple issues. There is also the Council's lack of transparency, which is probably the worst of the EU's three main bodies. Aside from set-piece meetings, almost all of what ministers decide is done either behind closed doors or in the myriad working groups mentioned earlier. That Lisbon decreed Council debates be held in public, and their votes published, makes little real difference.

New Council voting rules under Lisbon further dilute national accountability, shifting more power from smaller states to larger ones in line with their widely different populations. Its effect will be to nearly double the weight given to Germany's vote and more than halve that of the eight smallest EU members. France, Britain, Italy and Spain also gain significantly while almost everyone else loses.[21]

A more fundamental change is the removal of national vetoes from various categories of law-making. Many more decisions will now be made by qualified majority vote, which weakens the say of individual states. While Parliament identified 40 new areas of policy to which the new rule applies, Bonde found 68. Ministers, given yet more powers under the new treaty, may introduce yet more.[22]

Yet more accountability disappears in "trilogues", an increasingly common law-making approach involving Parliament, Council and Commission. The result is yet more of the EU's trademark speciality – taking decisions behind closed doors.

This is detailed stuff, but not impenetrable. We citizens must understand the EU in order to grasp the extent of its sovereignty grab. Trilogues are intended to break institutional deadlocks over new legislation. The price is lost scrutiny by the public and all bar a few

MEPs. Tony Bunyan, writing for Statewatch in 2007, said the problem was more than the weakening of parliamentary committees. "Much more important is the shift of decision-making from a public, accessible, forum to one which is secret and thus removed from public scrutiny, comment, debate and possible intervention."[23]

Lost transparency means lost accountability to voters. It opens the doors to covert influence on policy fine print by well-connected commercial interests, of which Brussels has legions.

Accountability problems don't stop with the EU's big three. The European Charter of Fundamental Rights, made binding under Lisbon, draws major judicial powers away from member state capitals and further from their citizens. The beneficiary is the European Court of Justice in Luxembourg, or rather its judges. The impact will become clear only with time, as judges decide how EU citizens' rights are interpreted under the Charter. The effects will be material, though, if existing judgments are anything to go by. These have constrained workers' rights to strike, to collective bargaining and to equal treatment within the European Union. In these cases, judges delivered legislative verdicts that stretched the scope of underlying laws.[24]

Many other rights now fall under the court's remit. We will have to wait and see what they deliver. While we do, we should also ask why distant judges are granted such powers. That they are chosen as "persons whose independence is beyond doubt", by common accord among member state governments, is hardly reassuring.[25]

Without doubt, Lisbon's combined effects damaged public accountability in the EU's political structures. The extent will become clear only with time.

It wasn't as if things were that great before.

One of the oldest European policies of all is the Common Agricultural Policy or CAP. It goes back almost as far as the Europe project itself. Founder members conceived the subsidy system in the 1950s for a continent still raw from the hunger and food shortages of World War

II. It has since proved remarkably resistant to reform or repeal, to the delight of larger farmers and their ancillary industries and the expense not just of European citizens but also of poor farmers the world over.

CAP supporters' enduring success in keeping hold of their cheques was never more spectacularly in evidence than in 2002. That was when French president Jacques Chirac, a former farm minister himself, met his German counterpart Gerhard Schroeder on the eve of critical enlargement talks between all EU leaders. In a half-hour meeting, the two struck a deal that kicked CAP reform into the well-subsidised long grass and mapped out farm spending through to 2013. They bounced their EU counterparts into pretty much that deal the next day, infuriating serially frustrated CAP reformers. What was a coup for Chirac, locking his country's farmers into the largest share of CAP spending for the next decade, gave the lie to claims that the EU might be in any way democratic or transparent.[26]

No one should be surprised if some version of the same thing happens as the 2013 deadline rolls around. The broad lines were already in place in the Commission's proposals of late 2011, which suggested subsidies stay at about €55 billion/year up to 2020 versus €53bn in 2011, the latter figure representing 45% of the total EU budget.[27]

Snail-paced CAP reforms, for all their defenders' crowing about them, mean farm spending remains the biggest EU budget item. The main beneficiaries are not those plucky peasant farmers CAP supporters like to trot out when arguing for their hand-outs but those with the biggest, most valuable farms. Recent rules requiring member states to release data on who gets the cash show that in 2008, French farmers and farm-related interests got €9.9 billion, of which nearly one half went to just a fifth of recipients.[28]

The same data showed Britain's Queen Elizabeth got £473,500 in farm aid for Sandringham Farms, her 20,000-acre retreat. The Duke of Westminster, Britain's third richest person with a fortune estimated at £6.5 billion, got £486,534.[29]

Europhile turned foul

Other direct beneficiaries include multinational food conglomerates, sugar manufacturers and distillers. None of them farm themselves. They qualify for agricultural export refunds to cover the difference between subsidised EU prices and the world market price. The money covers their purchase of more expensive EU produce they wouldn't otherwise be able to sell profitably outside the bloc. The mugs who pay the bill include EU citizens and all the people affected by the dumped produce.[30]

Given an idea of the subsidy recipients, it's plain to see whose interests are served by cosmetically reshuffling the CAP. It's also clear why learning about the EU's seemingly impenetrable structures should not be left to political science junkies. Typically, the burst of transparency allowing people to see where all the money went lasted only as long as it took those same European Court of Justice judges to strike down the disclosure requirement, which they did in late 2010.

No surprise then that Europeans know next to nothing about the CAP, even though it costs each household around €1000 a year. One of the few recent bright spots in reporting terms is the emergence of *Farmsubsidy.org*, a network of European journalists, researchers and activists trying to prise open the data mine on farmer handouts.[31]

The CAP's effects spill over into EU trade policy, both in international talks and day-to-day matters. The same issues of skewed accountability play out to the benefit of industrial farming interests and at the expense of ordinary people inside and outside the bloc. What is important for us is not just the complexity of trade issues but also how EU policy-making takes place, who decides it and in whose favour.

EU negotiating positions in international talks emerge from a miasma of competing commercial interests with near-zero input from civil society. Accountability on day-to-day EU trade matters is little better. Regular issues and broad policy are tackled in weekly meetings of a Council working group called the Article 133 Committee, with specialist versions convened to do the more technical stuff. What is critical in all this is who gets to influence the process, which means getting access, both to people and information.

David O'Sullivan, a senior Commission trade official, was frank enough on that during a civil society meeting in Brussels. Though he said his door was always open to nongovernmental organisations, he said he specifically sought out business contacts. "I do not apologise for that, this is the way it's going to be," he told the meeting.[32]

These are no courtesy calls but detailed, regular briefings and discussions on policy. They involve the highest ranks of the Commission and their corporate counterparts. Ex-trade commissioner Peter Mandelson, who held office for four years up until late 2008, proved a keen friend of the EU's biggest businesses. While in Brussels he oversaw the Global Europe framework for trade policy. The campaign group Corporate Europe Observatory described its creation as having involved "unparalleled participation" by industry.[33]

The result was a policy reflecting a single constituency's view of EU trade priorities, sidelining all the others. Among the excluded were development groups, environmentalists, trade unions, social and consumer bodies and even small and medium-sized firms. That's to say nothing of either the European public or the poor countries promised disproportionate benefits from new global trade talks to make up for what they lost in the round I covered during the 1990s.[34]

Accountability issues are as bad in EU justice and home affairs. The same minimal transparency and public consultation govern what are highly sensitive issues. These include cross-border police cooperation, counter-terrorism, immigration, asylum and border controls. Policy emerges from civil-society exclusion zones. The record is pretty consistent, beginning with the Schengen Convention of 1990, which abolished border controls across much of the bloc. It continued with the 2005 Prüm Treaty on cross-border exchange of DNA profiles, fingerprints and vehicle registration data.

Both Schengen and Prüm, agreements struck between a handful of EU governments committed to deepening cooperation, set the tone for laws that eventually spread in some form to the entire bloc.[35]

EU lawmakers went way beyond Washington's much-criticised Patriot Act in placing their citizens under surveillance. The rules now require mandatory fingerprinting of all EU passport, visa and residence permit holders, with Britain and Ireland as exceptions. They also mandate the retention – for general law enforcement purposes – of all telephone, e-mail and Internet usage records. Don't even think of boarding a plane.

The next five-year phase of justice and home affairs work, the so-called Stockholm Programme, promises worse still. "Under national laws implementing EU legislation, state agencies are beginning to build up a previously unimaginably detailed profile of the private and political lives of their citizens, often in the absence of any data protection standards, judicial or democratic controls," the European Civil Liberties Network said in a 2009 report on the work ahead. For all the Stockholm Programme's friendly noises about balancing respect for individual freedoms while guaranteeing European security, the priority is clearly security, security, security.[36]

A preparatory report by the Portuguese government under their Council presidency in late 2007 spoke breathlessly of a "tsunami" of personal data soon to become available to security forces. "In the near future most objects will generate streams of digital data about their location and use – revealing patterns and social behaviours which public security professionals can use to prevent or investigate incidents," it said. Those "objects" include data tracks on people's cars, mobile phones and even their clothes. Clothes? Yes, you read that correctly. The technology is called radio-frequency identification, or RFID, and it's coming soon to a pair of knickers near you if it hasn't got there already.[37]

There are EU laws governing personal data, the uses to which they can be put, who may access them and to whom they may be passed and for what purpose. Individuals to whom data refer have the right to view and correct those data.[38] Not for much longer according to Statewatch, which says this definition of "privacy" carried weight in the past but is virtually meaningless now and promises to get more so.

Franco Frattini, the then European Commissioner for Justice, Freedom and Security, made official security priorities clear during a Council meeting in May 2007. "There is a need to overcome the traditional dogma of seeing collective security and individual freedom as two opposed concepts which exclude each other. Individual rights can only flourish in an atmosphere of collective security," he said.[39]

So security first and let's see what's left of freedom once that's sorted. That mindset parallels the thinking in boardrooms of European arms makers and their post 9/11 incarnations as "homeland security" vendors, which is hardly surprising. The reason is clear from the EU's Security Research Programme, which unites EU officials with people from Europe's biggest arms and IT companies. Its advisory groups are chosen with no parliamentary consultation, national or European, or any civil society representation. That gives Thales, EADS, Finmeccanica, SAGEM and BAE Systems top table seats in determining subsidies to Europe's domestic security industry.[40]

The advisory groups give profit-making corporations official status in the EU, with direct influence not just on security research but also on policy. With justice and home affairs ministers intent on using all technology available to them to spy on their citizens, and arms companies directing the research traffic to produce that technology, the result was always a foregone conclusion. EU security policy frogmarches its citizens towards constant, high-tech surveillance and near total disregard for their personal liberties.

It makes sense to consult industry on research but not in the absence of scrutiny by parliaments or civil society. It is equal nonsense, from a democratic perspective, to give arms companies direct influence over the strategic development of a €1.4 billion EU research programme.[41]

Fans of ever intensifying surveillance invariably try to pacify critics with the double-edged line that those doing nothing wrong needn't worry. That ignores the extraordinary powers accruing to data holders over those whose data they hold. It ignores the wide availability of the soon-to-be-harvested data via multiple access points across the EU's 27 member states, half a million at the last count.[42]

That concerns every one of the EU's 500 million citizens as well as its 26.5 million or so third-country nationals, 18.5 million of them legally, the rest without documents.[43]

Europe's illegal immigrants keenly understand the implications of increased surveillance. Its legal ones, while entitled to go about their business, face ever more stringent checks and administrative hoops through which to jump, as do those organisations with whom they deal. Along with migrant populations, Europe's ethnic minorities, regardless of where they were born or how many generations their families have lived in their chosen country, will inevitably face more frequent and intrusive scrutiny as EU policies run their course. To them you can add the poor, the jobless and other benefit claimants anywhere across the continent. Civil disobedience activists the UK government routinely dub "extremists", to be bracketed alongside terrorists in the list of threats to national security, should also count themselves among targeted groups. Anyone considering direct action or protest in response to the EU's theft of their democratic rights should do so in full knowledge of the institutional weapons arrayed against them, legal and physical.

I returned to the question of EU legitimacy in 2007, as a reporter on my own account. Standing outside a Carcassonne court in southwest France, a 1000km south of Brussels, I witnessed one of countless fallouts from the EU's accountability vacuum. For all the complexity of Brussels procedures, it was simple enough to draw a line joining officials' approval for commercial planting of GM maize to the black-clad riot police outside a French court. The display of state power accompanied five accused men as they climbed the court steps to face charges of hindering work at a local plant of US crop giant Monsanto.

I asked myself what sort of democracy requires French peasant farmers to risk personal financial ruin and prison to stop an unpopular, unaccountable law from being enforced. Why was it that European Commission officials, civil servants remember, had pushed through the original approval despite wide public opposition and significant resistance from several EU member state governments?

The case was one tiny outcome of a law-making process driven by corporate and financial imperatives as opposed to popular ones. It carried particular resonance for me given I'd seen both ends of the process, the law-making in Belgium and law-breaking in France. It is the job of good journalism to make such links, to give the necessary context and background to explain how government takes place in our absence, without our knowledge or assent. The challenge ahead is how to create the necessary core of people with sufficient EU knowledge and reporting skills to build a body of stories making that problem clear to everyone.

The same disconnects between people and policies are obvious across much of EU law, some touched on here. All illustrate the same problem of unaccountable power and its capture by narrow, commercial interests at the expense of ordinary European citizens. The serial euro crises flaring up around the continent through 2011, and the unrest provoked by official remedies, are just the latest manifestations.

Those were not my thoughts as I left Brussels in September 1997. Back then, I still had more basic lessons to learn about the realities of our everyday governance and the journalism that accompanies it. Among those, the most personally painful emerged in the switch in UK government from Conservative to Labour, and the silky-tongued Tony Blair. I gleefully sucked up New Labour's "Things Can Only Get Better" campaign message, feeling excited about the mainstream political process for the first time in my life. I cheered at live TV coverage of Michael Portillo's loss of his Enfield Southgate seat to Labour's Stephen Twigg, the pantomime villain's defeat encapsulating his party's routing.

The irony of my Labour leanings was my idea the party would be more positive and engaged towards the European Union. I remained an EU enthusiast despite my misgivings on specific environmental and trade questions. I thought concerted EU action on the environment, a single currency and social protections would produce more benefits than if individual states acted alone. I thought the quality of Britain's domestic politics would improve under the influence of its neighbours, not least the Scandinavians who'd recently joined the club. I also liked Labour's promise to consider electoral reform at home, one of many manifesto pledges it would duly dump. What an idiot I would come to feel.

Those politics lessons were still to come as I packed up my life for London. My destination was the Reuters commodities desk and a job as precious metals correspondent. I'd wanted a move but not that one, which seemed further than ever from what I'd originally planned to do as a journalist.

Once more, the apparent promise of mainstream journalism had got the better of gut instincts suggesting I should try an alternative approach. I'd let myself be persuaded the job was an essential next step in my Reuters apprenticeship, ideal preparation for the serially postponed nirvana of more socially meaningful journalism.

Such dreaming would have to wait. It was time once more for me to take my medicine.

Chapter 3

Fear and greed correspondent

Two hundred Gray's Inn Road certainly looked the part of a major global news hub, its great glass façade giving on to flickering screens, TV studios, and several layers of journalists tapping away at computers. Alongside a few hundred Reuters staff, other tenants included the news operations of ITN and Channels 4 and 5. That meant sharing lifts with the likes of veteran newscasters Trevor McDonald and Jon Snow, their familiar faces standing out among the anonymous ranks of all bar a few of my new colleagues.

Being part of a bustling media hive made me feel a bit brighter about my new job while also rubbing my nose in the fact it was way nothing like what I wanted to be doing. I faced a minimum two years of writing about financial markets before graduating to anything approaching the foreign correspondent's job I'd imagined as a Reuters career. As yet, I'd no idea of the manoeuvrings and politicking it would take to get me out again.

It helped to be joining the commodities desk, a friendly bunch of people covering global markets in coffee, cocoa, base metals and various other physically traded goods. I was to write about daily moves in precious metals, mainly gold but also silver, platinum and palladium. The first two at least carried a whiff of excitement from their association with murder, intrigue and general bad behaviour down the ages. The others were more prosaic, basically expensive industrial metals plagued by opaque supply chains known only to a few well-placed insiders.

My goal was to do the job as well as I could for the shortest time required to get me posted back overseas. It felt like going to have a tooth pulled. I'd accepted the idea that to get on in Reuters I had to learn about financial markets. I supposed the precious metals post was as good a place to do that as any. In hindsight, it taught me a lot more than the market reporting skills I needed for Reuters. The real value was in its lessons on journalism's fundamental failures, even if I didn't appreciate them then.

The dominance of financial reporting for a news organisation like Reuters is not obvious from the outside. Those who know the company probably read its name on newspaper foreign pages or from its news and photos on the Internet. The Reuters of 1997, much the same as today despite its purchase by Thomson Corporation, was rather different from that public face. More than 90 percent of its income came from selling real-time price data and dealing screens to banks and other traders on global financial markets. So nine in every £10 of my salary was from traders and investors using Reuters tools to deal stocks and shares, currencies, bonds and all the rest. Lumped in with all that was our news, the text stories, video and photos that make up the company's media output.

I soon learned about the real version on joining the company in Brussels though it didn't sink in until I got to London. Sitting in the global headquarters of our news operation, the importance of financial market reporting was obvious just from the desk space given over to it. That change in editorial focus had lagged the company's evolution into a financial data and services powerhouse during the previous 25 years. Profits had ballooned with Reuters's spectacular success in selling screen-based financial data to traders. It began with the launch of Monitor Money Rates in 1973, a humble box carrying a few lines of green text and foreign currency prices. The product revolutionized real-time trading and made Reuters a pivotal part of an emerging global electronic marketplace. By the time I joined, those glory days were fading fast as nimbler competitors emerged. Part of the attempt to see them off was to refocus our news priorities towards theirs.

The effect was to shade all our news, more or less subtly, to reflect the interests of traders, bankers and financiers. Editors would endlessly push for our work to reflect "investor risk", meaning reporters should include at least a line or two in their stories about the financial implications for investors in any news event. My job as precious metals correspondent, tucked away by the smoking room in a corner of the fifth floor, was embedded even more deeply with its audience than that. I was part of a great pack of Reuters reporters worldwide dedicated solely to writing market-related stories for traders.

The main audience for my work was highly specialist, bar the rare occasions when major price swings or other news broadened its appeal to a wider public. Among the core readers were precious metals dealers, gold miners and their financiers, central banks and cross-market traders of bonds, foreign currencies and other financial instruments. Gold often moves in the opposite direction to currencies and stock markets, being seen as a "safe haven" investment in times of market turbulence. The idea is that if stocks fall, gold will gain, even if it's not always how things work.

On top of my direct audience were the derivatives traders. These secretive types were already beginning to make their presence felt across all the financial markets when I arrived in London, as I would soon learn. My daily work was to provide them all with regular reports explaining any moves in precious metals along with the results of twice-daily, gold-price fixings. The routine grind didn't leave much time for broader reflection or initiative reporting, even supposing the audience much wanted it.

Overshadowing the work was Bloomberg, our main competitor in financial news. Their swankier, client-friendly dealing terminals, and their often-snappier stories, were a big hit with traders. Their growing presence served as a constant pressure on us to give our specialist audiences the sort of news with which they could trade and make money. All editorial tinkerings were done with these specialist clients in mind. That idea was drummed into us by the requirement that we do regular customer feedback visits as part of our work.

Reuters has always liked to boast of the speed, accuracy and freedom from bias of its news. This client-oriented focus, while commercially logical, makes the last part of that claim impossible. Its market reporting efforts, an increasingly dominant part of its daily output, can never be free from bias. The news priorities that govern it are aimed four square at giving bankers and traders more of what they want to read about. They have nothing to do with being free from bias except in the narrowest possible frame of one bank or market versus another. Rarely does this news feature anything like balance as ordinary members of wider society would understand the term. Nor does it give much more than token space to wider ideals of social justice or the public good.

I would understand in time the academic perspective on how such commercially driven audience focus is bound to sideline public-interest perspectives. For the time being, I was limited to finding out how that inevitability played out in everyday financial journalism.

Journalists tend to brush off the idea that media ownership or income sources inevitably skew the news towards the agenda of whoever's paying. The concept jars with our grandiose self-images as guardians of the truth, righting wrongs and doing service to society. For Reuters, the company's income and ownership structure produce news that is heavily geared towards financial markets, bankers and listed companies. That means established power and money. The problem is both acute and widespread, affecting not just Reuters but the great bulk of financial markets reporting by all news media. Questions of wider public interest are ignored or tacked on only as an after thought. They are never the primary focus of sustained, detailed journalism written for ordinary people.

The inner workings of banking and finance are generally impenetrable to all bar those with a direct interest in learning them. That made starting from scratch highly intimidating, all the more so for the knowledge that most of my audience knew more about my assigned beat than I ever could. Having built my Brussels contacts and detailed specialist knowledge about the European Union over half a decade, I had to put them all aside to begin again from pretty much zero. It's standard practice for Reuters reporters, one that tends to make them highly adept at super-fast but often superficial treatment of many topics. They're far poorer analysts of the fundamentals of power.

My ignorance of precious metals and finance generally made me all the more vulnerable to another major hazard in news reporting, which concerns story sourcing. The people reporters call for information have huge influence on the news perspectives presented in stories. For specialist markets such as precious metals, the potential pool of insiders is tiny, leaving little room to broaden out the story presented. These sourcing effects on stories compound the ones imposed by media income and ownership, biasing story content and perspective further towards the interests of incumbent wealth and power.

Not only are markets highly technical, their members are often a tight-knit bunch of organisations and individuals. As a new reporter hoping to throw light on this world I depended on the patient help and explanations of these people to understand anything of what was going on. Sorcerer to my apprentice was Brian Spoors, my predecessor in the job, a fellow Scot whose genial humour meant no one took themselves too seriously. Brian was a master at landing us the convivial lunch dates with dealers and analysts that made our reporting lives possible. Such basic, human contacts, in what was acknowledged as one of the friendlier City sectors, hugely helped our chances of getting phone calls answered on the market's more hectic days.

Virtually all the material we put in daily reports came directly from market participants or live data streams – there was no other way to do the job. We were necessarily by the market, of the market, for the market. That wouldn't have mattered much if the only thing at stake had been wider public understanding of a small backwater in the global financial system. No one would have needed to worry. That wasn't the case even in 1997, before serial financial crises had blasted the world of banks and finance from newspaper business sections on to front pages around the globe. At that time, I saw speculative attacks on currencies, on poorer countries' economies and even whole regions as things that happened elsewhere. I reasoned even Black Wednesday in 1992, when the pound was forced from the European Exchange Rate Mechanism, was an aberration. The British government had made a policy mistake that was seized on by the market rather than the market having instigated a coup. My sense was still that market crises merely amplified underlying problems, that traders exploited weaknesses or acted in response to prevailing economic conditions. The evidence showing how speculation provokes crises, rather than being just a side effect, had yet to reach anything like today's tottering pile.

Neither speculators nor Reuters story bias were what bothered me most at the time about gold and financial markets more generally. I was more concerned about the effects of the precious metals industries themselves. I knew gold's story was not just about jewellery, sovereign coins and the antics of a few bullion traders in a handful of world financial centres. There were also pollution and land rights issues related to mining and even the question of what justification there could be for mining a metal with so few practical uses. The idea that gold could be hoarded for times of economic crisis or political upheaval was all clear enough even if it all seemed a bit far-fetched. I was aware of the argument that gold was a more reliable form of money than paper currencies but not at any deep level. Like most people, I knew that printing unlimited piles of paper money would send inflation through the roof and have us all pushing barrows of cash around to buy a loaf of bread. I didn't yet get how that related back to the fundamentals of money, the difference between a paper IOU note based on bank loans and debtor repayments versus something backed by a physical store of value such as gold.[44]

The problem I saw was more to do with how miners could make money while leaving the costs of clean up for others to pay for. I could see how our economic system encouraged and rewarded an activity that was so evidently pointless on a practical level, regardless of how profitable it might be for a select few. Bullion market traders themselves would happily joke about the absurdity of their business. Who wouldn't given the industry's basic activity? Miners blast tonnes of metal-bearing rock from beneath the earth, crush it to dust and then refine out tiny amounts of metal that is then stored back underground beneath the streets of places like Zurich. Though I lacked the basic economic vocabulary to make the case, I certainly saw the problem. The explanation is in fact very simple and goes way beyond gold.

That gold miners function and prosper for all their pointlessness is thanks to what economists call negative externalities or transaction spillovers. These are the costs of an action passed to parties who have neither agreed to the action nor draw benefit from it, or only to a small degree. The best-performing miners in financial terms are those who can minimise the costs that fall to them. That applies to basic mining operations, to surface processing of the ore with toxic cyanide or mercury, to refining and the sale of metal. Some miners are undoubtedly more skilled than others but that's only part of the equation. Key to their success is also how well they shuffle onto others the many costs they generate while also maximising the revenue they get from metal sales. That means paying governments as little as possible in royalties or for concessions, including compensation payments to any local people displaced by miners' digging. It entails squeezing workers' wages, their health and any other social benefits while limiting the costs of safety equipment, of environmental protections, site remediation and all the rest. It also means using whatever financial tools are available to cut company finance costs and to maximise gold sales returns, of which more later.

In essence, it's basic capitalism. The more cost passed to others, the more profit for mining companies and their shareholders. The poorer the country of operation, the more costs miners can leave behind. The losers are local workers, their communities, host governments and the environment. The citizens and civil societies of poorer countries usually have the fewest rights and most basic protections, leaving them most prone to abuse. The more criminally lawless an operating environment – places such as the Democratic Republic of the Congo, Mexico, Guatemala, El Salvador and Honduras – the more foreign miners can resort to extreme tactics in crushing any local opponents. It all keeps costs down. That said, the same basic formula applies everywhere gold mining takes place.[45]

I never got my reporting teeth into these issues in the couple of years I was stuck on precious metals. I certainly never wove these basic truths in my regular market reports or backgrounders on the bullion markets. I failed to get out on field trips for on-the-spot reports from mines themselves or in life-cycle analyses of the industry's basic absurdities. That was despite there being some great candidates for in-depth mining stories during my time on the job, the extent of which I grasped only as my broader understanding of both politics and journalism improved.

This shallowness in market reporting, and its lack of any broader context, causes no obvious professional damage to its authors. Those are not elements that the primary audiences, or editors, either ask for or expect.

Financial reporters aren't supposed to be system critics or mould breakers but quite the opposite. Their role is to reflect their market's activities back to the main participants and other interested parties. As it was for gold, so it is for the near totality of financial market coverage by all the big media organisations, Reuters included. In the rare cases when reporters do highlight looming market failures or allude to their structural causes, they generally fail to address or critique the underlying ideology that causes the problem. Perish the thought that they should do so and then take it a step further by routinely building the case for radical systemic reform into their stories. That would be "polemical" journalism, not freedom from bias at all. Any attempt to write it would have been edited out or caused the story to be re-written or "spiked", to use journo-speak for draft articles that don't get published.

Part of what was missing from my stories was that context and background from basic economics theory. Had I drawn on my previous work as an environmental reporter I wouldn't have gone too far wrong. I'd written before about how measures such as gross domestic product give perverse impressions of the underlying reality. A country's GDP rises in the event of an oil tanker disaster polluting its beaches, despite the havoc wrought on the natural world. Money spent on clean up would be chalked up as an economic positive, glossing over the obvious negatives. That same, perverse logic applies to gold mining, the positive of local jobs, income and royalties obscuring the giant costs miners leave behind or pass on to other parties.

No great fuss is made of journalists' routine failure to highlight such problems in stories, or certainly not by the people who determine their career prospects. It is totally normal and what's more, it keeps the clients happy. To start banging on about externalities and companies dumping their costs on society at large is to challenge capitalism itself. It's not an option for a financial markets reporter relying on market sources to do the job. The Reuters paying audience and its shareholders are convinced capitalists, an ideology running through their fabric like the lettering on a stick of candy rock. The dominant mindset of markets, their regulators and supposed media watchdogs is one of unbridled capitalism. It's not usually spelt out so baldly, people use more nuanced terms such as favouring deregulation or supporting "free" markets. What sort of sourpuss could be against freedom after all? The trap is in the Orwellian language, the conjuring of a benign fantasy of freedom when the reality of global markets is they aren't open, free or fair.[46]

Not least is the question of access to bullion markets and the information that drives them. In this, a few major banks and their favoured clients enjoy huge advantages over everyone else. The problem is at its worst in markets for over-the-counter (OTC) derivatives, the custom-designed trades between individual parties who operate outside more-closely regulated public exchanges. This is a huge problem for smaller financial markets such as gold.

The spillover effects of "free" market thinking were painfully clear to many people around the world in September 1997. I was not yet among them. I'd arrived in London with the Asian financial crisis already raging. The recently booming "tiger economies" of Thailand,

South Korea, Malaysia and Indonesia were suffering major shake downs. The market fallouts figured a bit in my work though I was pretty much oblivious to their scale. There were massive impacts and dislocations for people in the region, the poor being hardest hit for all the little they'd had to do with the original problems.

On a professional level, the Asian crisis certainly stretched my perspective on global markets. The Thai baht, having been pegged for years to the US dollar, had collapsed months earlier as currency speculators gambled against its prospects in the face of worsening local debt levels. That market coup triggered a wave of copycat attacks across Southeast Asia and up to South Korea. My beat was not the crisis itself but its impacts on bullion markets, which were relatively simple. Cash-strapped locals were selling their hoarded gold bars, jewellery and other trinkets to keep household incomes afloat as their economies and currencies tanked. The effect was to drive US dollar gold prices lower.

It was easy enough to grasp how more gold supply lowered prices. But there was another, more complicated downward pressure from within the market itself. Prices were also dropping amid sales of financial derivatives linked to gold, basically bets that paid out as gold prices fell. As a market reporter in 1997, you couldn't ignore derivatives. The exchange-traded varieties were relatively transparent due to the disclosure rules governing their operation. OTC contracts, struck in private between individual counterparties, were trickier if not impossible to track, despite their increasing popularity. Their allure was obvious, both for buyers and sellers. They gave buyers maximum flexibility, allowing them to bet on future price swings in shares, currencies, debt or commodities, alone or cross-combined. Sellers took a premium on every bet, just like bookies at the racecourse.

Financial derivatives make total sense in some real-world situations, allowing their holders to hedge against unexpected or unwelcome price swings. Farmers sowing winter crops might want to lock in the next summer's grain price to insure their harvest against potential losses on seed and chemical costs incurred months before. A mine company digging out gold one month, and incurring all the immediate costs it hadn't shunted on to others, might choose to lock in prices for metal delivered months later. For such markets to work, those risk hedgers need a counterparty to stake money on the opposite view. Like so many ideas in finance what began as a useful, specialised tool quickly became a money-making end in itself. For derivatives, what was designed as basic insurance quickly spiralled into global, casino-style speculation that overwhelmed the underlying markets it had been created to assist.

Gold-related derivatives were no different, both in offering miners insurance and in being abused by speculative trade from within the industry and by investment funds using piles of gambling chips built up with borrowed money. They posed miners their own version of the prisoner's dilemma – should they insure their future gold sales, guaranteeing revenues while forcing lower prices on their peers, or hold back to protect the price for everyone? Piled on top of insurance questions was simple greed, with some miners getting carried away with speculative trades that far exceeded any revenue protection. Hedging was always controversial, particularly among mine owners, whose approaches ranged from aggressive price speculation to none at all. Complicating matters was the variety of available bets, which was limited only by the creativity of the bankers confecting them and profiting from their sale. They ranged from simple forward trades, committing sellers to deliver metal at a certain price and date in the future, to increasingly complex, cross-market wagers on multiple moves in prices and interest rates.

Tracking these opaque trades and relating them to daily gold prices was a hit-and-miss affair, probably far more miss than hit. The best I could hope for was to piece together some sort of market picture by cross checking comments from different bullion dealers. All the while, I knew that even if what they said was what they thought or knew, they would invariably have a market position riding on the remarks. That problem is true of financial market reporting generally, not just precious metals.[47]

So at a simple, surface level, the market of September 1997 showed gold slipping lower on the combined effects of physical sales and bets made by miners and hedge funds that prices would drop further. The nature of gold derivatives means betting on lower prices can become a self-fulfilling prophecy as the mechanics of placing the bet usually depresses prices. In the two years I would spend on bullion, most of my time went on writing twice-daily reports on gold and other precious metals prices, their idling sideways or moves up or down. When I arrived gold was about $320 a troy ounce, an arcane measure of weight equal to about 31 grammes. When I left it was barely $20 lower though, luckily for my sanity, it had moved quite a bit between times. Price drivers throughout were rumoured or actual gold sales by central banks and the effects of derivatives trading. Central bank sales of their gold reserves, some done in public and others in secret, knocked prices to 20-year lows around $250. When banks announced plans to limit and coordinate sales while also throttling back their supply of gold for derivatives trading, prices snapped back into the mid $300s. The most notorious sales were undoubtedly the Bank of England's, though plenty of others were busy planning or doing much the same around that time.

For all the protests from miners and long-term gold investors, central bank selling was so much loose change on the scale of world financial markets. Britain's gold sales, ordered by the then chancellor Gordon Brown, raised around $4 billion between July 1999 and March 2002. The proceeds, a fraction of the same gold's value at 2011 prices, were puny compared to the derivatives trades by a single failed hedge fund from the same era. Long-Term Capital Management (LTCM) built its portfolio with $4.8 billion in capital, leveraged to $200 billion using borrowed money, for a fund whose notional value peaked at $1.25 trillion before it blew up completely. Derivatives trading lay at the heart of the whole fiasco.[48]

LTCM's meltdown, despite its eye-popping size at the time, was a mere warm up for the global financial crisis to be unleashed a decade later. Yet both collapses involved the exact same problems of mis-regulated derivatives trading. The first one even featured many of the same players who bombed world markets in 2007.

Derivatives trades form a critical link in the chain joining our financial markets to far broader questions about our political governance structures. Their impenetrability to the outside world, and the evident lack of understanding as to their nature and potential to cause massive economic harm, pose grave risks to our societies and our welfare. Speculative derivatives trading has cost ordinary people and their economies trillions of dollars in the last couple of decades. If that's not a subject for urgent treatment by our so-called democracies, it's hard to imagine what is.

For all the complexities of finance, the basics are startlingly simple. The 2007 crisis was built on failed gambles by a relatively tiny number of individuals, their stack of chips swollen with piles of borrowed money. The result was a gigantic bill for billions of people for years to come.

No one will ever know quite how big a bill. The IMF estimated crisis costs at $11.9 trillion in 2009, including capital injections pumped into collapsing banks, soaking up toxic assets and central bank debt guarantees and liquidity support. The Bank of England in January 2010 estimated governments around the world had spent or committed $14 trillion in a little over a year to prop up the financial system. It estimated indirect costs, those that hit global output, at between $60 trillion and $200 trillion for the world economy and between £1.8 trillion and £7.4 trillion for the UK alone. Abstract numbers are one thing, the reality is people who had nothing to do with the original bets losing jobs, homes and pensions and suffering cuts to their schools and hospitals and any manner of other publicly funded services.[49]

The rumblings of the derivatives meltdown and its mis-regulation were already around in the late 1990s. I even wrote about them occasionally albeit with no idea of their major significance. The first I heard of "regulatory arbitrage" for instance, a fancy term for how bankers shop around between legal jurisdictions for places to do things they can't do at home, was in 1998. The occasion was an interview with the then

London Bullion Market Association chairman Peter Fava, head of precious metals trading at HSBC Midland. He used the term positively, vaunting the City's advantages for bankers over Wall Street's heavier regulations. The reality is such "arbitrage" pumps risk into the global financial system by allowing bankers to evade rules put in place to reduce it. My limited grasp of governance issues meant I was in no position to put that point to Mr Fava. It's easier to see it now, the consequences of regulatory arbitrage being nowhere clearer than with the defunct Lehman Brothers. The Wall Street bank managed to hide its gargantuan, crisis-induced losses for months in 2007 courtesy of an accounting ruse deemed legal in London but not Stateside.[50]

I even wrote about LTCM as the backwash from its self-induced problems hit precious metals markets. The central banks and commercial banks lending gold to speculative hedge funds and miners were rattled by the debacle, fearing the collapse of one hedge fund might reveal a far wider problem in the burgeoning sector.

Faced with a potential systemic hit from a fire sale of LTCM's positions, the Federal Reserve Bank of New York convened a rescue team led by Goldman Sachs, Merrill Lynch and JP Morgan. The rescuers eventually included a dozen of the fund's other big creditors and counterparties, who paid $3.6 billion to keep it from immediate collapse and allow it to wind down its positions. Though not technically a bailout, and with no taxpayer funds used for the operation, the Fed's involvement drew brief criticism before the whole affair was brushed aside as an aberration. The US General Accounting Office said the rescue encouraged "moral hazard", its effects amounting to a massive public subsidy for risk-taking banks.[51]

That schoolmasterly term describes banks' tendency to be more reckless in taking risks when they know government-sponsored lifeboats are ready to pluck them from calamity. Typically for the problem that is moral hazard, the bankers soon shrugged off their worries about hedge funds and got back to selling and trading their gambling chips.

The dangers of moral hazard are nothing new for US regulators. The flawed Federal Reserve Act of 1913, and its failure to curb rampant speculation at that time, led eventually to the 1929 Wall Street Crash. The good news is regulators then got serious, putting in place a whole series of checks on bankers that kept them in their boxes until the 1970s, when rules unravelled once again. Regulators' problem isn't the gambling itself. The damage comes when bets are magnified with large amounts of cheap loans, transforming the work of consenting gamblers into system-wide risk. The result in 1913, once the Great War was out of the way, was a notorious asset-price bubble. Its puncture and collapse sparked multiple bank failures, corporate bankruptcies, mass unemployment and mass human misery in the Great Depression. It all sounds horribly familiar.

Examples of derivatives' potential to cause far-wider economic harm went further than LTCM. The problem, as always, came with bets more or less recklessly placed against the unexpected, those positions swollen with buckets of debt. Things went bad for LTCM when Russia defaulted on its sovereign debt repayments, triggering a market slide that left LTCM's positions deep under water. Another version of the unexpected struck the gold market in September 1999, when European central banks announced plans to coordinate sales of their reserves. The news put an immediate floor under gold prices, making bets on further falls suddenly far riskier than previously. At the same time, the central banks curbed their physical gold lending, a critical part of the derivatives merry-go-round, making the placing of bets much pricier.

So far so straightforward: central banks had changed their reserves policy, reversing downward price pressures just as many miners and other gold fans had begged them to do for years.

The problem, which took a few days to emerge, was that the ensuing price spike ripped the heart from the Ashanti Goldfields Corporation, one of Ghana's most valuable hard-currency assets. The mining house, 20 percent owned by the Ghana government, was listed in London, New York and Accra. It was the continent's biggest gold producer outside South Africa, its Obuasi mine in Ghana boasting proven and probable gold reserves of around 20 million ounces. It also held gold exploration properties in Tanzania, Guinea, Mali, Niger, Senegal, Zimbabwe, Eritrea and Ethiopia.[52]

Gold prices surging from $269 into the $320s an ounce within the trading week should have delighted any mine management, or so you'd have thought. Not so for Ashanti, whose chief executive Sam Jonah later admitted only to "recklessness" in the extent of the bets his company had placed on falling gold prices. Not content with simply hedging prices a few months ahead to insure current operating costs, Ashanti had turned from being mainly a miner to an out-and-out gold speculator. Jonah's company looked like it would sink under a mound of gold-based derivatives turned toxic by the price reverse. Had its 17 bank counterparties called in the $270 million in cash they were due as guarantees on failed bets totalling $570 million, it certainly would have done. But as those banks knew only too well, forcing Ashanti to pay out on its bets would have fired gold prices through the roof. The miner would have had to buy the physical gold required to close out its positions, endangering other miners with similar positions and probably some bankers and hedge funds in the process.[53]

It was echoes of LTCM once more albeit in a different country and a different part of the global financial system. The banks involved again got to call a market "time out" to limit the spread of damage from deals they themselves had arranged. Goldman Sachs was once more in the thick of it directly, on both sides of the Ashanti rescue in fact and in advisory relationships with central banks involved in the pact that sparked the price spike.

Goldman was not only the corporate adviser to Ashanti. It was also the mine company's biggest hedge counterparty thanks to contracts written by its commodity arm J. Aron, a trader on Goldman's account. So the investment bank earned fees advising Ashanti on its massive speculative hedge, in commission from selling the miner a stack of toxic derivatives and from profits made trading the market. Banks operate so-called "Chinese Walls" separating potentially conflicting activities. It beggars belief that all those interests could have been kept apart, not least given the market turmoil.[54]

Goldman profited once more from being a major beneficiary of the rescue it led. The operation landed the bank and its fellow counterparties the rights to the equivalent of Ashanti shares worth $4.75 apiece, less than half their value just days earlier. In return for potentially owning 15% of Ashanti, the banks granted the mining house a three-year waiver on calling in their right to cash deposits. It was expensive insurance for Ashanti given that by the time the deal was struck gold was back at $292 an ounce, meaning no cash deposits would have been due under its existing arrangements.[55]

Once the dust settled, questions remained about how Goldman's commodities arm had traded the market for the duration and what information its traders had known when. Not least of them was a heavy trade Aron made on October 5, before the waiver was agreed.[56]

The rotten smell didn't spread far given the story's complexity and the gold market's niche status. Ashanti counterparties all got a share of the carve up, with Goldman getting bumper servings despite having given the company such awful advice. Far more important for the market was that the rescuers had quietly defused a potential rocket under gold prices. That might have proved disastrous for their own derivatives positions, either directly or through additional counterparty risks from other clients who'd also bet on lower prices. Goldman reportedly kept the Bank of England, the supposed bullion market regulator, up to speed on the Ashanti rescue. That would suggest the regulator wasn't much bothered by the investment bank's multiple roles. You could almost imagine their nods and winks that client pillage and market manipulation were dandy, just as long as it was done in an orderly and discreet fashion.

Goldman and the other counterparty banks came out on top, as did Sam Jonah. Ashanti's minority shareholders were well and truly mugged while ordinary Ghanaians lost a great chunk of their national wealth. Holders of physical gold, having sat through years of falling prices caused by derivatives-driven sales, also lost out on higher prices. The sorry tale concluded in 2004 when AngloGold bought Ashanti for the equivalent of $1.4 billion, or $10.89 per Ashanti share, down from an all-time peak more than double that.[57]

Jonah joined AngloGold's board, his lawyers eventually settling out of court a US class action accusing him of deceiving investors over the state of Ashanti's hedging. The $15 million settlement filing listed the hurdles, potential costs and risks of failure in the way of securing anything more substantial. That pitiful sum, just $0.15 per share equivalent after legal and administration costs, was more than other minority holders got, not to mention ordinary Ghanaians.[58]

From the overall perspective of both journalism and governance questions, Ashanti's was a small story, for all its costs to Ghanaian citizens and Ashanti shareholders around the world. While neither Goldman, its fellow bullion banks, the Bank of England nor Reuters would pretend to owe the injured parties any duty of care, I can certainly imagine Reuters editors attempting to justify the freedom from bias of our news coverage. From the perspective of ordinary people, that certainly wasn't the case.

That is pretty much typical of financial news agencies such as Thomson Reuters, or rather inevitable given the effects of income, ownership and sourcing choices coupled with a baseline ideology that "free" markets can't be wrong. The same is true of its media peers, organisations such as Bloomberg or Dow Jones. Without resolute editorial ambition and resources in the shape of reporters with the time and budget to investigate, it is impossible to get to the bottom of such complicated, multi-country stories. My own reporting was part of that inglorious whole, being superficial and bound by the little time I had to give the story alongside all my routine market reporting duties. Bullion traders would have known straightaway the broad lines of exactly what had happened, where the bodies were buried and how they'd all been saved from having the market blow up in their faces. They had nothing to gain by explaining those realities to the outside world by spilling the beans to pesky journalists.

For my part, nearing the end of my precious metals stint, I was left pondering the mismatch between Ashanti's public statements and what subsequently transpired. Though I didn't write it, I knew the miner's minority interest holders had somehow been royally shafted. The story series planted another question in my mind about what journalism should be doing rather than what it did. As for others in the media, the *FT* wrote an atmospheric account of Ashanti's meltdown. Its piece highlighted Goldman's multiple roles in the affair, though not as a criticism. In glowing prose it described what it saw as the bank's consummate skill in negotiating the rescue despite multiple conflicts of interest, one questionable trade notwithstanding.

The story might have disappeared into the fat file of examples labelled "Westerners gull credulous Africans out of their resources with the help of a few locals" were it not for multiple replays of the same in other markets over the subsequent decade. Some even featured the same conflicted positions of Goldman Sachs, its own-account trading in direct opposition to client interests.

Those conflicts emerged in their most spectacular form in Goldman's dealings with AIG, the insurance giant that all but destroyed itself during the 2007 financial crisis. Its near-death experience came from selling insurance on packages of poor-quality US home loans to Goldman, Société Générale, Deutsche Bank and Merrill Lynch, before markets collapsed. Its $182 billion rescue by the government, the biggest Federal bailout in US history, included some $13 billion paid to Goldman. US citizens paid the Wall Street bank full value for its bets on home loan defaults.[59]

AIG was undoubtedly the major cause of its own meltdown, just like LTCM and Ashanti had been. It was helped on its way by Goldman, whom AIG staff accused of lying about the quality of mortgage deals for which the investment bank sought insurance. Their claims will never get to court – AIG's bailout required that the insurer forfeit its rights to sue creditor banks for any irregularities in the mortgage securities it insured.[60]

AIG was the most spectacular example of some highly questionable practices at Goldman, there have been plenty of others. Matt Taibbi, a swearing, horse-sperm-pie-throwing, pill-popping former pro-basketball player, has been among the best at nailing it all down so far. No really, I mean it. He began one *Rolling Stone* article by describing Goldman as "a great vampire squid wrapped around the face of humanity, relentlessly jamming its blood funnel into anything that smells like money". That certainly wouldn't pass muster with Reuters editors, which is fair enough, though it certainly got his point across.

Maybe wider society doesn't need the vivid imagery of Taibbi-style journalism. It desperately does need more mainstream media coverage that incorporates the systemic critique his work encapsulates. The problem is that none of the major financial news organisations, Reuters included, is doing anything close to that job. Taibbi's book *Griftopia,* ostensibly about the capture of US society by the narrow interests of major money, repeatedly features Goldman. A recurring theme is the bank's record of inflating debt-fuelled bubbles then running off with bags of cash just as the onlookers close their eyes for the bang. Reuters would never attempt such a hatchet job on a valued client, still less expose the underlying problem as being far more wide-ranging than any one bank's antics.[61]

It would be easy but wrong to demonise Goldman while ignoring the wider problems. They include wholesale regulatory failure allied to the associated uselessness and ideological complicity of the politicians who are meant to govern the regulators on our behalf. What's more, those same politicians rely on the donations of bankers and hedge fund owners to fund their political campaigns and party operations. Journalism has to go deeper into the underlying issues rather than skate around on top. Populist stories about bankers' pay and bonuses, and politicians' half-hearted attempts to temper bankers' ongoing smash-and-grab of publicly funded credit and market liquidity, are easy cop-outs. Far worse, they are critical distractions from the more entrenched problems of regulatory failure and political capture. Those two, most obvious in the supine argument that markets should decide, typify governments' surrender of control over what should be significant levers of power at the service of all their citizens.

For all the problems with banks, they are executives of their owners' and wealthier clients' orders, which are basically to make as much money as possible in whatever way they can get away with. That entails speculative bets on global financial markets, on national economies, whole industries or commodity classes. They drive prices up or down as best suits their in-house trading positions and business interests. Ordinary citizens are left helplessly to watch their assets, income and livelihoods get shredded.

It is little comfort that regulators land occasional victories. Goldman paid $550 million in 2010 to settle a crisis-related securities fraud complaint brought by the US Securities and Exchange Commission. The scale of its profits versus such trifling no-fault *civil* penalties, civil meaning no jail time for anyone, makes the odd fraud settlement nothing more than a business cost and public relations blip.[62]

None of this is secret yet we rarely get these details folded in as background or context in regular news stories on the crisis aftermath or banks' ongoing activities. Nor does banks' behaviour drive news priorities or allocation of reporting resources, just as I discovered when the Ashanti story broke. Coverage is superficial, giving the bare bones based on public statements or quotes from the few parties who are prepared to comment. What editorial bravery there might be is hopelessly constrained by Britain's defamation laws and the lack of editorial budget to take stories forward. The news herd's focus quickly moves on. That leaves the fundamental, systemic problems barely disturbed and certainly unexamined or explored in the sort of depth that might bring about any radical change. Specialist investigative journalism operations such as *ProPublica* do a fine job of digging out and amassing evidence of wrongdoing and summarising the charge sheets. Thanks to them, and a few individual reporters and authors elsewhere, we know more than we might have done in crises past. While that's all fine, we need much more. *ProPublica* reporters don't take things the several steps further required to spur fundamental change to the politics or ideology at the root of our misgovernment. That would need broader treatment of the political context in stories, making clear the roadblocks preventing regulatory action and highlighting how moneyed interests hobble political processes at every stage. Their work is no substitute for the sustained supply of context-rich stories for mass audiences that might actually change the way things are.[63]

More people need to start doing that job, either existing journalists or would-be ones driven by a desire to free our societies from the grip of banks and financial markets. The scale of problems means we must learn to join the dots linking banks, financial systems and their regulators to the wider economy. They go to the heart of how we are governed and explain our currently pitiful level of influence over the process. Learning the required politics and journalism is a pressing task for existing journalists and those who aspire to bring about change. It's something I've found tough, both for the complexities involved and because understanding what's involved required me to change so much of what I'd thought before.

Reporting on precious metals, coming on top of the governance questions I'd begun to raise in Brussels, was part of that gradual evolution. By the time I'd witnessed Ashanti's plunder and the end of gold's speculatively driven slump to 20-year lows, prices were back pretty much where they were when I arrived. It was time to get out.

I'd already applied for postings to South America and Asia, still eager to get to a foreign bureau not dominated by financial news reporting. Moving within Reuters was always a lottery, meaning you had to keep fighting to get the jobs you wanted. With no better offer in sight I switched to the London equities desk for what I was promised would be a one-year stint before going back overseas. It was a joyless move, leavened again by good colleagues and the buzz of covering the global bubble in dotcom and technology shares. That sweetened the pill but changed nothing of my underlying frustration. Five and a half years into my Reuters career, a decade on from first dreaming of a job in journalism, my progress felt decidedly mixed.

104

I was no innocent party to the market frenzy, having bought a few shares myself in the months before being assigned to my new job. I was well aware of the potential conflict of interest and told my new editor the first time he asked me to write about one of the companies whose shares I held. The rule at Reuters is that reporters mustn't trade a stock they write about in the month before or after their reports, and that they tell their editors when writing about a stock they own. I complied with all that, though I thought it a lax constraint given the impossibility of not being biased towards such a stock, at the very least unconsciously. Such scruples clearly didn't bother the *Daily Mirror's* self-styled City Slickers, Anil Bhoyrul and James Hipwel. We wrote up the effects of their share tips on little-known tech shares, whose prices often jumped on the day of any mention. It all went wrong when they were found to be buying the shares themselves before tipping them, a crime that got them fired in early 2000 and subsequently convicted.

The two certainly broke the law, as well as the UK Press Complaints Commission's toothless Code of Practice. There's no question of them having been the only ones. Others who sailed very close to illegality were Piers Morgan and Tina Weaver, the two reporters' editor and deputy editor respectively.[64]

As *Guardian* business journalist Paul Murphy rightly remarked in 2005, after Bhoyrul and Hipwel's convictions, hundreds if not thousands of dud companies were floated on stock markets on both sides of the Atlantic during the dotcom bubble. Their shares were puffed to the rafters only to crash when the bubble burst. While US authorities found dozens of cases of illogical optimism crossing into illegality, British regulators proved spectacularly less able or keen-sighted. "Unbelievable as it may sound, the only act of state retribution against those who duped the British public out of so many billions has been through this trial of two young clowns, caught punting with inside knowledge," Murphy wrote.[65]

Their offences were tiny compared with the confidence tricks pulled by banks and start-up companies in some of the share listings during that period, most notoriously in the United States. That included ditching the requirement for companies to show past performance or profitability, a complete break with previous practice in share flotations. Advisory banks went from requiring three years of prior profitability in the companies they backed to one, then just a quarter, then no profitability for the foreseeable future. Compounding the bubble-machine effect were investment bankers' efforts to inflate company valuations and pump their launches. That included practices called price "laddering" and "spinning", what ordinary people would understand better as illegal price manipulation and bribery. The bankers didn't escape entirely unscathed, though again the penalties were mere slaps on the wrists. Goldman settled one such suit with the US Securities and Exchange Commission in 2005, paying $40 million in civil penalties without admitting guilt.[66]

Owning some shares at least put me on a par with most of the people I spoke to each day on the phone, with a tiny financial interest in the subject at hand. The routine was once again writing regular market reports through the day, usually dominated by tech stocks' boom and subsequent bust. Aside from that, the stand-out story from my year of FTSE reporting was one that left me highly cynical about UK regulators and the regulated.

The story, about Granada Media, was again no huge deal in the bigger market picture. It was hugely instructive though. On a personal level, it woke me up to the murky world of information flows between companies, analysts and brokers, much of it highly price sensitive. It is a world apart from ordinary investors and the wider public, as well as most reporters. The story basics were that Granada's shares dropped nearly a quarter in three trading days in September 2000, wiping £2.9 billion off the company's market value. Accompanying the fall were a couple of earnings downgrades by analysts at two banks, Merrill Lynch on day two and ABN Amro on day three. Bank analysts routinely rate publicly quoted companies, recommending to their clients that they buy, hold or sell shares based on their reports. Granada then announced a warning itself, just as its share price bottomed out.

I phoned all three parties, who denied having been in contact over the information. It was not hard to dig out furious, if unattributable, comment from others in the market accusing them of just that. The London Stock Exchange, which has powers to probe unusual stock price movements, gave its usual "no comment on individual cases" in response to my telephoned questions. Needless to say, nothing more was ever heard from them.

Some analysts did fall foul of the law after the dot.com boom went bust though their bosses most certainly did not. Among them was Henry Blodget, a senior research analyst at Merrill Lynch. The Motley Fool investor site later described his name as synonymous with "what amounted to a near-larceny of billions of dollars of shareholder assets". Blodget was censured in 2003, permanently barred from the securities industry and made to pay $4 million to settle charges of misrepresentation. Within an absurdly short space of time, he'd remade himself as an acidic market commentator and guide for small-time investors. So while vast amounts of money can hang on star analysts' opinions and recommendations, the penalties they pay for breaking the law are nothing like as severe or personally brutalising as those faced by conventional criminals guilty of far smaller-scale thieving.[67]

This is not just a question of protecting retail investors, although that's a part of it. More broadly, it is the question of how to regulate financial markets that trade trillions of dollars every working day. Those markets support bets that often have nothing to do with underlying economic rationale. The risks they take place often-inexorable pressure on national policies in countries the world over. All the while, the gamblers are accountable to no one other than their major shareholders, sometimes not even them.[68]

How these markets could be regulated, not to say constrained or even shut down, is the major question not just for specialist regulators and politicians but more vitally for we ordinary citizens. Our societies need journalism that helps citizens to understand the stakes and to build pressure for real democratic reforms and regulation. Such ideas rarely, if ever, figured on the lips of colleagues or editors during my time as a financial markets reporter. Nor did they much feature on our newswires or those of our mainstream competitors. They were on some people's lips, for certain, just not the ones we usually quoted in routine, day-to-day coverage. They certainly didn't inspire our daily news priorities or frame our stories. The views of such powerless non-people, no matter what their numerical strength, just don't rate on news radars.

Any staff journalist thinking otherwise is in for some fun. Framing their everyday work around such perspectives would draw immediate accusations of being "polemical", or having "gone native". Their work would be canned or re-written to fit the status quo, what Reuters calls "freedom from bias". For freelance journalists attempting the same, their commissions would dry up. A rare few, ones like the *Guardian's* George Monbiot, get space in specialist columns. Yet their work runs alongside a flood of daily stories printed without the necessary framing, context or background to give readers the full picture.

During all my time as a stocks reporter, I kept my eyes on the calendar, always looking for an exit. My badgering at last began to have an effect. I got a two-week reporting stint in the Thai capital in July 2000 but failed to get the permanent post. I began learning Spanish in anticipation of a four-month assignment to Buenos Aires though again, with no guarantee of a formal job at the end of it. Finally, I was offered the position of deputy bureau chief in Malaysia, scheduled to last the full three years of a standard posting. Having scrambled for the reference books to find out something about the place, I grabbed at the chance.

The prospect of once again rebooting my reporter's knowledge base postponed any deeper processing of what I'd learnt about financial markets reporting. I'd certainly got a sense of the loaded dice favouring insiders, how hard it was to get beyond the superficial, and markets' impacts and importance for society. I'd yet to build the incidents of poor governance and regulatory failure into any wider critique of democracy or journalism.

Big parts of the puzzle were still missing. I still believed in the basic quality of our democracies even though I could gripe with the best of them about individual politicians and their parties. I still thought elections a fair means to decide which individuals got to govern a country and that the differences between political parties made such contests worthwhile. My faith in all that took a beating during my last months in London as I watched George W Bush and Al Gore's infamous battle for the US presidency.

It began with the live election-night results I watched during daylight hours in the Reuters London bureau. Our US coverage, like that of all the major news organisations tracking the outcome, swung from calling the election first Gore's way then flipping it to Bush after his startling victory in Florida. Those doubts got worse in the following weeks of contested counts, re-counts and endless tussles between opposing legal teams. Bush's eventual victory, courtesy of a Republican-friendly Supreme Court in December 2000, drove home my sense of the whole sorry spectacle. If that was the state of the world's most powerful democracy then look out the rest of us. That impression only got worse with revelations about the systematic scrubbing of voter lists to cut potential Democrat support in Florida, a state governed by Bush's fellow Republican and brother Jeb.[69]

For all their critical importance globally, US domestic politics were a world away from where I was going. At last, I thought, I was heading for something like the foreign correspondent's job I'd first imagined in the university careers office. Of the little I knew about what lay ahead, I was certain it would give me a better sense of what it was like being on the wrong end of financial markets.

As things turned out, that wasn't even the half of it.

Chapter 4

Malaysian awakenings

Waking up after my first night in the modern heart of Kuala Lumpur, though befuddled by jet lag, I definitely heard a cockerel crowing. Out in the cityscape stretched far below my hotel window, hidden among multi-storey blocks dominated by the steepling, steel columns of the Petronas Twin Towers, was a chicken.

It was my first taste of what would be a common experience during three-and-a-half years in Malaysia, that of having my pre-conceived ideas dumped firmly on their heads. What seemed initially to be one thing would then prove to be its opposite before finally turning out to be a bit of both at once. Malaysians seemed to revel in the associated confusion and ambiguity, even when they themselves were its victims. They even had a word for it – *sandiwara* – meaning charade or farce. They used it most often in reference to their politics and politicians, when things weren't exactly what they first seemed. Here was my introduction to it, high up in a luxury hotel room in the country's capital, lying alongside an apparently poverty-stricken Malay settlement called *Kampung Baru*, home to my inadvertent alarm clock. I soon learnt the capital was neither as wealthy as it seemed nor the settlement as poor, the latter's residents having refused multi-million-dollar enticements to develop their land.

Though it was hard to start with, I got used to this permanent state of uncertainty over the coming years. What made it tricky in the beginning, which added to the disorientation, was the little I knew about the place. Bar some weeks reporting in Thailand the previous year, and a short holiday tacked on the end, I had zero experience and little more knowledge of Southeast Asia, its myriad cultures, histories and politics. What homework I'd done was limited to some hastily bought and digested books, not least because just a couple of months before I'd been learning Spanish and mugging up on Argentina. Nearly seven years with Reuters, split equally between Brussels and London, seemed little help to me now.

My situation was normal, if not without its damaging effects. Reporters who arrive badly prepared in foreign countries are prone to doing, saying and writing the most crassly ill-informed things. Their ignorance can last for months or longer on postings that may not stretch beyond three years. It's worse for short-stay assignments and the emergency journalism of war zones. It means reporters rely heavily on local experts, Western diplomats and market analysts, using their views and intelligence to camouflage their own ignorance, inevitably colouring their stories. Local reporting staff help save new arrivals some of their blushes. They supply contacts, stories, quotes and colour from their long-term or native knowledge of a country. Their work feeds into stories written from a Western perspective, drafted or re-written by the newcomer and edited on regional news desks, in my case Singapore.

The effect is to homogenise global news, placing minority, rich-world views over majority, poorer ones. It bolsters the flaws, imbalances and inequities of existing power structures. This was my world.

An example that unfolded as I arrived in Malaysia concerned political cronyism and corruption. Local Malaysian conglomerates habitually work closely with government, muddying the line between business and politics. We wrote plenty of critical articles on that theme, pitched as ever with foreign investors in mind. There was no shortage of material. The hypocrisy of beating up on Malaysian practices in isolation became clear in the coming months. US energy giant Enron's sudden collapse from stock-market superstar into bankruptcy, and its close relations with the George W Bush administration, outshone in sheer chutzpah anything Malaysia could ever produce. Somehow the tenor of Reuters coverage never reflected that. We never allowed ourselves the same critical licence in the United States as we did in Malaysia or other such countries, casually linking business shenanigans to government. The contrast was striking. More important for me, watching events from Malaysia gave a jolt to my idea that crony capitalism was somehow limited to developing countries.

I was due a similar lesson on environmental issues. Inevitable tensions arose from Malaysia's efforts to grow and develop versus the damage that growth wrought on its tropical forests and their spectacular store of endemic species. European customers gladly bought Malaysian raw materials – wood pulp, palm oil and crude oil – while being quick to criticise its development practices. Malaysians legitimately complained of EU countries' hypocrisy in demanding that they protect their natural wealth despite the Europeans having long-ago destroyed most of their own in getting rich themselves. That was to say nothing of Europeans' rapacious demand for stuff, made from the very same resources they told Malaysia not to exploit. And there was me thinking EU countries were the good guys, at least versus the United States.

Even with the best preparation in the world, which is rare for journalists, the complexities of Malaysia and its neighbours would have taken some getting used to. My own compatriots, including at least one near relative, were partly to blame. Britain's rule over Malaya, one of its richest colonies, suffuses the place to this day. The British brought in Chinese and Indian coolie labour to work their tin mines and rubber plantations. They mixed new cultures, languages and traditions into the existing ones of majority Muslim Malays. Understanding the politics of these different populations from my conventional Western perspective on democracy and journalism would keep me busy throughout the posting. The frequent confusion I experienced, though at times profoundly unsettling, was a gift that left little place for complacency.

Supreme among the sources of confusion was the ever-reliable Mahathir Mohamad, whose 22 years as prime minister came to a voluntary end while I was there. The at-times irascible, then charming, then tearful former medical doctor, of fierce intelligence and personal drive, was a dream journalistic assignment. During frequent speeches or otherwise tedious ceremonies to launch this or that product or conference, Mahathir's targets for verbal skewerings were nothing if not varied. One day it might be his fellow Malays or other Malaysians.

Another it would be neighbouring arch-rival Singapore or perhaps the world's Muslims, Jews, Americans, British or Australians. A favourite was the outriders of global speculative capital, typified by the likes of George Soros. What's more, the prime minister would often take reporters' questions, meaning frequent treks out of the office to whatever event he was at, just to get an official line on the day's story.

The sheer variety of targets, and the gap between Mahathir's arguments and the investor-friendly perspective at Reuters, meant much of what he said went unreported. I had various explanations for that, perhaps the main one being he'd said similar things before so there was little new to report. Mahathir's own contradictions, that he would castigate others while clamping down on his political opponents, also damaged his credibility. Another was that his comments clashed so obviously with the status-quo, Western thinking that they could simply be ignored. Whether I wrote up all of Mahathir's speeches or not, I benefited from hearing them. They were a good education in how the world's poorer states generally see the richer ones.

For all the criticisms of Mahathir's heavy-handed tactics at home, he was lionised in the Muslim world and in poorer countries seeking to emulate Malaysia's robust economic and social progress. Admirers lauded his record in developing the country and lifting millions of its people out of poverty, helped by a decade of 8 percent annual growth through to 1997. They particularly praised his handling of the Asian financial crisis, including Malaysia's unique approach to fending off speculative attacks on its currency. The country refused IMF demands for deregulation and privatisations in return for emergency help and asset firesales to foreigners. That Mahathir repeatedly and caustically derided global currency dealers and hedge funds, constituencies that usually either terrify politicians or co-opt them, was all to his credit.

Compared with Mahathir's fiery tongue, most other Malaysian official sources were pitiful. That was if they could be reached at all let alone coaxed into saying anything. Partly that was the natural, modest reticence of Malays. Mainly it was because of an atmosphere of fear pervading the country when matters turned remotely political or controversial. Those fears were legitimate, fuelled by the real danger, and past examples, of official censure.

The effect was to paralyse Malaysian media almost totally. Reinforcing the effect were media ownership structures, leading directly or indirectly back to government, to state-friendly businesses, or both. I found the newspapers useful for picking up basic facts, and clues about what was really happening, but not much else. Had I been able to read any of the Chinese, Malay or Tamil ones I would have done a bit better. Reading or watching the English-language news was like blocking your nose while emptying the rubbish, an essential chore to be endured. Stories followed government lines, puffing up the establishment while ignoring or denigrating opposition figures and their arguments. I hadn't clocked how Reuters did much the same thing on a bigger scale, albeit with far greater subtlety, its unwavering loyalty being towards the interests of global finance. Rare alternatives such as the online *malaysiakini* or the opposition's *Harakah* shone out from their peers. Reporters from both paid the price, suffering insults at government news conferences, houndings in their daily work and threats delivered via the columns of other publications.

As a newly arrived and under-informed foreign journalist, I found it hard to know where reporting boundaries lay. Just weeks into my assignment, Mahathir was lambasting both local and foreign media. He slammed *malaysiakini* staff as a bunch of traitors. They'd allegedly taken money from some funding body set up by the hated Soros, by then the poster-boy bogeyman for financial crises the world over. At the same time, the Malaysian Home Ministry blocked circulation of two foreign news magazines for criticising the country and portraying Mahathir as tired and politically out of touch. Not helping matters was the critical foreign media coverage of inter-racial clashes between Malays and Indians. The reality was that any coverage would have angered the authorities. Six people killed and 30 more wounded in a poor area outside Kuala Lumpur was not the news they wanted reported about Malaysia. Ministers and government-friendly newspapers joined in the sledging of foreign media and their locally hired staff.

A few insults and some lost magazine sales were one thing, what I found hard to know was what will to act lay behind all the bluster.

Malaysia was clearly nothing like the *Killing Fields* scenario of nearby Cambodia, either for the local population or for journalists. Nor did it present anything of the dangers run by reporters or civilians in war zones or the more murderous environments of Central and South America and elsewhere. Things clearly weren't that great though. The country scored a pretty miserable 110th among 139 countries surveyed in the Reporters Without Borders Press Freedom Index of 2002.

Whatever the real level of threat, it was always going to be most acute for local reporters. We foreigners always knew we could just leave if ever things got too hairy.[70]

Using relentless insults, threats, occasional arrest and accompanying physical violence on media critics is an unfailingly effective tactic. It works not just in midway autocratic regimes such as Malaysia's but also in far more violent ones. Attacks on the media, by governments and their supporters, have real-time, all-pervasive effects. They choke down the number and tone of critical stories. They certainly affected our daily operations early on during my Kuala Lumpur posting, albeit not as acutely as they did local media. Not least was that articles took far longer to report, to write and to edit in the face of aggressive responses to even the slightest error or misplaced nuance in their production.

The process of neutering establishment-critical media is subtler in the world's most powerful representative democracies. It works on multiple levels in the face of people's real, hard-fought freedoms to speak, to protest and to organise. Among its daily expressions is the way most commercial media select and frame their stories in ways that legitimise the status quo. Established power structures and their representatives get the air time and column inches to pump their case, often without critical context. Alternative, more socially progressive or non-establishment perspectives get pushed to the margins, their treatment accompanied by more aggressive questioning and critical framing within stories.

My journalism at Reuters was a tiny bit-part of that neutering process. Most of what I'd done to date was a long way shy of my original ambition to do socially progressive reporting as a foreign correspondent. I'd written endless stories about the European Union and financial markets, barely any of them relevant to what I'd planned. Now that I'd got to Malaysia, and a job more like I'd imagined, I was forced to think more critically about that ambition and its consequences. Until then, I'd ignored how vacuous and irrelevant the bulk of my work had been. The occasional flashes of doubt I'd had, about governance issues or the quality of Reuters reporting, should have woken me up to the broader problem. Instead, I'd pushed the doubts aside, comforting myself with the idea that I was heading in the right general direction. Malaysia's more aggressive reporting environment forced me back to first principles, rebooting my ideas about both politics and journalism.

Stories on crony capitalism and the environment certainly highlighted the contradictions in my own politics. They also made me start thinking about how such contradictions conditioned my journalism, how they made me a part of a process that skewed the output of mainstream media towards the interests of established power.

A clear example was how I used to cite various US State Department reports criticising the Malaysian government's rights record. They would detail the abuses and list various laws the government had used to clamp down on dissent. Most of the latter were legacies of British colonial rule, covering sedition, official secrets and defamation. I was to fall foul of the last one myself before leaving Malaysia, getting sued for libel over a story about the national carmaker Proton.[71]

There was nothing wrong with US criticisms, they were bang on the mark. Where I and my Reuters colleagues routinely fell down was in our failure to balance them. We should have put some context about Washington's own human rights record since World War II, particularly in its foreign policy. Republican and Democratic presidents alike over that period had tried to overthrow democratically elected governments around the world, or grossly interfere in their elections.

For decades, they'd backed many of the most brutal dictators, installing some of them in office and keeping them there against popular will. All that before US invasions of Afghanistan and Iraq under the guise of Washington's perpetual "war on terror".[72]

A sense of that US rights record to qualify State Department criticisms would have brought some much-needed balance to my stories. I didn't think to put it in, blind as I somehow was to its direct relevance. Nor did my editors make good the error, as they would certainly have done had the story been about lesser powers criticising other countries or the United States itself.

Such unthinking omission is no rank carelessness. Reuters is not in the business of system critique. Its role is to transmit accurately and quickly the words and deeds of the powerful and to frame its stories according to their world view, even if that's not what's written on the packet. Those Reuters reporters or editors who stray from official narratives, and some certainly do, soon face accusations of "bias" or of having somehow gone native. It's easier to blot out the logical contradictions than take a path that leads inevitably to conventional career suicide. That phenomenon is an effect of what media critics call "flak", the process by which reporters or media outlets who question establishment positions are discouraged or discredited. It is far more insidious, and far less known or acknowledged, than the straight-out intimidation or arrest of reporters in more obviously media-hostile regimes such as Malaysia.

Without that balancing context, my reports of US criticisms would have rung hollow for those who are alive to the double standards of Western governments and media. If Reuters stories out of Washington had been similarly critical of US government abuses abroad, that would have helped balance our file of stories. That barely ever happened and certainly not to the extent that US actions would have justified. The bar for critical Reuters coverage of the United States stood far higher than the one for Malaysia.

Better still would be consistent reporting of rights issues across the world according to a universal scale of abuse. News cover would reflect the extent and severity of all abuses committed by governments, at home and abroad, directly or via proxies. That would give a far clearer perspective of reality, endowing the journalism with accuracy and fairness.

Such a yardstick would drop Malaysia way off the scale in any global table. Washington and friends, the United Kingdom included, would remain much nearer the top, even before their scatter-gun responses to the 9/11 attacks.

Such gross inconsistencies, not to say the hypocrisy they betrayed, were what made Mahathir so furious with his Western critics, including foreign reporters. While Washington's record didn't excuse the Mahathir government's rights abuses, it was directly relevant context that begged inclusion in our stories. He was justified in being angry.

Such poor journalism serves none other than the rights abusers themselves. They are quick to highlight the double standards. Consciously or not, that's pretty much what we had at Reuters, certainly for our Malaysian human rights stories of early 2001.

It was an example of how mainstream media skate over or bury those truths that are inconvenient to powerful elites in major representative democracies. Vital background facts never make it as "boiler-plate" paragraphs, the recurring sound bites or snippets of information recycled endlessly in running stories. You would never read: *"The United States government, itself guilty of human rights abuses domestically and in dozens of countries around the world in recent decades, criticised XYZ".*

Complaints about such double standards arose all the time in Malaysia. What was true for our human rights coverage held good for other topics, including the way we covered elections and questions of democracy. Despite George W Bush's farcical election in 2000, there was rarely any reference to the illegitimacy of his victory in news stories during his presidency. Imagine the qualifying paragraphs in stories about Venezuela's Hugo Chavez or even Mahathir had something

119

similar happened in their elections. The legitimacy point should at least have figured as context in stories about the Bush government's frequent claims to be acting in the interests of freedom and democracy. Something like: *"Our aim is to bring democracy and free elections to the people of Iraq," said Bush. The US President, handed power by a Republican-friendly Supreme Court that ignored major voting irregularities in Florida, is a poor champion of democracy.*

Not likely.

The nuances of media coverage weren't the biggest concern of Mahathir's domestic opponents during my time in the country. His ex-deputy Anwar Ibrahim was in prison on highly dubious charges of corruption and sodomy. Four months into my posting, in April 2001, seven of his supporters joined him behind bars. Police arrested them under British-era internal security laws allowing detention without trial. Their alleged crimes included possessing explosives for use at an upcoming public rally.

It was typical that to get any official comment on arrests reporters had to troop off to the day's Mahathir engagement, which proved to be a classic of its kind. A large press pack turned out for what would normally have been a mundane event, the launch of a Malaysian dental amalgam product. We sat through dull speeches, a sound-and-light show featuring a giant model molar and even a live tooth filling – I couldn't help but think of the torture scene from *Marathon Man*. Only then did we get to question the prime minister. In the scrum around Mahathir, who sat serenely in an armchair, I asked for a comment on the recent arrests. He never missed a beat, firing back that police, not human rights groups, were responsible for national security.

"The foreign media will bash at us. They have never said anything (good) about us even if we are very nice. So we have a duty to the people, our country. They can go and fry their faces," he replied.

It took me all my time not to laugh out loud while also trying to scribble down the quote. Three more arrests followed in the days after, bringing the total to 10 people, the majority of them being pro-Anwar opposition figures. Despite the serious charges, the government never produced the evidence to support them. Authorities released two men within weeks, another couple won their releases via the courts while the rest stayed in jail for the full two years.[73]

The arrests, and threats of more to follow, dealt a huge blow to Anwar's camp. They marked a trademark Mahathir response to political opponents who risked becoming an effective force against him. It was a reminder that anyone could be detained at any time, for any reason, or even for no reason at all.

I found it ironic that Mahathir's genuine success in improving the lives of Malaysians generally, his fellow Malays particularly, should then crash into its inevitable consequence. Malaysia's wealthier, better-educated citizenry was agitating for more political freedom. Mahathir seemed unable either to appreciate the pressures he himself had generated or to accommodate them. Just that point was made to me a couple of months later during an interview with Harun Mahmud Hashim, vice chairman of the-then-one-year-old Human Rights Commission of Malaysia.

"We have got to that level where people are asking for freedom of expression, freedom of assembly, all these various freedoms," said Harun, a former judge. His Commission's biggest challenge was to change mindsets, those of the authorities most of all. For all that's changed in Malaysia since, he might as well have been speaking in 2011, a whole decade and two prime ministers later.

That failure to accommodate opposing views is typical of leaders grown used to high office. Once in power, bedazzled by their sense of self, they spend their time doing everything they can to stay there. For outright dictators, that means crushing opponents and their views by all means available. Mahathir's version was less brutal, allowing regular elections that were won by his ruling coalition to leave him in power just the same. He clamped down on whatever looked like threatening that. The majority of local media were loyal to his coalition, meaning opposition figures struggled to get their messages out to the electorate.

When the opposition did make any inroads, their leaders were imprisoned, neutering their efforts.

Malaysia-style democracies can expect sustained, external criticisms of their political regimes – justifiably so. Western politicians lecture them on how to do better and their national media write up the comments as news. Those politicians' choice of targets – hector Malaysia, say nothing rude about Saudi Arabia or Israel – influences which countries get written about most critically. The likes of Britain and the United States, for all their out-sized impacts on the rest of the world, get nothing like the same treatment. Those same politicians who criticize other countries would bridle at such impertinent scrutiny of their own systems. Not the same thing at all, they'd say. Those same reporters who might write about Malaysia's democratic shortcomings are less ready to consider their own governments' lack of popular accountability.

I hadn't yet made the connection between the poor quality of Western-style democracy and its light-touch media treatment, deep as I was in Malaysia's. My first direct taste of the local version came in state elections in the Borneo island state of Sarawak. I went there for a week just prior to the September 11 suicide attacks, with the state vote due later that same month.

Fallout from the bombings rippled instantly into the politics of a place ruled by Abdul Taib bin Mahmud since 1981. Before the attacks, opposition parties looked likely to deny the chief minister his habitual walkover. Even the government-friendly *New Straits Times* predicted that 10 of the 62 contested seats might fall to the opposition. My research for a package of stories – on state politics, jungle biopharmaceuticals, a controversial hydroelectric dam and rainforest logging – all threw up the same thing. Everywhere were complaints about native land title and profound dissatisfaction with the state government's development record.

A regal Taib brushed that all aside as so much "hot propaganda" when I met him in his gilt-edged state offices. Same thing for the suggestion that Sarawak's natural wealth was heaped on well-connected oil palm planters, rainforest loggers, politicians and their families. The mismatch between what I'd seen and what Taib said felt surreal. Out front, his driver touched up the tyres of his vintage ministerial Rolls with dabs of black paint.

Taib's confidence proved emphatically well placed in the vote a couple of weeks later. He won in a landslide. Malaysia's ruling powers had made full use of the 9/11 attacks to tar their opponents as Muslim extremists. Government supporters from Mahathir downwards raised the spectre of militancy, painting the opposition as being bent on a *jihad* or holy struggle against them. The alliance lost only one seat.[74]

Watching it all was pretty dispiriting, not least the mismatch between what government and ordinary people said. September 11 pretty much set the tone for Malaysian domestic politics until well after I left in August 2004, including for the government general election victory of that year. Authorities kept up their drumbeat allegations of militancy, arresting dozens of suspects. Their frequent accusations, maybe some even justified, we could never tell, made the opposition's chances of electoral success pretty much nil.

Sarawak was the classic example of the government's advantages, exaggerated by its outsize allocation of national parliamentary seats. The use of state personnel for campaigning, and government cars, boats and helicopters to ferry ruling party candidates around, all played their parts in the win. Manipulation of the electoral system, media bias and outright vote buying also helped tremendously.[75]

Sowing fear to silence or discredit would-be reformers and critics is an effective tactic for any government. Journalists must always be on guard against it. I got a taste of it myself just hours after the 9/11 attacks, phoning a news alert to our Singapore desk before evacuating our office along with everyone else in the Petronas Towers. What police first described as a routine fire drill turned out to have been an opportunistic bomb hoax. By then, I'd already scampered down 32 floors in what at the time was the world's tallest building, images of exploding airliners from the previous night's live TV coverage crowding my mind.

The event turned a giant spotlight on several running debates not just in Malaysia but throughout the Islamic world. Among the most controversial was how sacred Islamic law or *sharia* should apply to family matters and in the treatment of women. Those questions had struck me as I first landed in Malaysia to see the head scarves or *tudungs* worn by so many Malay women. Local politicians, mostly men, would muddy the lines between politics and religion, opposition ones more even than those in government. I found the co-mingling of private faith and public policy unsettling, as I would have done regardless of the religion. Raised in a post-1960s Europe, my view is that divorce, adultery, rape, domestic violence and women's dress should be kept separate from electoral politics. For unapologetically male-dominated societies such as Malaysia's, that was all the more important. Among the rare Malaysians to tackle the debate head on was Zainah Anwar, executive director of the local campaign group Sisters in Islam.[76]

Reuters, like most Western media organisations, is poorly equipped and even less disposed to tackle inter-faith questions or spirituality. It generally did a decent job on the Pope and Catholicism but that was pretty much as far as it went. It is a big blind spot given the polarisation of debate since 9/11, not least the wholesale demonising of Muslims and Islam.

The point was brought home to me during the Malaysian general elections of 2004. I'd interviewed a senior figure from the opposition Pan-Malaysian Islamic Party (PAS) only to see the article stagnate on the desk for days. It was then canned by one of my news editors in Singapore. Nik Abdul Aziz bin Nik Mat, an old-style rural Malay cleric, had been characteristically critical of the West, not least the United States. Not for us, said the editor, who decided unilaterally to keep the interview from the Reuters news file. "Why should we give some bit-part politician free hits at United States?" the editor asked. It was an indefensible call, helping to maintain the chronic imbalance of our output. We would gladly cover Western leaders' habitual talk about the alleged, all-pervasive threat of radical Islam. It was far harder to cover what people said in reply, even senior politicians.

My professional frustrations in covering Malaysian politics were nothing compared with those of ordinary citizens. They got no chance of the more pluralistic governance structures that may have been possible with the help of more balanced media coverage. I wouldn't say the PAS candidates I met would necessarily have been better than the incumbents. Their religious zeal always unsettled the sizeable non-Muslim Chinese and Indian constituencies of Malaysia's multi-faith electorate. Malaysia's stilted political conversation meant poorer political options all round.

The very personal upside was the workshop I got in representative democracy's easy malleability and potential for abuse. I saw for myself how periodic votes in elections supposedly free and fair could hide all manner of tricks to keep existing elites in power. It opened the way for me to look further, to consider how little real power the ballot box gives ordinary voters in electoral democracies the world over. Could it be that middle-income, developing countries such as Malaysia were not the exception but the rule?

There are various causes for this gap between democratic illusions and reality. A big one concerns the flaws inherent in all systems of representative government: everything that's lost in transit between the wishes of we the people and the actions of our governors.

A second is in the gradual convergence of thinking among supposedly different political parties in the world's dominant Western powers, particularly the United States and Britain. For all the apparent differences, opposing parties favour similar versions of supposedly unfettered competition, market deregulation and reduction of government. Those politics apply not just domestically but also in their foreign policy goals. Behind such policies lies the insidious, unelected and rarely acknowledged power of global financial markets and corporations. Greasing the wheel are their permanent facilitators in selected global bureaucracies such as the International Monetary Fund and the World Trade Organisation.

I was far more attuned to the second factor than to the first, the result of having steeped myself in both financial market and global trade reporting by the time I got to Malaysia. Mahathir's many speeches on the unchecked power of markets over sovereign governments made for an extended tutorial. There were plenty of sympathetic echoes from the heads of state and government who visited the country. Among them was long-time Cuban leader Fidel Castro, who hailed Mahathir as a fellow rebel in May 2001. He called on his Latin American neighbours to emulate the Malaysian prime minister's example. Far better they do that, he said, than bending to the political winds out of Washington and its ideological enforcers at the IMF and World Bank.

I sat patiently through Castro's 45-minute speech and the hour and a half he spent answering just three questions from the floor. All the while, I itched to put some of my own. While I agreed with much of what the ageing revolutionary had said about globalisation, I was keen to ask about his treatment of domestic opponents. More particularly, I wanted to know how it was that both Cuba and Malaysia could champion the world's poor majority on global issues while simultaneously clamping down on domestic dissidents.

I reworked potential questions in my mind, translating them into my rudimentary Spanish in the hope of waylaying one of the late 20th century's political icons. What I wanted to avoid was garbling out some softball, star-struck questions.

It pretty much worked, though no thanks to my Spanish – Castro's interpreter having to re-translate my request for a moment of *El Presidente's* time as he marched for the exits. Pressed in by fellow reporters and camera crews, I put my questions standing face to face with their target. Castro is tall, standing several inches higher than six feet. That meant I had to juggle my notebook and brain while glancing up to put more questions and stop him leaving. Though he seemed relaxed enough, he punctuated comments on the qualities of Cuban democracy with measured prods of his finger to my chest.

"In no country of the world is the population more participatory than it is in our country... They are very well informed by the media," he said. It would have helped to have had to hand a copy of the 2002 Press Freedom Index. It put Cuba 134th, blaming the country's lack of news diversity and routine imprisonment of journalists.

My brush with Castro wasn't so different from trying to winkle answers from the other political leaders and lesser politicians I approached over the years. They routinely dodged the issues or denied enough time for discussion or follow-up questions.

Trying to question Russia's Vladimir Putin in Malaysia got me shoved aside by his giant security guards. "You're lucky I did not break your legs," said a blond one in thickly accented English after his boss had swept by, all smiles.

I got much the same, minus the direct menace of physical harm, trying to waylay Bill Clinton during a walkabout in the Dutch town of Delft. I made it half way into a question about Monica Lewinsky before a presidential guard cut me off with a bark of "no press".

Set-piece political news conferences, one of the few chances for reporters to question leaders directly, are often little better. If you manage to get picked to ask something there is often little chance of a follow-up if the target dodges the question, as they so often do. My sense of White House and Downing Street news conferences, I never did any myself, is that the chances of straight answers are no better.

At least Castro's answers got me thinking. He contrasted Malaysia and Cuba's social measures of infant mortality, life expectancy and literacy with those of the Latin American countries who followed Western development models. His argument stood up then and stands today, not just in Cuba's own back yard. Such initially hopeful beacons of democratic emancipation as South Africa are a case in point. Multi-racial elections in place since 1994 put it among the world's 115 democracies in the widely cited Freedom House survey of 2010, yet social progress stagnated.[77]

Two decades since Nelson Mandela's joyous walk from prison, democracy for his country had brought limited practical gains for everyday citizens. The development measures Castro cited make for ugly reading in Pretoria, despite the country's vast mineral wealth. Cuba's two-man dictatorship under the Castros, since 1959, managed the world's 51st best human development score in 2007. South Africa came 129th despite its voters being on average nearly half as wealthy again per head than Cubans. IMF-style deregulation and privatisation, in cahoots with the old elite, have a lot to answer for in that.[78]

This was a complex debate to have broached during an impromptu interview with Castro. I was doomed to end up frustrated. It was a useful encounter though. I realised elections were of little use if they left most citizens in poverty and most of the money in the pockets of a tiny few.

Castro's set-piece speech had included serial digs at the Free Trade Area of the Americas, an embryonic agreement to reduce trade barriers between all countries in the Americas, bar Cuba.[79] Here at last was a national leader giving coherent counter arguments to the ones I'd glimpsed back in Brussels, half a world away and nearly a decade past. Developing countries had learnt by experience how rich-countries' promises of benefits for all from increased global trade had been so much rubbish. The division of spoils was decidedly skewed towards those same rich countries, or rather the senior staff and shareholders of their multinational corporations.

Castro's arguments enjoyed wide currency in the developing world for all their relative rarity on the pages and airwaves of Western media such as Reuters. Similar points were made by the array of protesters who'd help stymie new trade talks in Seattle in 1999 and in plenty of other cities since. The emergent global justice movement rightly lumped together the WTO, the IMF and World Bank as major parts of the problem.

Building these perspectives into regular coverage of trade and other global issues was near impossible at Reuters. While fall out from global misgovernment is everywhere, its extent and underlying causes are tackled only fitfully in mainstream media. Policies that promote corporate tax dodges, deregulation, privatization and the unrestrained global flow of speculative capital – all sold under the banner of "free" markets – are of huge benefit to transnational corporations. The big winners are the bankers and traders who provide the bulk of earnings for a company such as today's Thomson Reuters. Neither the financial news agency nor its advertising-dependent media clients ever carry more than token nips to the hands that feed them and never with the necessary depth and context as it relates to our governance. To do so would be to transgress editorial rules requiring that stories carry establishment or corporate voices as "balance". It would risk "flak" attacks on the coverage itself, and on its writers, while affronting editorial ideologies.

A story I wrote in September 2001 was a neat-if-unexceptional example. With Castro and Mahathir's remarks ringing in my ears, I was on the hunt for Reuters-acceptable stories in this vein. The best I managed from my Kuala Lumpur dateline was a piece on business executives struggling for a corporate response to the global justice movement. It featured a series of quotes from confused, big-brand executives from the likes of Shell and the corporate umbrella group, the World Council for Sustainable Business Development.

I was by now much better aware of the underlying issues and counter arguments in the global trade debate. I'd witnessed Western governments' habitual hypocrisy in global negotiations over the years. I'd also read up on the non-corporate perspective in the likes of Naomi Klein's classic *No Logo*.

The lure of Reuters, for me, had always been what I'd thought was its multicultural perspective. I'd imagined a melting pot of different ideas and views in a company with reporting bureaus dotted across the globe. As a Scotsman in England, I had never felt satisfied by the Anglo-centric perspective of London-based media, another reason I'd been attracted to Reuters as an alternative in the first place. In Brussels, I'd wondered at the possibility of an English-language media organisation that represented the breadth of popular political opinion across all EU countries, doing something more substantial than the British press. Back in London, on international financial markets, I quickly grew frustrated at the pro-market bias of Reuters cover and that of its peers. I wanted to work in a place that represented fairly, substantially and consistently the plight and points of view of those affected by financial markets, not just the ones of markets' major beneficiaries. The communities displaced or polluted by gold mining operations were one, pinprick example. Here I was in Malaysia, surrounded by substantial critics of corporate-driven globalisation but with little chance, time or editorial encouragement to do anything like justice to their points of view.

Those arguments are worth briefly summarising, not least as a tiny counter to the generous space usually given to advocates of "free" markets. The status quo views are endlessly quoted directly or endorsed implicitly in the everyday stories, story angles and background paragraphs put out by most mass media. Mahathir spoke often about globalisation, a trend he accepted as inevitable and unstoppable in our world of instant communications and rapid travel. His complaint lay in the term's default interpretation.

"Ostensibly, it is about the efficient giving of the best at the lowest cost. But in reality, it is about establishing the monopoly of the strongest and the biggest," he said in September 2002 in what were typical remarks. He saw globalisation's narrowest interpretation boiling down to freeing up capital movement by lifting all regulations, rules, conditions and controls on its flow.[80]

Enforcers of that scorched-earth approach include the IMF and World Bank. Both are subject to US controlling votes and all that means in terms of Wall Street lobbying power in Washington, on Republicans and Democrats alike. Mahathir defied them all in September 1998 by imposing capital controls to fend off speculative attacks on the Malaysian ringgit. Western banks and ratings agencies slammed his mould-breaking approach at the time, as did the one Reuters editor I spoke to on the subject when I arrived in Asia a couple of years later. That editor, a veteran of foreign exchange markets and speculative runs on various major currencies over the years, resolutely backed the IMF approach over Mahathir's. No wonder our news coverage took the same line. It was clear my fundamental politics and ideas were edging away from those of my senior colleagues. A time was coming when I would either have to put up and shut up or get out.

For all Mahathir's detractors, his formula won more supporters and gained in credibility over the years as Malaysia rapidly recovered. Among them was Joseph Stiglitz, former chief economist at the World Bank and adviser to Bill Clinton. He laid a large share of blame for the Asian financial crisis and its after effects on IMF deregulators.

"The IMF policies in East Asia had exactly the consequences that have brought globalisation under attack. The failures of the international institutions in poor developing countries were long standing; but these failures did not grab the headlines. The East Asia crisis made vivid to those in the more-developed world some of the dissatisfaction that those in the developing world had long felt," he wrote in *Globalization and its Discontents,* a book he published in 2002.

Were Stiglitz to revisit the question now, a decade or so later, he could add a long and growing list of countries similarly blighted by the effects of global financial deregulation and self-defeating remedies. The main difference is that richer, more-developed countries are joining the line of victims.[81]

Regulating financial flows is a long-standing question, dating back at least as far as the IMF's inception, in 1944. The Fund's two main architects, Harry Dexter White and John Maynard Keynes, were certainly alive to the issue. They argued for restraints on the cross-border flow of funds and their destabilising effects on countries' economies. Among their suggestions was that recipient countries help enforce controls, even refusing to receive funds without the necessary information on their source. Their proposals met fierce resistance from

US bankers, who succeeded in crushing their ideas. The evidence was plain in the IMF's final Articles of Agreement, which carried only watered-down measures. They said co-operation between countries to control capital flows should be permitted, not required.[82]

Today's IMF articles are even weaker, allowing members to exercise "such controls as are necessary to regulate international capital movements" but not so as to restrict payments for current transactions or unduly delay transfers of funds in settlement of commitments.[83]

The issue concerns not just money crashing across borders as financial speculation but also what is called capital flight. The term covers all illicit financial flows, those not captured in official data on international trade. It includes monies pocketed by companies that underprice, overprice, mis-invoice or make up transactions, typically between subsidiaries of the same multinational. The goal is to avoid tax and manipulate profit figures for different centres of operation to the mother company's best advantage. The bulk of illicit flows relate to commercial tax evasion, accounting for maybe two thirds of transactions. The rest are mainly from criminal activity with a lesser amount from bribery or theft by governments and their officials.

Keep that hierarchy in mind next time a business executive mentions burdensome regulations or the need to avoid double taxation. Their ultimate goal is no regulation at all and no taxation. Businesses pursue this double dividend by relentlessly lobbying against all checks on their affairs and tireless construction of labyrinthine company structures across multiple jurisdictions.

Bear in mind those same figures next time anyone says Africa's problems all boil down to endemic corruption among its elite ruling classes. Far more critical is those countries' ongoing pillage by rich Westerners, the proceeds shipped out via secrecy jurisdictions.

It is a chronic and economically debilitating problem for the world's poorer countries, the worst-off, most-indebted ones being African. Data for 40 Sub-Saharan countries together estimated capital flight at $420 billion (in 2004 dollars) for the period 1970-2004. Imputed interest would take that to $607 billion in 2004 money. That compares with those countries' combined external debt at the time of $398 billion. So the continent was a net creditor to the rest of the world, not such an economic basket case after all.[84]

Lax capital controls persist thanks to enduringly profitable lobbying over decades by bankers, financiers and their corporate and private clients. The World Bank estimates annual cross-border flows from criminal activities, corruption and tax evasion at $1,000-$1,600 billion. Of that, half comes from developing and transitional economies. That compares with OECD countries' $100 billion or so annual payments of foreign aid.[85]

Stemming such flows would give poor countries a chance of developing on their own terms. They could then escape the strings-attached aid and loans that lock them into policies of perpetual disaster-prevention and asset plunder. It would also help to insulate them from the predations of short-term money flows intended to exploit or create domestic financial and economic instability.

Mahathir went beyond mere rhetorical attacks on speculators and their supporters in international bodies and Western governments – he suggested remedies. They included mandating more transparency in foreign currency trading, limiting volumes and taxing speculative transactions. Once again, such ideas gradually won more support. Even the IMF gave them an endorsement of sorts in 2010, voicing qualified support for currency controls in some instances.[86]

Arguing for regulatory change is one thing, making it happen is quite another. The pitiful state of our global and national governance systems is a major barrier to change, as is the poor general quality of our journalism. Vested interests and their effective lock-down on policy-making is still another. Suggested tinkerings to the rules bob between various global summits without result, despite the increasing scale and severity of financial crises and the damage they cause. Those who have flirted with the issue include the Group of Eight rich-country leaders, the broader Group of 20 (G20), the IMF and bodies such as the Organisation for Economic Co-operation and Development.

The prospect of substantial change emerging from any of them is next to nil, regardless of what seductive promises they might make. Far more likely is the sort of manoeuvring described by ex-IMF chief economist Simon Johnson. He called the G20's post-global-financial-crisis reform proposals a "sophisticated delaying action" by the masters of economic policy spin.[87]

Johnson identified the standard summit ploy of kicking politically hot issues, such as capital controls, banker salaries or capital requirements, into the long-grass equivalent of technical committees.

By the time officials report back, their recommendations are watery versions of anything that might work and the momentum for putting them into force has long gone. "There will be some minor changes, and these will be much trumpeted. But what will really change in or around the power structure of global finance – as it plays out in the United States, Western Europe, or anywhere else? Nothing," says Johnson. And that's an ex-insider talking.

That sort of critical perspective might occasionally feature in a one-off news story from the likes of Reuters, or carried as a quote in a report. It will rarely inform the basic assumptions of mainstream journalists, far less their news organisations.

The World Bank, while not always as ideologically brazen as the Fund, is nevertheless a doughty champion of deregulation and privatisation. Both form a central plank of the Washington-inspired policies Castro singled out during his Malaysia visit. The Bank's own data bear out his arguments. Between 1990 and 2003, 120 developing countries pushed through nearly 8,000 privatizations, raising $410 billion in revenue. Latin America made nearly half the total in 1,300 deals. For all those sales, little benefit reached ordinary citizens. From 1980 to 2000, Latin America's income per person grew only 9 percent, with a further one percent registered in 2000-2005.[88]

Mark Weisbrot, co-director of the Washington-based Center for Economic and Policy Research, highlights the effects of different policy approaches. He compares the minimal growth during quarter of a century with the 82 percent rise in two decades leading up to 1980. That was before the IMF and World Bank began making aid and loans conditional on their deregulatory policies.

"To find a growth performance in Latin America that is even close to the failure of the last 25 years, one has to go back more than a century, and choose a 25-year period that includes both World War I and the start of the Great Depression."[89]

Again, that sort of perspective features all too rarely in Reuters news or that of its peers. It most certainly doesn't drive the general thrust of everyday economic coverage or feature as explanatory background or context to stories. That's not our job, the editors would say. Don't call yourself free from bias then, would be my reply.

Even if there were momentum for World Bank and IMF reform, the US government can strangle any attempts at change. For both bodies, Washington dominates their core stratagems and wields most influence over senior staff appointments. Once again, there is little hope for reform from within.

The same is true of the WTO, despite it having a governance structure that seems to be far more broadly based.[90] Mahathir would often argue that poorer states should get a fairer say in trade regulation. He advocated a handicap system to help them develop outside the full force of international competition. That would be no more than what all of today's richer countries enjoyed, he argued.

Malaysia's trade minister, Rafidah Aziz, put it more bluntly.

She criticised the likes of European Union countries and the United States for talking a good game on free trade while piling up de facto trade barriers to their competitors. "The market is open, it is very open, but it's not possible to bring your products in at competitive prices because there are so many things you need to do." She cited the veterinary controls and punitive duties rich countries used to stymie their poorer, less legally agile competitors.

Speaking in October 2002, Rafidah correctly predicted ongoing stalemate in global talks under the Doha round. The core cause, then as now, was Western countries' refusal to budge on their massive farm subsidies or the terms of trade offered to poorer countries. It wasn't that Rafidah had any special powers of prediction, she just described things as they were. Her views are common in majority-world countries, even if they are little aired in richer ones and still-less understood by those countries' citizens. Not helping that ignorance is the biased and incomplete coverage of conventional media.

I reported her remarks on several occasions as news stories but that was about the end of it. Reuters trade coverage included endless stories quoting ministers, officials and business leaders on the potential benefits of increased global trade. It made far less noise about the structural imbalances bolted in by the rules, the sticking points in talks or who was to blame for their lock down. Nor did it much highlight how moribund trade talks were just fine for the world's richer countries and their corporations. For all that they might say otherwise, most benefit famously from existing rules.

Today's global trade regime is broadly the same one whose birth I'd witnessed from Brussels during the early 1990s. Back then, the United States and European Union had more diplomatic heft in talks than they do today. That was before poorer countries' coming-out party in Seattle, a debut made to the beat of mass protests on the city's streets. For all the noise, today's rules remain stuck in the last century, with built-in inequity favouring rich over poor.

Lori Wallach is director of the US Public Citizen's Global Trade Watch and a long-time trade justice campaigner. She gives a sweeping account of how the WTO's tentacles extend beyond simple acts of buying and selling. She likens its effects to "a slow-motion coup d'etat" against all levels of elected government the world over. That was locked into the WTO's DNA at birth in 800-plus pages of one-size-fits-all rules.[91]

Members must make their domestic laws conform with their WTO commitments. It's no easy feat given the always-on threat of legal attack for having "illegal trade barriers". Merely the risk kills many, potentially progressive policies at birth, with rarely a whimper of protest, including the EU fur-trap ban I'd covered in Brussels. Actual challenges activate WTO tribunals presided over by three, pre-approved judges who meet in secret. For the losers, who are almost always the defendants, the choice is either to make their laws WTO-compliant or face permanent trade sanctions.

"Taken as a whole, the WTO and its agreements are a powerful mechanism for spreading and locking in corporate-led globalization," says Wallach. "The WTO is a mechanism to bring every country in the world – ready or not – into an existing global market designed by corporations, and to take the practices those corporations invented willy-nilly – which, of course, suit their needs – and set them in stone as 'WTO rules'".

This is not the sort of routine context to be found in stories by the *Financial Times*, the *Economist* or Reuters. It might feature in quotes made by trade reform campaigners or the odd poor-country minister but not as a base assumption in coverage. The words and perspectives of the powerful drive and shape what gets written, those of weaker ones trail in behind. That translates as WTO-style global trade rules being the gold standard, promising "free" trade for all. Benefits will come from increased global growth. It sidelines systemic inequities and the way talks are loaded against poorer countries.

That the rules need radical reform should be glaringly obvious. Trade is a major potential motor for development, one of humankind's oldest practices. Whether a revamped WTO should be part of that overhaul is another question. Walden Bello, senior analyst at the Philippines-based think-tank Focus on the Global South, thinks not.

"Reform is a viable strategy when the system in question is fundamentally fair but has simply been corrupted, such as the case with some democracies. It is not a viable strategy when a system is so fundamentally unequal in purposes, principles, and processes as the WTO," he wrote in the late 1990s. Nothing much has changed since.[92]

Bello advocates instead that civil society, in rich and poor countries alike, should work to cut back radically the WTO's powers. At the same time, activist groups should fight for change via other global institutions, via environmental and labour agreements and the evolving regional trade blocs in South America, Africa and Asia.

"It is in such a more fluid, less structured, more pluralistic world with multiple checks and balances that the nations and communities of the South will be able to carve out the space to develop based on their values, their rhythms, and the strategies of their choice."

Such a manifesto could apply just as well to the IMF and World Bank regimes. It could apply equally to less-known, more opaque governance bodies. Those include the International Organization of Securities Commissions,[93] the Basel Committee of the Bank for International Settlements,[94] the International Association of Insurance Supervisors[95] and the International Accounting Standards Board.[96]

Don't bet on it happening, not least because the debate barely features in coverage by our main sources of news and opinion. Yet reform is vital and urgent, across-the-board, if we are to get any sort of public accountability into the global governance process.

Opportunities to address such issues were few in Malaysia, something I found frustrating. Not only were there few easy opportunities, I lacked the time to work up anything more substantial. Making it all the more difficult was the lack of appetite among Singapore editors, who were generally either uninterested in the issues or plain uncomprehending. Instead, they made endless requests for improvements to the bureau's equities and economic cover to ensure our stories beat those of Bloomberg and the rest. One request, relayed to me by my bureau chief, I plain, point blank refused. I was asked to report more about Malaysia's economy as part of my regular work. I said I hadn't come all the way out to Malaysia to do that and so wouldn't. I was increasingly mutinous, the evident mismatch between my journalistic priorities and those of Reuters inexorably widening.

I took what chances came my way to tackle global governance questions. One presented itself in the form of Malaysian diplomat Razali Ismail, an ex-president of the United Nations General Assembly. He agreed to an interview just weeks after US forces attacked Iraq in March 2003.

Razali was by then the ill-starred UN special envoy to Burma, or Myanmar if you wished to be polite to the country's ruling junta. He'd made his diplomatic name in 1997 with a proposal to reform the Security Council. The Iraq invasion, without a UN mandate, showed the problem was current as ever.

"The Security Council cannot be involved in huge issues that deal with security and the lives of people on the basis of its present structure. That surely must be clear to everybody," he said.

"There are people who are alarmed or even disgusted at what's happened. Even people working in the government of the United States, some of them that I know, are quite aghast at what has happened. We cannot accept: 'If it ain't broke, don't fix it'. In many ways the UN is broken. We have to fix it."

Clear as that need might have been, the unreformed United Nations made no difference to US invasion plans. Given Washington's desire to remove Saddam Hussein perhaps no sort of UN could have stopped it. Maybe the UN's main value in 2003 was to demonstrate the sorry state of international law, exposing the Security Council's fundamental lack of credibility to the widest possible audience. Its failure helped fuel discussion of the invasion as a war of aggression and therefore a crime against peace under the Nuremberg Principles.

Iraq made for a depressing and frustrating time to be a journalist, Reuters or otherwise. For me, it was the worst example of global governance failure, trumping all the ones I'd begun to identify in relation to trade, financial markets, the environment and all the rest. I had little to do with the story bar covering the odd ministerial speech or protest outside the US embassy in Kuala Lumpur. The spurious link between the 9/11 attacks and Saddam, confected by the Bush administration and maintained by Tony Blair's, became spectacularly more obvious the further you stood from Washington. In majority Muslim countries such as Malaysia, well-practised in spotting the *sandiwaras* of their own politicians, the idea was contemptible.[97]

There were plenty of other things to keep my mind off the war in daily, routine work. After my refusal to morph into a straight-out economics reporter, I was tasked to seek out interviews with media-shy Malaysian business leaders. There was also the endless editing and filing of local colleagues' stories plus the administrative and management chores that piled up during my bureau chief's frequent absences.

The work became less and less satisfying – journalistically pointless stories and endless office grunt jobs were not what I'd had in mind when joining Reuters. I organised our reporting cover for UN-led talks on global species extinctions, which took place in Malaysia in February 2004. Editors' interest was never more than tepid.

I was pessimistic about the chances of anything better elsewhere in the company. What I was seeing in Malaysia seemed pretty much standard, modern Reuters. Colleagues and friends dotted elsewhere around the world reported much the same problems. Rather than pitch for what would usually have been my next rung up, a bureau chief's job, I changed tack completely. I pushed editors instead to create the job of globalisation correspondent, building it out of our existing trade post in the WTO's home city of Geneva.

Through Brussels, London and now Malaysia, I'd come to realise how our news coverage was blind to the depth and breadth of globalisation issues. We ignored the accountability problems of bodies such as the IMF and World Bank, their lock-step with rich-country agendas at the expense of the world's majority poor. In reams of stories to media clients and screen traders, we gave little space to the case for reform.

No one seemed to think this was a problem.

News editor priorities were obsessively focused on serving financial market clients and weaving questions of investor risk into all stories. Anything else was to be fitted in, if at all, once the spadework of market-sensitive reporting was done. I argued that Reuters, of all major media, should be tackling global governance failures from a worldwide perspective. We could own the story, drawing on the deep, collective knowledge in our network of local and international reporters. We could report the human effects of economic crises where they happened and link back to the financial centres where traders drove the contagions and gambled on their outcomes. I suggested our wall-to-wall cover of summits between world leaders, bankers and finance ministers include a major focus on structural reform and regulation. That would mean something more than tokenistic hat tips to global justice activists and their arguments in stories framed around the agendas of Western governments and finance.

All I needed to do, so I thought, was to convince some suitably senior editors of the arguments. They'd then let me address them, coordinating a network of other reporters working along the same lines. It was not such an outlandish suggestion – I myself was already part of a network of environmental reporters producing both ad hoc news reports and event-led feature stories.

The nub of the reply was: "Nice idea, fat chance."

The news was at least delivered by a sympathetic editor who had the wit to get what I was talking about. He said the editorial budget for 2004 could stretch no further than an extra half-post for a currency market reporter in Tokyo. Reuters news in a nutshell.

I'd had enough of banging my head against a wall with ideas I knew were sound. This final, pathetic act of faith turned out to be my liberation: I no longer loved Big Brother. I was ready to dump the organisation that had captured my heart all those years before as an eager undergraduate.

Around the same time, I'd been trying to negotiate a bonus payment for being de-facto bureau chief for most of the previous six months.

The flat-out refusal I got, accompanied by not so much as an acknowledgment of the extra work I'd done, pushed me to take a decision I'd been mulling for months. Rather than resign straight out – I'd been warned that to quit on assignment meant personally footing the bill to get home – I asked to be posted back to London.

What could have been a disappointing end to my Malaysia posting was leavened by getting what amounted to an exit interview with Mahathir, by then retired from office. It proved a neat example of my frustrations with Reuters. From almost as high up as you could get in the 88-storey Petronas Twin Towers, the ex-prime minister held forth on far more than global governance, the topic I'd asked him to address. Once I'd rushed out stories on all the time- and market-sensitive remarks he'd made, there was little appetite from the desk for much on globalisation.

Though I left Malaysia laden with uncertainties about my planned exit from Reuters, I wasn't totally downbeat. I felt enormous gratitude to the country and to its people for what together they'd taught me, deliberately or not. It helped sustain me through what turned out to be another nine months with Reuters, working 24/7 reporting and editing shifts for the UK online service in London.

Rather than resign on arrival, I was advised on subtler ways to leave an employer. Instead of a petulant: 'I quit and you'll be sorry!' I said I wasn't so happy with my new job back in London and would consider any redundancies going. Two weeks later, my new boss announced a third of the posts on my desk were to go. I grabbed the chance of an exit cheque. Rather than leave with nothing, Reuters would pay me to depart. I'd got my bonus after all.

Helpful as the money would be, I now had to decide what to do next. I'd called my own bluff, dumping my regular salary and all the other perks of working for an established multi-national news organisation. That was to say nothing of the excellent colleagues I'd had and the many friends I'd made, in bureaus and on reporting assignments over years. There was nothing to gain by staying. My challenge was to make sense of the decision professionally, to make clear for myself why I'd fallen out of love with Reuters but not with journalism.

I had no interest in conventional jobs with other mainstream media. None suggested I'd find the global, non-partisan perspective I'd mistakenly hoped for and failed to find at Reuters. My thinking about what journalism I did want was hopelessly abstract, something based on the idea of serving democracy. How to do that was not obvious in a practical sense. What quickly became clear was my basic ignorance about both conventional journalism and democracy, the brass tacks of their history and theory if not their modern practice.

Whatever the future held for me in April 2005, when I left Reuters, I knew it would need much more study, and practical trial and error.

Chapter 5

Democracy now?

The first time I met Brian Haw, in January 2006, he'd just finished talking to his lawyer through a hole in the top of his sleeping bag. He told me to fuck off and let him go back to sleep. I ignored the rebuff, waiting in flurries of snow on London's Parliament Square for when he emerged from his tarpaulin cocoon. I wanted to find out why he'd given up on conventional politics, something I was pondering myself. A few sworn insults weren't going to put me off.

Haw's home of five years had been a pavement, its iconic views of Big Ben and the Houses of Parliament spoilt only by the rumble and fumes of passing traffic. His one-man demonstration began as a call to end sanctions against Iraq, which were estimated to have killed hundreds of thousands of ordinary Iraqis. It broadened in 2003 to include opposition to the Iraq invasion, and Britain's hand in it. The war killed at least as many people as had the sanctions, possibly several times more according to some estimates.

That Haw had left his wife and children for full-time, open-ended political protest seemed incredible to me, for all the killings and injustice he was trying to highlight and stop. It made me reflect on what little I was doing about anything, not least in my stalled reporting.

My politics, having shifted over the years, were resolutely blocked in frustration. Political structures seemed immune to the influence of ordinary people, let alone individual protesters. It made me question the point of journalism. That was true for governments of the so-called left or right, most obviously for me in Britain but also the United States and elsewhere. Iraq, a cooked-up war fought in defiance of public opinion, was a spectacular example. There were countless lesser ones from my years as a reporter. I knew public accountability was inextricably bound up with democracy, I just wasn't yet sure exactly how, or where and when the relationship broke down.

Nailing that question was fundamental to the others I faced, which was what sort of journalism to do and how. It wasn't as simple as just ditching the editorial agenda of an employer whose goal was to please its banking and financial markets clients. I needed to define my own agenda, what topics to prioritise, and work out how to pursue it.

I thought talking to Haw might help clarify those questions. I hoped to do a video interview about his protest to put on the Internet, an attempt at some sort of alternative journalism, while also asking him about democracy. That way people could at least get an idea of the man and his arguments on camera, which they'd have struggled to find in conventional media coverage.

The process took me nearly a whole year. Our first meeting, once Haw did emerge from his sleeping bag, did little more than establish basic contact. It was a small step towards building some sort of trust. Clearly he was sick of journalists dropping by for a choice quote when it suited them while ignoring the broader context of his protest. They were happy to harvest soundbites but never to give the issues he raised any space or depth. I left him after an hour or so in the January cold after my first meeting, shaking bodily despite my thick gloves and outdoor jacket. It felt pitiful that I should bolt in a blink of discomfort. Haw, of course, remained at his station.

By the time I'd reached Parliament Square I was already several months on from Reuters. I had pages of notes attempting to map out journalism's relationship with democracy. None seemed to stick. I was clear the journalism I wanted to do should be about making governments fully accountable to their citizens – I just couldn't quite see how.

It was complicated. Fifteen years as a reporter had taught me that getting politicians to be accountable for anything was hard enough.

146

Doing the same for cross-border or global issues was harder still. Challenge enough was working out which politicians to hold to account and on whose behalf.

Each issue I wanted to tackle, the ones I saw as most urgent, was ultimately linked to the overwhelming political influence of globally mobile capital and business. Most crossed national borders in their impacts and potential remedies, an inevitable result of the increasing globalisation of all business and politics. I'd thought for years Reuters was the place to do journalism addressing those sorts of issues. I'd finally realised it wasn't and maybe never had been.

The mistake was mine, not theirs, as I was at last beginning to understand. I'd learnt how the Reuters news priorities, as defined by its staffing, story choice and presentation, were closely tied to what suited the bankers, traders and investors who paid its bills. That realisation helped me start to see similar biases in other media. They included not just other news agencies but also financial publications such as *The Economist*, the *Financial Times* and *Wall Street Journal*. It was an important realisation for my emerging idea of doing journalism that somehow served democracy. In plain terms: if a media organisation's paymasters are bankers and financial markets, or major businesses buying ads, it won't champion ordinary citizens' interests over those of its clients.

The same constraint applies pretty much identically for state-funded news services, whatever their public service remit, with few exceptions. Their ultimate "clients" are unaccountable governments, or sanitised committees of the great and good whose tenure depends on politicians. They are never the ultimate audiences – those same governments' disenfranchised voters.

That bias towards client interests need not be explicit or even obvious in stories – far better that it isn't. Editors and reporters incorporate the necessary perspectives into their news priorities and story choices, usually without thinking. They accept bogus concepts such as "free" markets, which in practice are far more likely to create dominant monopolies. They treat economic growth as the supreme measure of

147

national progress, ignoring the sheer, mathematical impossibility of its endless rise on a finite planet. They quote business leaders chirruping about "de-regulation" without stopping to ask what that means in practice, which is often no regulation at all.

Whatever their editorial boasts, conventional news organisations must survive financially. The traditional media revenue model is advertising sales boosted by channel subscriptions or cover price charges. While the shift online scrambled that model it did nothing to alter the influence of revenue sources and ownership on output. If my idea of doing journalism that held governments accountable to their citizens was to have a chance, I would need to think about the funding problem from the start.

Journalists habitually ignore this glaringly obvious point, or simply won't entertain that it biases their work. The same is generally true for their audiences. I struggled with it myself. Yet it explained my difficulty in imagining any other mainstream news organisation to go to. None seemed to promise anything better than what I'd just left.

If I was to stay a journalist rather than drift into something else I would have to find a better model.

Luckily, help was at hand. Part of my voluntary severance from Reuters was a couple of thousand pounds to spend on training, useable within a year of leaving. Here was my chance to find some political and journalistic alternatives. I crossed the Atlantic to Boston, Massachusetts, taking a bus north to Woods Hole, home of the Z Media Institute.

Z Media's near-annual courses involve a few dozen people, mainly young North Americans. Its 2005 edition introduced me to far more radical thinking than I'd been used to, shining some light on all the questions I'd been wrestling with on my own.[98]

ZMI teachers have decades of protest actions to support their theorising about democracy and the news. Among them is Noam Chomsky, co-author of *Manufacturing Consent*. His propaganda model dissects mainstream media's routine failure to critique existing power structures in Western democracies, the United States in particular. The analysis extends to the editorial effects of media income and ownership, ramming home what I'd gradually realised with experience.

Another teacher was Michael Albert, originator of participatory economics, or parecon. His proposed political system aims explicitly for more social justice and less inherent violence than free-market capitalism, the bedrock credo of Reuters and its clients. Not much mention of that one on the news file I remembered, or indeed much criticism of capitalism. Others included Chip Berlet, a reporter who made his name investigating US race hate groups, and Amy Goodman, co-presenter of *Democracy Now!'s* award-winning daily TV show the War and Peace report.

Faculty members presented media and politics perspectives from across the spectrum of social justice movements, ones I'd only rarely touched as a journalist up until then. They ranged across movements for peace, civil rights, black power, Native Americans, ecology and the rights struggles of workers, women, gays and lesbians. It was a rich mix for a single week, turbo charging my thoughts about democracy and journalism and bringing home the extent of failures in both.

For all the bigger names, the most intriguing people I met were Brian Dominick and Jessica Azulay, members of a journalism collective publishing *The NewStandard* online newspaper. Their aim was to provide an alternative to profit-focused news, resolutely pitched in the public interest and funded solely by readers. That approach governed story choice as well as their organization as an egalitarian, participatory workplace. In plain terms: no bosses and everyone gets a say in how things ran. Maybe that could be a model for the future, I thought.[99]

Returning to England, I kept coming back to the question of democracy. Though I still felt journalism should somehow serve democracy, I now had more questions. What if democracy itself was failing, routinely promoting narrow, minority interests over those of the large majority of constituents? What should journalism do then?

And what should it do about a democracy's negative effects beyond its borders? Not just obvious ones such as wars but subtler, more complicated ones. Things like the effects of EU and US farm subsidies and the associated dumping of their surpluses on other countries, trashing markets for local produce and ruining small-scale farmers?

My thinking by now was that journalists should bypass ideas of "democracy" to focus directly on the interests of democracy's constituents, which is to say ordinary people. Given the scope and scale of our biggest political stories – serial financial crises, food price hikes, growling climate change and a seemingly open-ended "war on terror" – those ordinary people could not be limited to any one country. Nor should questions of race or religion favour one group over another. Any genuine public-interest journalism would have to cross borders and stretch to the defence of all human beings as well as their home, Planet Earth.

I hadn't given up on the idea of democracy itself, just put it on probation while I worked out where it was going wrong. I couldn't simply dump the system of government most people I knew considered the pinnacle of political ambition for all rational beings.

Translating these ideas into journalism practice suggested a potentially massive project that I wasn't yet ready to get into. It wasn't outlandish though. I already knew of the Zapatistas, a Mexican rebel group, from years spent writing the global trade story. They had declared war on global capitalism in 1994 as the North American Free Trade Agreement came into force. They'd announced their aims over the Internet as their indigenous armies briefly took control of several cities. What provoked them was a legal threat to their rights to communally own land, pushed through in the name of "free" trade. It opened the door to private land ownership and their inevitable expulsion.

The Zapatistas inspired social justice movements around the globe, appealing beyond barriers of race, culture, language and geography. Among the effects of their provocative-cum-playful appeals to the world was the galvanising of cooperation between previously unconnected movements. That took physical form in various mass global justice protests around the millennium, most famously the one in late 1999 that closed down world trade talks in Seattle. That same protest launched the *Independent Media Center* or *Indymedia*, which quickly spawned a global network of alternative reporters.

I already knew and liked the idea of *Indymedia* but steered clear of it for the moment. I still needed to get my head around democracy and accountability and how conventional journalism ignored that. I had to get beyond the idea of regular elections and conventional political parties being automatic guarantors of good governance. I knew they weren't – the Bush victory of 2000 being just the most glaring example. That nine ageing lawyers had guillotined the outcome was bad enough. They hadn't even looked at the doctoring of electoral rolls and ballot card designs to swing the result his way.[100]

Faced with such serious doubts about democracy, not just the US version, my reporter's instinct suggested I ask ordinary people what they thought. A chance came when spending the last of my retraining budget learning to shoot, edit and publish short video reports. The course took place in Brussels just days before Belgian local elections, so I decided just to interview people on the street.

For all the randomness of the process, many who talked gave deeply considered replies. Two even sheepishly admitted, halfway through, to being candidates themselves. An older Flemish man, who wasn't a candidate, blamed democracy's accountability problem on "economic powers" outside the process. He said they must be integrated into democratic systems rather than standing apart, minding their own capital. How to do that was another matter, he laughed.

A French speaker, hair tumbling over a black T-shirt with fluorescent pink skull-and-crossbones, was initially reluctant to talk. When I coaxed him on, he said local elections were by far the most interesting and accountable versions of democracy. They allowed different groups to be represented and more regular switches in personnel.

For elections more generally, he predicted computers and the Internet would change everything, driving a re-emergence of democracy thanks to instant communications. "Elections and democracy will be reinvented by groups that don't have much to do with what we know as political power today," he said. Boy is he proving right.[101]

I agreed with much of what I heard but still wasn't satisfied. How to reflect those ideas with sustained, practical, credible journalism? And why wasn't there more of that happening already?

By now I'd moved with my family to France, returning to the UK only for odd visits. It was on one of these that I finally landed the interview with Brian Haw, armed with my new video skills. Having tackled ordinary voters in Belgium, I was now chasing the protest vote. I wanted to know why it was that people abandoned elections for more direct action. I suggested to Brian that I run part of the interview as some sort of alternative to the Queen's speech. My edit landed a day before the conventional one.[102]

Poised on the kerb, the roar of Christmas traffic in the background, I finally got some idea of Haw's thinking on democracy. He cited the example of MPs' scrutiny, in March 2003, of the government's case for invading Iraq. He compared the few hours they'd debated Iraq with the hundreds spent banning Britain's peculiar practice of fox hunting.[103]

"They didn't even have a vote about war or peace, did they? That wasn't what the vote was about. The vote they had over there was: 'Have we talked enough about this? Are we tired of talking?' A whole seven hours I'm told they spoke about war – seven, whole, hours. I'm also told they spoke seven hundred hours regarding fox hunting. That's our debating priority is it? Is this sick or what?"[104]

The debate he referred to took place on March 18th 2003, ending with 412 MPs for war versus 149 against.[105] Aerial bombardments officially began two days later, launching the invasion. By August 2007, the attack our MPs supported was estimated by one count to have killed more than a million Iraqis, injured millions more and contaminated their land with radioactive dust and debris.[106]

Polls in the months before found that 90 percent of Britons opposed any war fought "unilaterally by America and its allies", a far cry from the MPs' vote.[107] The gulf between governors and governed was clearest in the millions of anti-war demonstrators out on London's streets and elsewhere around the world, days before the invasion.[108]

Tony Blair had spoken at his theatrical best in the pre-invasion debate, one he was bound to win given the opposition Conservatives' support. His performance was pure public relations, not least in the cloyingly uncritical news coverage he enjoyed through into the next day, with the rarest of exceptions. That Blair repeated many of his lies of the preceding months, some of them already publicly challenged, didn't seem to bother his media cheerleaders.[109]

No one could argue this was a parliament accountable to its people or journalism in the service of citizens.

Talking to Haw, and cross checking his remarks later, took me deeper into British divisions over a war I'd watched mainly from Malaysia, with its Muslim majority. It reminded me of my own tiny part in the UK process, a vote for Labour during the 1997 election that brought Blair to power. What I experienced back then as a joyful ousting of the Conservatives, the party of power through all my adult life, had turned to disgust and confusion over the fundamentals of Britain's political system. The act of voting seemed futile to me if not an insult to the intelligence. What was the point if both main parties had the same discredited policies, not just on Iraq but also in their bias towards business and finance interests over all else? Added to that bleak view was its professional implications – what sort of journalism made sense in the face of such structurally embedded political hopelessness?

I admired Haw's determined campaign against Britain's military and foreign policy misadventures. But I needed more, to answer questions that extended to the whole system of government in Britain, the one I knew best of any. While the Bush election had made me doubt Western democracy's grandest claims, Blair's behaviour alerted me to the unaccountable powers of British prime ministers. As a believer in "democracy", whatever its flaws and however vaguely defined, I'd never bothered with what seemed like quirky political trivia. The rituals and pageantry of Westminster, its state openings of parliament and rowdy question times, had blinded me to questions of who held power on whose behalf. Iraq changed all that.

What I wanted were some political basics, facts I'd ignored through my professional life and during undergraduate studies as an engineer. Iraq taught me British leaders could declare war without asking parliament, so the debate of March 2003 really had been a charade. I learnt that prime ministers could negotiate and ratify treaties, hire and fire ministers, recommend dissolutions of parliament, grant pardons, peerages, honours and patronage and senior judicial appointments.[110]

That concentration of power in one person's hands follows England's complicated political history, its centuries-long shuffle away from uncontested royal rule to something more popularly accountable. From the Magna Carta of 1215 onwards, crown powers leaked away to the nobility and clergy and then to politicians. Centuries of halting evolution, wars, weddings and union treaties brought us the present-day Westminster within a United Kingdom. British prime ministerial powers are among the many peculiarities of a nation with no formal constitution. Britain lacks the single, consolidated document or statement of subjects' basic political rights, the sort most modern states and their citizens take for granted, most famously the United States.

My entry-level politics lesson made me think back to all the elections in which I'd voted since the 1980s. Seen from the present day, my various votes seemed irrelevant to what policies the victors then pursued. That was as true whether I'd backed winners or losers, so it wasn't just sour grapes. While Iraq was the most blatant mismatch, others included government policies on transport, privatisation, schools, health and various environmental issues.

I wasn't alone. The 2006 *Power Inquiry* held an extensive investigation into people's attitude towards politics. It found popular alienation towards British politicians, the main political parties and key political institutions to be "extremely high and widespread".[111]

Our media routinely ignore this gulf between voter preferences and policy, giving no sense of it in their politics stories. Instead, they obsess over personalities, and differences within and between the members of the main parties, principally Labour and the Conservatives. They run endless opinion polls and extrapolate their findings to future general elections, rating one party or political leader over another in vapid popularity contests. They sidestep the near-identical agendas of each side on all major issues, playing up rhetorical differences. Here was my clue to the accountability gap, democracy's failure to represent its constituents and journalists' failure to capture that.

When Blair left office in 2007 his powers passed straight to Gordon Brown with some ceremonial nods from Labour party members but no new mandate from voters. From Brown, powers passed to David Cameron in the closed-door shenanigans following the 2010 election's hung result. Politicians and journalists used financial market skittishness to argue for a quick deal – bulldozing through the result's complex implications. In their haste, they buried a rare opportunity for real political change with little fuss from anyone. No change there.

For all people's alienation and dissatisfaction with politics and political parties, no one raised much of a stink. That collective failure epitomised our general hopelessness and lack of political imagination, not least on the part of conventional media. It also made clear the scale of problems facing anyone seeking positive change and structural reform.

Brian Haw held his stand throughout the circus, showing what little he thought of changing guards at the head of national government. British foreign and military policy remained the same throughout. Lung cancer eventually stopped his protest towards the end of 2010 then killed him a few months later, in June 2011.

The many obituaries included a parody of Haw's speaking style by *The Economist*. It finally gave some play to his campaign, the story now sanitised by death. The hugely influential weekly even mentioned genocidal war crimes and the lies of Bush and Blair, the killing of Iraqi children by war, sanctions and contamination from shells tipped with armour-piercing depleted uranium. The story was all cordoned off though, tucked away from the main news section, so many whispered condolences in the obituaries section. No need to bother the standard news stream with such unconventional talk.[112]

Haw would have scoffed at the coverage, demanding to know where it had been while he lived. When had *The Economist* ever run cover stories giving serious and sustained treatment to those same arguments? When had other mainstream media included them as routine background paragraphs or context in their stories about Iraq or about Bush or Blair's activities since leaving office? Most of Haw's media treatment had concerned authorities' persistent attempts to move him on. It failed to convey his persistent, illegal harassment by police let alone the bigger picture of his protest.

My video of Haw at least gave him an extended hearing on camera. That meant anyone with Internet access could judge his arguments for themselves. It was a tiny example of the sort of journalism I'd started to envisage, which included treating political activists and their arguments more seriously. That meant taking time to understand their protests, letting them make their points without cutting them off or short-changing their points in scripts, pictures and video-edit choices. People who are prepared to risk personal safety, arrest and even their lives in support of reasoned arguments for change deserve our attention. A good journalist must find out why they fight. Only then can they know if a person's actions bear scrutiny and whether or not to write them up.

Reporters may make mistakes by covering the odd charlatan, that is a hazard of the job. They could hardly do worse than today's mainstream journalists, who routinely fail even to talk to protesters or address the issues they raise. Yet they jump to attention for government ministers, civil servants, business leaders and the police, no legitimacy questions there. Too many reporters wrote Haw off without a second thought. We have to do better.

This was what I attempted with my next video report, in March 2007. My aim was to ask the French activist-turned-presidential candidate José Bové about democracy. Having failed to arrange a meeting, I went for a sure-fire date, one of his many court appearances. Bové was one among five people on trial in Carcassonne, southwest France, for a protest against genetically modified organisms (GMOs). All were charged with preventing Monsanto employees from going about their work by conducting a citizens' inspection of company premises.

I wanted to know what sort of people became activists and why. What did their efforts say about the state of French democracy, and the effects ceding sovereign powers to the European Union and the WTO? Why had they abandoned more conventional routes towards policy influence? Bové proved impossible to get so I caught one of his co-accused instead, the small-scale beef farmer Michel David.

"We believe that our fight is legitimate, even if it is not legal. We are making tomorrow's laws and we think that as long as the law is not fair regarding the state of GMOs… we will fight by committing acts of civil disobedience," he told me.

David cited Gandhi as inspiration, saying there were causes for which it is worth running the risk of prison to take them forward. It was not the first time he'd been in court during the campaign. Each time he risked jail and losing what few assets he had, as others before him had done already.[113]

David's choice of civil disobedience honoured a tradition of protest by the powerless that echoes around the world. The spark for the maize case came in April 1998, when the EU cleared the contested Monsanto maize variety for cultivation in European fields. David had various objections, shared with several thousand fellow *faucheurs volontaires* or rebel reapers. They included risks of uncontrolled cross-pollination with other plants, the untested health effects on humans and a tightening of corporate control over the farming industry by way of seed patents and monopolisation.

Such arguments failed in Brussels just as they'd done in Washington. The demands of economics, business and growth had trumped any worries about damage to nature, human health or the world's small-holder economies. The result left Monsanto's shareholders free to reap the benefits while others paid for any damage done.

My previous experience of GMOs had been in Brussels in the late 1990s. Carcassonne was my chance to look at the other end of the policy chain. Reporters following policy-makers in Brussels and other major capitals rarely do that. They seldom get the time or budget to explore the real-world effects of the policies they cover. It's far easier, and cheaper, to stick with diaried news conferences and other events geared to those same policy-makers' agendas. For me, I was intrigued to see grannies, mothers and children marching the streets in the weekday rain in protest.

The French state's position was clear. Prosecution arguments and the ranks of riot police glowering from courtroom steps made sure of that. For all the weakness of the legal case, which soon collapsed, the display of force had its uses. It drove home the power of a multi-tiered, multinational policy process stretching far beyond most ordinary people's imagination, let alone their influence. David and friends were impressively bold to stand in its way in defence of their principles.

Europe's GMO policy is one of an increasing number that undermine the very idea of accountable government. Mainstream journalism, the source of most people's daily information, doesn't seem much bothered by that.

Had I still been at Reuters, the story might have just made our file as a brief news item. Maybe it would have stretched to a wider feature story on GMOs or the presidential hopeful Bové. The involvement of Monsanto, a giant, publicly listed US agro-chemical firm could have fired editors' interest though probably only from the perspective of investor risk. Probably none would have been compelling enough for editors to hire a TV crew locally or to send one down from Paris. The same would be true for opposition outlets Bloomberg, AP and most other foreign media in France. Among French ones – only regional and local organisations would have paid much attention and even then only from their narrower, national perspective. The broader, global view, the story of pitiful political accountability at many levels, would sit stuck on the margins.

These stories must be told if we are to understand the failures in our governance structures, the chasms between us and the decision-makers. Journalism that fails to do this job is no journalism at all. This is the void that what I would call public-interest journalists and journalism must fill. It sorely needs our attention.

News agendas, the daily assignment of reporting priorities, are never designed to test governments' accountability to citizens as their principal goal. Reporters' jobs are to chase down established powers in politics or business, to harvest their quotes and follow or react to their news agendas. Putting the popular accountability of government as journalists' main concern would transform our news. We would see and read much more of the Brian Haws and Michel Davids of this world, their words and actions pitched in their full context. We would understand what they were doing and why, not simply brush them off as some naïve or hopeless wasters. We would see their efforts and those of countless others for what they truly are, red flashing lights warning us of governance systems in dire health.

My research and training, plus some activist chasing, gave me ideas about what might make a different sort of reporting. I still lacked a vision for what a different sort of politics could mean. I knew from personal and professional experience how ordinary people were locked out of day-to-day decision-making and any real influence over their politicians. I hadn't quite piled the evidence together to see the problem lay with Western government itself.

That was coming though. Increasingly, I found myself using quote marks when writing or talking about "democracy". Somehow, that still didn't feel quite right. It jarred with the idea that people had struggled and died for the right to vote over centuries. Had all those landless men, those women, blacks and colonised countries been wrong? Or was it just me, deluding myself about democracy's apparent problems?

I got further into that question in my next report, an interview with French activist and long-time political prisoner Charlie Bauer. I questioned him the day after a local screening of *Marathonien de l'espoir*, a documentary on his extraordinary life. It included the 25 years he'd spent in prison for what were deemed political crimes. We talked about democracy in the context of the upcoming presidential elections, which he criticised for the lamentable quality of candidates.[114]

Bauer paid genuine homage to the principle of universal suffrage and the struggles it took for people to win the vote. His deep, gravely voice and melodramatic delivery rang home the endorsement. But he derided the way "democracy" was now imposed on people in countries such as France. Notions of left or right were irrelevant to him given how no candidate addressed the problem of the millions of French people living in dire poverty.

The ex-inmate was by now a sociologist and social critic. He rejected the idea of backing some lesser candidate in the hope of winning token political improvements. Better to argue for radical change to the status quo, a reinvention of democracy as an idea and as a practice. Prefixing "evolution" with the "r" from rage or *rêve*, the French word for dream, gave "revolution", he observed. It needn't mean Kalashnikovs but did demand something way beyond the current system. Even the best candidates are polluted by power, he said, so another sort of politics was necessary.

He'd certainly have got my vote.

If journalism were to support that sort of change, which I believe it should, it will have to change itself. Part of that would be to produce something other than our conventional coverage of elections. It would ignore the main contenders' merry-go-round of made-to-measure stunts and news conferences. Public-interest journalism would focus instead on ordinary people's needs and interests, not tired re-runs of the same old political horse race. Conventional media, driven by their tacit income-generation or state-service remits, won't ever do that. It will require another type of journalist, maybe self-appointed ones and possibly self-trained to start with. If those journalists bother with conventional elections at all, it should be in mocking candidates' stunts and spoofing their sound bites. They could then lay bare the most spectacular stunt of them all: the elections themselves.

Talking to Bauer made clear the narrowness of my political thinking. The idea that democracy was all about elections and majorities of voters choosing their governments was too lazy and incomplete. It had taken me a decade and more in various forms of journalism to realize this gaping hole in my understanding. My education taught me no more than the basics, a pitiful state. Just as poor was that my ignorance had never seemed to harm my chances of work. It was a perfect example, on a painfully personal scale, of the truism that we get the governments we deserve.

I'd previously have thought most people knew something about democracy's meaning and origins. Given what I was finding about my own case, I was no longer so sure. More likely is that people know enough to get by. Maybe indifference, hopelessness or something else prevents them finding out more. What conversations they might have about democracy probably end with British wartime leader Winston Churchill's line about it being "the worst form of government except all those other forms that have been tried from time to time".[115]

Basic definitions

Churchill's quip was no longer good enough for me. I wanted to know democracy's root definition and descriptions of its practice from 2,500 years ago in Ancient Greece. *Democratia* comes from *demos* "the people" and *kratia* "power or rule". For me, that was a revelation. The original meaning of democracy meant people were sovereign, governing themselves rather than choosing their 'rulers' by any sort of process, elections or otherwise. So not just occasional voting then.

I found Churchill's "other forms" were described pretty well by those same Greeks, the philosopher Aristotle among them. He looked not just at systems of government but also participants' ethics, roles and responsibilities. He defined citizens as those involved in both the judicial and deliberative decisions of their cities – which is to say their legal judgments and policy making.

Centuries later, Britain allows its voters a sporadic judicial function in jury service but no deliberative role at all. Perhaps that shouldn't surprise us given leaders' typical disdain for electorates. Take Churchill's less-known quote that the best argument against democracy is a five-minute conversation with the average voter.[116]

We would be kidding ourselves to think such attitudes apply only to past political leaders. Present ones, for all their slick marketing, are as bad if not worse. More important is what we average voters think. We should all ask ourselves if we personally believe in a system that values our views only as much as our neighbour's. Perhaps in our hearts we would prefer that "democracy" mean government heed our views while ignoring those of that stupid/clever/white/black/fat/thin/rich/poor/Jewish/Christian/Muslim/gay/straight/ whatever person living across the road. If it's that, we shouldn't pretend we want democracy. Knowingly or not, we fancy something more tyrannical.

It's not a flippant question for journalists or would-be ones to ask themselves. The reality is that many probably share their elite targets' disdain for ordinary voters. That makes it easier for them to collude with the political theatre that keeps things just the way they are. Were they to change their views, one of the questions journalists could ask is this: if Britain isn't a democracy in the sense of people governing themselves – what exactly is it?

Aristotle looked at dozens of governments in Greek city states, rating them good or bad depending on whether they served common interests or rulers' selfish ones. He said good and bad systems could involve one, a few or many people as rulers. The three possible good ones were monarchy, aristocracy and what he called polity. The poor or corrupt ones were tyranny, oligarchy and democracy, the last being least bad of the three. So Athens-style democracy scored fourth out of a possible six, not great for a term that was later to become a worldwide rallying cry.[117]

Britain certainly wouldn't qualify as a democracy. Its mismatch between voters' wishes and government policy decisions is all the worse for the minority governments thrown up by its first-past-the-post elections. That winner-takes-all approach gives seats to candidates with the most votes, discarding those of all the rest. Paul Cartledge, Professor of Greek culture at Cambridge University, is scornful of modern Britain's distribution of powers. He calls it a disguised oligarchy bordering on tyranny.[118]

"Rule by crown powers from the prime minister, ministers, and EU directives, bypasses all accountability to the people's elected representatives and invalidates parliament's role of holding power to account. This is a form of tyranny… paraded by the establishment as democracy," Cartledge wrote after Blair's election victory in 2001. That means people don't elect their leader or influence policy in any way. Their only indirect control is to choose between minority elites in the next elections.

For all the noise around Britain's Alternative Vote debate in 2011, it was so much cosmetic fluff. A "yes" would merely have tinkered with seat allocations in elections, leaving the oligarchs firmly in control.

British media are quick to spray around the term "oligarch" in reference to Russia's political and business elites. They are rarely as loose lipped when it comes to their own. Insisting on simple accuracy in language, and consistency in its application, should be the iron rule for public-interest journalism. Applying such discipline to the labels we stick on our governance systems would have a major effect on our understanding of them, opening the way for their radical overhaul.

Aristotle was pessimistic about ever achieving any of the three good systems of government he described. He considered something balancing the dangers of oligarchy with those of democracy as offering the best hope of workable compromise. His thinking, summarised by the academic Richard Kraut, was nothing if not pragmatic:

"Elites and masses must learn how to work with each other, each party using its mistrust of the other to ensure that the injustices so common in political life do not get out of hand."[119]

This tension between rich and poor, so clearly seen by Aristotle if never resolved, has smouldered down the centuries in all talk of government, democratic or otherwise. To ignore it in favour of minutiae such as voting systems, the broadness of multi-party elections or turnout rates, obscures this core question. Yet minutiae are the overwhelming concerns of modern, mainstream debates about democracy, not least when it comes to media coverage.

This tension is the bedrock question. It should be declared in bold, up front as part of public-interest journalism's mission to expose and explore. Such clarity of focus would do wonders for demystifying the sound-bite factories that are our modern political parties. The base measure of all party promises and their execution would be the predicted justice and fairness of the proposals, how they might play out for elites versus the masses. In that, journalists would be resolute defenders of we the people. They would not be today's privileged "insiders" to us "outsiders" or daily scrutineers of a perpetual horse race between competing political parties serving the elite.[120]

That might bring us a step nearer the first democracies, adapted to modern societal values by including all eligible men and women, children even. The original term described a specific, popularly accountable mode of government used in dozens of Greek city states, Athens being the best known. Today's "representative democracies", usually called democracies without qualification, are nation-state governance systems that give only token powers to their people.

Democracy gets representative

I found the research helpful, but still couldn't see how democracy had become the loose-fitting label for today's most globally sought-after form of government. What happened on the road from Ancient Greece is rarely spelled out, still less widely known.

I had more work to do.

The term and its practice pretty much disappeared with the eclipse of Greek cities by Rome in the second century BC. When it re-emerged into European elite consciousness in the 1200s, it did so only as a description of mob rule. That was pretty much how the United States founding fathers viewed it when drafting the US Constitution five centuries later.[121]

The founders' political thinking, fired by their experiences of British colonial rule and taxation, inspired the three branches of government we know to this day. They are the executive office of president, law-makers in two houses of Congress and the judiciary. They aimed to limit government power over individuals while also protecting them from control by majorities. The founders called their system a "republic" – from the Latin "*res*" and "*publica*", meaning something like "a public affair" – not "democracy".

That meant a governance system based on fundamental ideas of individual equality and equal right to life. It built in freedoms of thought, expression and the pursuit of happiness, kept in check by a government subject to rule by the people.

Keeping a lid on the tyranny of many is a big challenge for all political systems. Tyrannical majorities were certainly a risk in Ancient Greece from what we know. Those original democracies had flaws and certainly produced bad decisions, not least the philosopher Socrates's sentence to death by majority vote. Yet blaming Athens-style democracy is absurd. The supposed antidote system, born in the USA and expressly designed to guard against tyrannical majorities, is one of today's most eager executioners. Any worthwhile political system, any just or fair one, must certainly guarantee minorities' protection from majorities. Today's bigger challenge is to prevent minorities from tyrannising the majority, Occupy's infamous 1% versus the 99%.[122]

Founders' choice of "republic" over "democracy" spurred endless debate on the relative attractions of each. Far more critical is the failed accountability of today's Western governments, democracies and republics alike. To counter that, public-interest reporters must always be alert to whose interests are best served in any political decision.

Taking that approach with US history throws up where founders laid the base for today's accountability problems. While Alexander Hamilton argued for representative government James Madison warned of majority factions crushing the will of minorities. The minority he meant is clear from historical records of the closed-door constitutional debates. There he argued for the planned Senate to be designed for permanence and stability. Specifically, he wanted it to "secure the permanent interests of the country against innovation". That meant protecting property owners from any future, popular pressure for land redistribution. "They ought to be so constituted as to protect the minority of the opulent against the majority," he said.[123]

Madison and company certainly got their wish, namely stability and protection of the rich. Popular elections for senators, introduced later, changed little given the barriers to office imposed by money. The global reach of US power today extends the effects of founders' designs way beyond domestic politics.

The US Senate's climate-change veto, which hung over both Kyoto and Copenhagen, is just one example of senators' elephantine influence. Legislation intended to cap US citizens' bulging per capita greenhouse gas emissions staggered through the House of Representatives in 2009. The price of its passage was major loopholes and giant concessions to the business interests affected. The Senate equivalent needed tens of billions of dollars more in promised sweeteners for industry to get anywhere near adoption a full year later, before it failed entirely.[124] What's true for climate applies also to US foreign diplomacy, to domestic healthcare reform, to regulation of banks and finance, to tax, to military spending and research – to pretty much any policy you care to mention.

Money's capture of US politics is not limited to the Senate. It engulfs each arm of government in different ways – the House of Representatives, the presidency and the judiciary.

The problem is most obvious in campaign finance, the money candidates and backers lavish on TV ads and elsewhere to pull in the votes. The 2008 election cycle saw House of Representative incumbents raise $1.4 million on average versus senators' $8.7 million.[125] The total for the same year's presidential campaign topped $1 billion for the first time – you read that correctly, $1,000 million dollars for an election campaign. President Obama talked of raising a $1 billion in funds for his 2012 run.[126]

Donors don't give their money for fun, they're buying political influence. If that channel fails, a second one exists in the revolving doors connecting government to business. Changing administrations provide a merry-go-round of interests that pitches individuals from US government into business, finance and the law and out again, depending on who's in power. Today's regulators become tomorrow's regulated and vice versa, muddying questions of public accountability, transparency of interests and influence.

Britain's accountability issues are less structurally overt and cheaper to buy into. They're just as easy to read in policy outcomes. The heft of banks and finance was clear right through the Blair, Brown and Cameron governments. Each in turn soft-shoe shuffled on regulating the City – before, during and since the global financial crisis.[127]

Perhaps we would be telling a different story about democracy today had France's masses succeeded with their more ambitious project to unseat their elite. The 1789 revolution, unlike the US one, took direct and explicit aim at inequalities between the rich and poor.

Historian John Dunn characterises the French and US revolutions as a battle between the orders of equality and egoism. US reformers favoured property rights in their broadest sense at the expense of greater equity, made good in theory by representative government. French ones envisioned more direct democracy, inspired by the philosopher Jean-Jacques Rousseau, versus Madison's systemic defences against faction and tyrant majorities. At stake were both the word "democracy" and the system of government laying claim to it.

For Dunn, on each count, the US versions categorically thumped their opposition. Who could disagree?[128]

The result was that Washington's representative government usurped the mental space available for Athenian *demokratia* – which is to say participatory, deliberative democracy. At the same time, it claimed squatter's rights to the word itself.

The US take on democracy, the official, rhetorical version, dominates most casual notions of the idea, certainly those without quote marks round the word. Typical is the definition by Samuel Huntington, a Harvard political scientist and sometime government adviser. His widely cited definition of democracy is profoundly unambitious. He defines it as a system whose most powerful decision-makers are chosen through fair, honest and periodic elections. Candidates may freely compete for the votes of virtually all adults. Such societies allow popular freedoms to speak, publish, assemble and organise.

It seems not bad on the face of it – those are liberties anyone would be happy to have and remain beyond a large section of humanity even today. For all that, Huntington's democracy is nothing like what we could enjoy with truly accountable governance, something we deny ourselves by accepting his democracy-lite version.

The definition seems fine until you consider what it leaves out. Huntington calls "classical" notions of democracy, such as power in the hands of the people, rationalistic, idealistic and utopian. He defends his definition as pragmatic, allowing easy comparison of countries' governance qualities. "Elections, open, free and fair, are the essence of democracy, the inescapable *sine qua non*," he argues.

Yet city-states in Ancient Greece had complex systems of assemblies, courts and councils as their governments. They used selection by lottery as the default for allocating political office. Elections took place only for posts with military or financial responsibilities. Citizens' wishes were live and ever-present, not locked behind bars for brief expression in occasional ballots. Ancient Greeks thought elections favoured the elite, people already notable by birth, education or wealth. Those advantages all but guaranteed unequal opportunity and outcome in ballots, leading inevitably to oligarchy. For elected posts, winners remained under popular control, subject to instant recall, office term limits and an obligation to provide regular accounts of their work.[129]

Why something similar should be beyond modern nation states, at the very least for lower tiers of government, is a mystery. Public-interest journalists should make it a priority to look into why that should be.

Huntington's definition, which has been remarkably effective at blanking out more accountable alternatives, traces its roots to the birth of the United States. Its model of representative government launched what he calls democracy's "first wave". The definition's wide acceptance presents a critical challenge to anyone thinking "democracy" should mean power in the hands of a majority of the people, even better a deliberative majority.[130]

Reclaiming democracy as a word and practice should be the mission of all public-interest journalists. US ones should remember their founders' Declaration of Independence, which proclaimed the right to revolution and consent of the governed. The neutered constitution that ensued has proved enduringly effective at keeping political control with the wealthy few at the expense of the poorer many, albeit with the odd reverse. The political structure designed by lawyers, merchants, planters, land and securities speculators, civil servants and politicians is creaking badly. Its durability and influence mean similar problems face the representative governments it inspired all around the world. More than two centuries after its birth, it is long overdue radical change.[131]

Journalists should highlight the limited reality of modern representative democracy versus its hyped-up hopes. They should make their core editorial aim to kick-start informed debates for radical reform. That shouldn't be some short-term, academic, elitist or ad-driven exercise to boost audience numbers – the effects of unaccountable government are far too serious and too entrenched for that. If my own poor knowledge of democracy is anything to go by, an important job would be to gather basic materials that give a proper perspective on democracy. They should be shared as widely as possible, offered for free online, without copyright protection, for anyone who wants them. Lack of money should not deny people access to the debate.

My shallow trawl through democracy's history at last gave me a sense of where "democracy" had lost its original meaning to an upstart alternative. It helped me understand political accountability as the critical problem with our governments, planting the seeds of a personal editorial manifesto.

Before taking that on, I thought it worth looking at the quality of existing representative democracies.

For all Washington's global power and influence, it can't claim anything like the world number one spot. With all the usual caveats over definitions, the best one is probably Norway.

The Economist Intelligence Unit's democracy index is better than most. It defines four categories of regime – full or flawed democracy, hybrid or authoritarian – assigning countries individual rankings. The 2011 one identified only 25 "full" democracies. It measured electoral process and pluralism, the functioning of government, political participation, political culture and civil liberties. Norway scored 9.80 out of a possible 10, followed by three of its Nordic neighbours plus New Zealand and Australia. The United States managed 8.11 points or 19th, with Britain a place above. Other G7 powers, the world's richest countries, stretched from Canada in 8th position to the "flawed democracy" of France and Italy at 29th and 31st respectively.[132]

While the EIU index is certainly subtler than the much-quoted one by Freedom House, it still takes no account of the economic or social well-being of countries' citizens. That yields the significant problem of mis-comparison between people's real lives and ignores wealth disparity within societies. So South Africa ranks 28th in the EIU list of

167 states, among the highest-ranked "flawed democracies". Cuba sits at 126, down among the authoritarian ones, its far superior development indicators counting for nothing.

Could it be that the government of a country the US State Department describes as "a totalitarian communist state" is more accountable to its people than many countries ranked above it? It's a worthwhile question public-interest journalists should consider when filtering rhetoric from reality. Cuban authorities certainly think they should rank much higher, of course. They are not without their reasoned external supporters.[133]

Neither the EIU or Freedom House scores for the effects of a country's policies on others. That matters enormously for the likes of the United States, with its multiple military interventions abroad. So too for the global banks and corporations Washington and other major capitals fail to regulate for their human rights abuses, pollution or worker exploitation. Neither markets, consumers or the media can act as regulators in governments' absence – it just won't happen. We need governments that are far more accountable to their citizens. The effects of making that happen would resonate beyond national borders, just as they could have done had rich-country leaders followed their citizens' wishes in writing off poor-country debts or by acting on climate change. A fuller index would mark the fall-out from regulatory failure and unconstrained militarism as strong, net-negatives on national scores.

Britain's mark would suffer by virtue of its role as a major hub of global offshore finance, to the severe detriment of both its own and other countries' governance quality. The City of London sits astride a global web of secrecy jurisdictions. The twilight regulatory zones of British overseas territories and crown dependencies constantly feed business and capital into London from all the secret accounts, shell companies and other tax-haven dodges that they harbour.[134]

Offshore finance is a no-man's land stretching from the dubious-if-legal to the outright criminal, running unchecked by truly accountable government. Its secret deposits and the illicit financial flows it allows are not victimless events. The losers are domestic tax authorities and their hapless onshore constituencies, the latter suffering heavier taxes and state budget cuts as a result.[135]

The good news is that Washington's ideological dominance over the meaning and practice of democracy is weakening. Space is opening up for what looks like a global flowering of democratic alternatives. Some extend existing practice, such as ballot initiatives and referenda. Others are strikingly new and more fundamental in the changes they represent. They include the participatory budgets of places such Brazil's Porto Allegre, which have transformed civic governance. Citizens' assemblies and deliberative juries are also taking root.[136]

All offer story opportunities for public-interest journalism by anyone dreaming that democracy should be more radical than "elections free and fair". Interviewing the protagonists, explaining the initiatives and how they play out should be reporters' regular beat. Comparing the status quo with more accountable alternatives should be a benchmark of coverage.

Experiments are underway in established and emerging democracies alike, meaning plenty of reporting work to go around. One is Sweden's Demoex, which grew out of students' frustrations with right-left polarizations in politics and their pessimism about the prospects of ever wielding influence. They built a mix of direct and representative democracy in which elected candidates – well candidate for the moment, they only have one – follow Demoex members' directions in local government votes.[137]

Another is the Transition Network, a UK-inspired, global movement of community-based efforts preparing for the twin challenges of peak oil and climate change. In just a few years, the ideas of co-founder Rob Hopkins and others have spread from southwest England to inspire more than a thousand offshoots in Britain and around the world.[138]

Whether Transition participants realise it or not, their various efforts are inherently political. They presage a leakage of power and responsibility away from formal structures of government and elected politicians. A backlash seems inevitable. Power gained by one party comes from another, a transfer that rarely happens lightly.

It begs the question of tactics. Should social change seekers engage with existing powers, facing the accompanying risk of co-option and neutralisation? Should they confront incumbent structures directly or simply operate without reference to them? These are legitimate questions for which there aren't hard-and-fast answers. Journalists should be in the thick of debates, doing their best to reflect the depth and richness of the conversation.[139]

Transition efforts are currently limited to local or regional levels in a few countries. None is anywhere near the nation-state level despite the urgencies of both climate change and peak oil. One initiative that has made the step up is Sweden's grassroots Active Democracy Party. It fought parliamentary elections in 2006 and 2010, failing completely to win much more than some media airtime. Its promise was that successful candidates would become "button-pushers" for their electorates, bound to vote in parliament according to citizens' wishes. Australia has a similar thing in its Senator On-Line party, though it too is only tiny so far.[140]

Swedes and Australians are lucky already to have the fourth and sixth best electoral democracies respectively, according to the EIU. The rest of us shouldn't leave such experiments to them, we should explore some of our own for ourselves. This is another job for public-interest journalism – exploring the possibilities for similar systems at local government levels in reporters' home communities. Independent local media could host alternative political discussion arenas to find out how participatory systems of government might work.

Scoring well among world democracies is no reason for complacency, as Iceland and Ireland have discovered. Despite being second and 12th respectively among the EIU's "full democracies", both were wrecked by the global financial crisis. Their domestic governance qualities proved no protection from the effects of under-regulated local and global banks and finance. Though personal debt binges played their parts in both countries' downfall, they were not the main causes. The real blame lay in the political and regulatory failures that left the doors wide open to debt speculators. Their citizens now face bills and service cuts to make up asset piles that disappeared to who knows where? So far, so familiar – dozens of countries have suffered market beatings over the years. What set Ireland and Iceland apart is how popular dissent at least spurred some efforts at formal political reforms.[141]

Where are the reforms in the countries that hosted the ongoing financial crisis and its major players? Where in Britain or the United States are these public accountability questions being asked? The answer is pretty much nowhere among politicians and hardly much more anywhere else. At least, that was, until Occupy movements sprang up on parks and pavements in Wall Street, the City and dozens of other places in late 2011. Those protests, inspired by grassroots political surges in Tunisia, Egypt and elsewhere, suggest a pent-up appetite for tackling the fundamental inequalities produced by our unaccountable political systems. Whether occupations and their associated actions will spur deep-rooted reforms is too early to say. What is already clear is the creative energy they have attracted, not least among activist media makers and tech specialists.

Any public-interest media project needs to tap into that spirit, putting questions of political accountability and reform at the top of its editorial priorities. A major part of its work would be to do news and features that unpick conventional thinking about economic growth and finance, exploring alternatives and efforts to bring them into being. Reporters could write about the basics of money – how it is conjured into being each time commercial banks make loans, adding to a global pool of debts that leads inevitably to speculative booms and busts. They could look at Transition Network initiatives intended to re-localise economic activity in the UK by creating alternative currencies such as the Totnes and Brixton pounds.[142]

Getting from popular disgust at the global financial crisis to political action requires sustained mental effort and dogged hard work on the part of activists. The same applies to reporters. Most of the latter will need to reboot their conventional thinking and ways of working so as to build up some credibility with their politically disaffected audiences.

The underlying theme to all this work is the state of our political structures themselves. This should be the central pillar of public-interest media, infusing all its stories. Whatever topics reporters might pursue, their coverage should refer to the existing political structures that govern the issue in question. They should reflect on how structures themselves skew political outcomes towards the interests of a rich elite at the expense of the poor majority.

In seeking out alternatives, reporters should consider the potential policy effects of having Athens-style direct democracies in place of today's less-than-representative governments. No such structures yet exist anywhere in the world for conventional national politics though there are significant smaller-scale attempts. None is more striking than the efforts of the Zapatistas in southeastern Mexico's Chiapas state, or rather the parts of it controlled by their indigenous Zapatista Army of National Liberation.[143]

For fans of political accountability what startles is the Zapatista army's relationship with power and the way its communities govern themselves. That was evident in the Zapatistas' original call, in January 1994, for the right to select their own administrative authorities. They briefly fought, negotiated with then finally bypassed the federal government in pursuit of those rights. Today, governments in their autonomous areas use rotational systems to select political office holders, not unlike the way juries are picked in countries such as England. The Zapatistas, despite facing chronic low-intensity warfare, draw clear lines separating the army hierarchy from civilian politics. Supporters point to improved women's rights and better education, health and nutrition since the 1994 uprising. While no one claims the movement is perfect, its efforts have inspired countless other global justice campaigners in the years since.[144]

Accountability deficits are the common theme inspiring various experiments in democracy stretching from local governments around the world to the global level itself.[145] For the European Union's 27 members, an additional barrier to popular political influence exists in the Brussels institutions and the EU Treaties. This gulf between people's expectations of democracy and their daily experiences is a potentially powerful motor for change, magnified by the Internet's burgeoning communications power. The promise is not for some Twitter- or Facebook-inspired political brush fire but a deeper-set, longer-burning affair. Taken as a whole, what looms is the possibility of a far more hopeful vision for democracy's future, fundamentally transformed to reflect popular accountability.

Journalists who adopt the role of accountability champions could play a critical part in keeping that process on the road. An ill-defined sense of that possibility lured me from Reuters in 2005. While I could only guess at the political changes to come I could feel the rumbling of something politically significant and fundamental underway. I knew I would struggle to explore or understand it from within my very conventional news bubble.

Nearly seven years on, a combination of political study and reporting experiments have clarified my thinking. In addition to the activists I put on video were many others I met and interviewed. People such as Sandor Dus, or Cosmo to his friends, a singer-songwriting English teacher living in Cardiff. Twice he landed in a Scottish jail during the 2005 Gleneagles summit of world leaders. His crime was to have tried to dance in a field in attempted protest at leaders' pitiful efforts at poor-country debt relief.

The activists I met were a minute sample of those around the world who are waking up to the unaccountability of governments we lazily dub democracies. Their actions involve varying degrees of engagement, personal discomfort and risk – some far greater than others. Their efforts link them back to the people throughout history who have struggled for political systems that are more directly accountable to the governed and more apt to foster justice.

For all the obstacles people face, their efforts do sometimes succeed. One of the most inspiring people I saw during the Copenhagen climate talks in 2009 was Maldives President Mohamed Nasheed. As a victim of beatings, torture and six years in prison and work camps, he could claim to have suffered more than most in the name of democracy. Yet he got his prize, the Maldives' liberation from Maumoon Gayoom, de facto dictator of 30 years.

"The dictatorship had the guns, bombs and tanks. We had no weapons other than the power of our words, and the moral clarity of our cause. Many democracy activists like us had vanished, forgotten by history, their struggle a failure," he told a rapt audience.[146]

Despite the victory, Nasheed and his island-nation electorate face a threat to their existence no local ballot box can counter – that of rising sea levels driven by global climate change. For all Nasheed's faith in democracy, his prize risks disappearing along with the country's coconut palms and white sand beaches.[147]

Would-be governance reformers and public-interest journalists should pay heed to his story. It shows the impotence of representative democracy in the face of critical global problems such as climate change. For that, we need a functioning global governance mechanism that includes fair and transparent negotiating processes. The severity of government accountability problems, not just in the United States, kills off all chance of a just or equitable policy emerging. Bleating about the intransigence of emerging powers such as China, India or Brazil is a dishonest distraction from the basic history of the problem.

A second point to take from Nasheed is how his case highlights the attention and seriousness reporters must give activists and their efforts to address our accountability deficits. I watched Nasheed speak in the warmth of a modern conference hall because he'd won his struggle and escaped from prison to lead his country. Most of my time in Copenhagen was spent in the cold with activists, the former Nasheed's equivalents, not with negotiators. I deliberately broke conventional journalists' norms of objectivity because those norms are so much bunk, tying us to status quo sources. We shouldn't shy from civil disobedience actions that help our audiences understand the idea of public accountability. First-hand reporting as a demonstrator, direct audits of police behaviour, is a valid part of that exercise.

It's a lesson to take to other global meetings and institutions, the United Nations, IMF or meetings of G7 or more leaders from major nations. If reporters must attend such made-for-media events they should leave their newsrooms to find alternative stories. Whatever they write should highlight accountability issues. They should look at the political access business lobbyists get versus the treatment meted out to activists trying to represent civil society.

Another point about Nasheed is that while his country faces graver threats than most other newly liberated states, which is to say its total destruction, all are inherently vulnerable. Their electorates are at constant risk of losing their political freedoms to the more-restrictive forms of government from which they have just escaped. They quickly discover the constraints on popular power and influence presented even by their newly minted versions of representative democracy. None is more pervasive, or less subject to influence, than globally mobile private and corporate capital acting via international financial markets. If a new government's powers and policies aren't tightly bound by the demands of capital from the outset, the speculators have the levers to bring them quickly to heel or even topple them. Their effective powers challenge the dreams of democracy and voter sovereignty that inspire Nasheed and his like.[148]

For all the euphoria of Tunisians, Egyptians and Libyans as their long-time dictators fall from power, these are the realities that await. Reporters covering reformers' efforts should keep in mind the limitations of Huntington's democracy-lite definition, keeping alert for more accountable alternatives pursued by the new governments.

The EIU launched its 2010 democracy index with talk of democracy having gone into retreat around the world, a year before Tunisians opened another, hopeful chapter for themselves and others. It blamed the global financial crisis for having accentuated certain "existing negative trends in political development". It made no attempt to factor in the national governance implications of governments failing to regulate international banks and finance.[149]

That shallowness is typical of conventional media cover. Most fail even to consider exposing the failures of representative democracy let alone suggest remedies or explore its mis-definition. Few venture near democracy activists for anything beyond the colour quote, the brief and superficial. They rarely if ever give proper context to activists' efforts, or make the necessary links with elsewhere. That means the gathering democratic revolution of which those activists are a part remains unappreciated and still less understood.

Human governance and freedoms have spread worldwide since Pericles eulogised the democratic qualities of ancient Athens. Both have required the best of our ancestors to risk bloody revolution, war, protest, imprisonment, torture and death. What progress there has been is tempered by the enormity of what remains to be done. Not least of the tasks is more fairly sharing the world's finite resources among a human population of seven billion people and counting. To do that, we must transform the quality of our debates about democracy and its practice. We must challenge the claims of representative democracy's advocates that their half-cooked system is the end of an affair begun thousands of years ago, even before the Greeks.

We face a massive task that comes with the added complication of being an urgent one. Evidence of representative democracy's failures is unanswerable at the same time as being chronically under discussed. It is particularly acute when it comes to the regulation of global banks, finance and resource extraction companies. Our conventional media deserve a large slice of blame. Their reporters and editors are too bedazzled by their VIP sources and constrained by pressures from their owners and income sources. Institutionally and personally they are too limited in their outlooks, too incurious and too frightened for their professional futures. Public-interest journalists must take on the job their conventional peers fail to do and plunge into the yawning governance gulf they leave unexplored.

That means doing stories that use basic, tangible, human measures to illustrate the state of our societies, unpicking the abstractions of economic growth and gross domestic product. Things like the quality of people's health, housing, literacy and life expectancy, coupled with data on disparities in their access to the means to improve them.

We are unquestionably at a time of hope but also great potential peril in the world. There are progressive responses underway. Some alone or together with others might ease or even resolve our fundamental governance crises and the problems they create. We need to hear much more about them, their whos, whats, whys, whens and wheres. That is where journalism comes in.

The journalistic vision required to explore and encourage the necessary governance revolution is just emerging. It risks derailment by journalists' ignorance, their professional pride and social or cultural separation from the victims of poor governance. Reporters are addicted to novelty, obsessed with the sensationalist, teaching audiences to want the same. What we need goes past that, beyond the diary-led storytelling of conventional media workdays. If journalism is to have worth or purpose, it must become an unwavering champion of good governance at every level of politics. That means an all-encompassing vision for public-interest journalists, and cooperation among them, building from the many locals to our one-and-only global. Existing reporters would be welcome to join if they can get their heads around the necessary change of mindset. Many could be young hopefuls at the point of entry into the profession. More broadly, they could include determinedly curious and honest people from communities all over the world, ones who with some training could produce all the public-interest journalism our societies need.

They could be you.

Conclusions

It's easy enough to criticise the status quo of modern politics and journalism – many of us do it all the time – far harder to suggest coherent solutions that might work. Critiques of our governance systems, the flaws in our media or both tend to peter out when they get to their conclusions, their authors seemingly too exhausted or timid to topple status-quo convictions. They shy away from joining the dots and following through with radical, practical proposals. It is understandable – the problems seem so vast and entrenched as to beggar possible alternatives. It is a mistake, though, and a wasted opportunity to help fundamentally transform our governance systems from their current, pitifully unaccountable states.

So, conscious of the enormity of the challenge and its urgency, I offer here my answers. Some are my own, others I have adapted or adopted wholesale from elsewhere. They stretch from the personal and practical to the collective and networked. I don't pretend to have a complete solution, *the* answer, but I do think the ideas can help. Their unifying aim is to promote and to practise public-interest journalism to make our governors and governance systems more accountable to us all.

Those systems, nested like so many Russian dolls from local to global levels, separate we the governed from our governors as never before in collective human history. Their workings are lost to ordinary people in a tangle of more or less-known and still-less-understood institutions and regulatory bodies. Many operate in near obscurity behind serial walls – physical, operational or technical – making them all but immune to our influence. Neither elected politicians nor civil servants, even those with the best possible intentions, exercise the necessary duty of care on our behalf. Conventional journalists and their employers are similarly incompetent public guardians, with rare exceptions. That opens the gates to elite interests whose motives are certainly not the collective good. The effect is to concentrate wealth in the hands of a tiny few at the expense of the global many. That leaves the job of governance watchdog and champion to us, the world's mis-governed, ordinary members of global civil society.

This huge task is far beyond the capacities of individuals acting alone in one country. To tackle it we need the sustained, determined focus of many people, acting alone and together in groups and networks.

Some are already doing it. They include social and political justice activists around the world focused on the many public accountability holes in our governments. More will emerge from among journalism students and novices, those whose professional vision has yet to be polluted by, or hard-wired into, conventional news production models. Others could be current or former professional reporters or even their news organisations, though not without them re-ordering their editorial thinking and revamping their revenue models. Many, many more will be ordinary people who have picked up the necessary knowledge and reporting skills on the run. Their work may be ad hoc or part-time, as circumstances allow, but no less effective for that.

Together, the shared editorial objective of all these people would be to do public-interest journalism. Its core aim would be to produce work that helps make our existing governments and governance bodies become radically more accountable to us or be shunted aside by alternatives. Their collective task would be to fill the void left untouched by the chatter of conventional media coverage.

This is not an abstract concept but a resolutely practical one. My personal response to the problems I saw with democracy and journalism was to go back to basics for both. I began experimenting with journalism to highlight the realities of representative democracy and explore positive examples of alternatives. I started on a local scale to show what's possible, always with an eye to scaling it up and stretching it wider in due course. Before even opening a notebook, I had to re-evaluate my professional habits and personal politics. I looked at my existing idea of journalism's role, which was that it support the healthy functioning of democracy. I soon found things weren't as simple as that. That vague definition threw up a whole series of other questions, such as what "democracy" meant, how to gauge the quality of one country's over another's and how to tackle issues stretching across several governance layers. The search exposed the limits of my own political knowledge while also giving some specific pointers towards the sort of journalism I wanted to do and why.

The result is simple enough – my aim is to do journalism that helps radically transform our governance systems. It is not a neutral process but a fiercely partisan one, totally committed to the public good rather than blindly accepting the political status quo on misplaced grounds of neutrality or objectivity.

A first step for any would-be public-interest journalist is to sketch out the various conventional political systems that govern people's lives in their local communities.

Where I live, in southwest France, those structures begin with the local commune and mayor then climb through several layers of authority to the national government in Paris. On beyond lie the European Union in Brussels and global bodies such as the World Trade Organisation and the IMF, in Geneva and Washington respectively. For all the apparent distance from the bigger ones, their decisions play out daily in local policy, directly affecting governance quality and accountability. Taken together, they influence our housing, health, education, farming, transport, care for the elderly, Internet provision, policing, in fact, pretty much everything.

Being a public-interest journalist doesn't mean you have to bury yourself in detailed knowledge of all the different political structures and their powers. It would help to have some basic understanding and awareness, coupled with a preparedness to learn more. I was lucky to know their official stories, roles and responsibilities, from my salaried work in the past. My problem was in being too biased towards their versions of reality, too unquestioning of their legitimacy and enamoured by their representatives.

Building politics into communities

Tackling that knowledge gap is a vital first step in any public-interest journalism project. It matters as much for would-be journalists as for their audiences.

Awareness of my own ignorance inspired one of my earliest alternative journalism efforts. It concerned watching and learning more than reporting. The idea was simple – to host regular, free documentary screenings, and occasional items of locally produced video, on the second Friday of every month. The evenings bring local people together to learn about a chosen political topic, to discuss it and share a meal. The act of assembly, open to all and tackling politically controversial topics, reinforces the general knowledge of politics. It introduces us to people we might not ordinarily meet, building community. Collective viewing and discussion contrasts with our usual, isolated acts as individuals or families in separate households. The range of content and its communal presentation is beyond the imagination or capacity of conventional media. It is as radical as fellow human beings with no prior relationship coming together, addressing tricky political issues and not killing one another. It is a small seed of real democracy, a precursor to reasoned, informed debate about concrete political issues in the local area. It is a vital part of any broader public-journalism project – both for its openness to the outside and the opportunity it gives for informal learning. Without sound political knowledge and understanding we are powerless to change anything.

Five or so years of regular monthly screenings have created all manner of bonds and connections between those who attend. It hints at possibilities for various future projects to be done together. Several professional film-makers have presented their work in person. The numbers attending have steadily grown over the years, reaching more than 50 on occasions in an area with a sparse and dispersed rural

Conclusions

population. Other such micro screenings have taken root nearby in what has always been a politically engaged and non-mainstream part of France. Together, screenings build a live audience for budding activist-journalists as well as a pool of potential reporters. Each evening holds the promise of positive feedback loops of engagement, collaboration and improved political understanding. They spill over into improved local accountability and showcase the potential for local, practical initiatives using journalism to improve our politics.

One evening, themed on water, combined local reporting, publishing and politics. I screened a video I'd made on the ecology of water and sewage treatment along with a longer documentary about the politics of water. It featured Uruguayans' rejection of water privatisation in a national referendum. The audience, which included local councillors and the mayor, learnt and talked about water issues together. It was a valuable exercise, preparing the ground for what will be expensive sanitation works due in our village in the coming years. The evening put down a marker for future debates and eventual public consultations over the work, including such taboo ideas as waterless composting toilets.

Our use of water, and the politics and economics that govern it, is a universally relevant subject. Shooting a video report gave the screening audience a bigger picture of the issue. It also provided a document for a wider francophone audience on the Internet. The report was nothing spectacular, yielding just a couple of thousand Internet views in three years, though it usefully contributed to local debate on managing our environmental impact.

This is public-interest journalism, reporting work that focuses on specific issues with the idea that we all have a right to determine how they are tackled. It explores alternatives to the obvious, status-quo approach, finding authoritative figures with no political or monetary interest in specific outcomes and airing their views.[150]

On top of the practical reporting, even on the micro-scale described here, comes the question of how to build genuinely democratic political cultures. My life so far has taken me through many different countries. The experience has convinced me people have a very acute sense of the "political", even if the status quo of their politicians inclines them to tune out or turn off. Anyone wanting genuine, participatory democracy, something in the style of Ancient Athens made modern, must believe in their fellow humans. Otherwise they should forget any ideas of power in the hands of the people and accept more dictatorial modes of government, such as our current ones. You can't have it both ways. For those hesitating over the choice, and let's face it, we all have our inner bigots, it helps to look at the evidence of people's qualities rather than trusting to personal prejudice. Get out there and meet people who are trying to make a difference. I always find it inspiring, for all its inevitable messiness.

The British modernist writer Virginia Woolf imagined collective political thought as some "shapeless jelly of human stuff", wobbling this way or that according to whatever instinct of hate, revenge or admiration bubbled up beneath it. Such haughty disdain is as common and pervasive today as it is misplaced. People may sometimes lack the language, historical depth or formal education to express their political arguments. That doesn't mean they have no innate wisdom, no true sense of justice or capacity to discriminate in matters political. Quite the opposite, in fact.[151]

Teaching and learning public-interest journalism

No one is so smart that a little more learning would harm them. That is certainly the case when it comes to understanding our political systems. Rather than wait for our representative democracies to catch up, by recognising real political education and journalism as public goods, we must provide them for ourselves.

As far as journalism is concerned, I know from experience the time, money and access barriers facing anyone who wants to work for conventional news providers. That is to say nothing of the constraints facing those who then succeed. Running free video journalism

186

workshops, in schools and the communities in which people live, helps tackle those problems. Practical training exercises can be themed around democracy – the two are bound together so why not use one to explore the other? As local skills sets grow, a network of journalists tackling local political issues will emerge, forming the kernel of a more sustained video reporting culture. While much of the content will remain local, it will still resonate with audiences elsewhere – politics is always politics. France already has *Les Vidéos des Pays et des Quartiers*, a limited network of participatory TV organisations, which is active both in rural areas and cities. Their members train others, producing and projecting their work to the communities in which they live. In the face of local commercial media's collapse or monopolisation, community alternatives could offer more public-focused journalism. These are not unique to France, in fact the place is probably behind the curve internationally in its alternative media, as with so many things Internet, despite its general culture of deep political thinking.[152]

Mathieu Gilles is a video activist with MO-TV, the local, participatory television service of Marennes-Oleron, western France. A big part of his work is public outreach, teaching local people the rudiments of video film production. I met him en route to Copenhagen climate talks in December 2009. We made the round trip together on a bus powered by recycled chip oil collected from his local community. A year later he gave a free video training workshop for around a half dozen people from my local area.

Mathieu taught people the basics of how to plan, shoot and record a video report, helping them to get started. Participants chipped in for transport costs and brought food to share. They took turns using the camera, mikes and doing shot planning. It was a much cheaper version of the video training I'd had myself a few years earlier in Brussels, mine having come courtesy of the retraining budget I got in my Reuters redundancy package.

Lowering the barriers to entry for would-be reporters is a critical requirement for building up public-interest journalism. Short videos are probably one of the most effective ways to communicate governance issues, bringing them alive with audio and moving images in a way that speaks to ordinary people. Language barriers can be overcome with subtitling, something easily done with modern video edit packages. The advent of crowd-sourced subtitling and subtitle translation, ones such as the Universal Subtitles project, will help the most powerful reports travel further.[153]

The output was a short video I edited from what participants had filmed. What it lacked in overall sound and image quality was made up for in its richness of content, all from local events that happened during the weekend. It clearly showed the potential for public-interest journalism even in such a small, out-of-the-way-part of rural France. Among the things covered was a local collective gardening project, its plots available to all comers. Another element featured an associative food-processing centre while yet another covered a charity art auction to support a Palestinian refugee camp in Gaza.

Any one of those strands could have been broken out to illustrate the global made local. The content could have been extended, subtitled and enriched to broaden its appeal and deepen its context. Each was a seed from which more public-interest journalism efforts could grow, projects stretching to other parts of France and abroad. They showed what's possible in the face of our political status quo. One gave an answer to our chronic reliance on fossil-fuel-powered farming, the next an alternative to our monopolised commercial food chains and the third highlighted the chronic indifference of our politicians towards seeking a just solution to the Israeli-Palestinian conflict. All participants had ideas of video projects they hoped to explore.

The weekend's training was nowhere near enough to learn all the skills required for effective public-interest journalism. What's needed is far more than plan, point, shoot, edit and publish. But it was a start for those who attended, giving them a base from which to build. Future workshops will aim to extend their expertise, and to pass it on to other local activists and to school children. Many people in the area are keen to prepare the community for the effects of climate change and peak oil, inspired by the UK's Transition Initiatives concept. That is another likely source of video project ideas and enthusiasts.

The idea of free video training is nothing revolutionary. The UK non-profit organisation *Undercurrents* was launched in 1993 to offer media support to grassroots direct action campaign groups. It won a series of international awards for its documentaries and alternative news videos before morphing into the online TV news channel *visionOntv* in 2008. Its work includes offering free training workshops and resources for would-be citizen TV reporters, part of its aim to promote and distribute video for social change. Technical excellence, or at least reasonable competence, is an essential part of getting social-change messages across. The added idea from *Fraudcast News* is to help citizen reporters grasp the fundamentals of those messages, to underpin their new-found practical skills with a political substructure grounded in accountable governance.

Replacing objectivity with declared subjectivity

One of the many things missing from my French workshop agenda was the question of what reporters should or shouldn't cover. The issue came up of its own accord during the weekend itself. Participants went to the local, volunteer-run Sunday market, an important weekly event in community life, where they did interviews and gathered visuals for the final edit. Those working the kit at one point decided not to film a full, stand-up row between some stallholders and the person allocating places. The energetic shouting match took place to the backdrop of a visual gift, a black and white poster of a smiling Gandhi. The row, which could have been edited to protect people's identities, was a great counterpoint to the picture of progressive, rural harmony presented by other events. It would have shown the trickiness of attempting alternative modes of living and doing business, keeping a check on reality.

All reporting runs the risk of sliding into outright propaganda, a major switch-off for audiences. We already have enough of it with the way our mainstream news covers officialdom. Such work insults audience intelligence, ultimately discrediting its producers. The best defence is to aim for accuracy and fairness, first in reporting but then also in story writing and production. Personally, I would have recorded the row, even if I'd subsequently decided not to use it. Not filming it meant denying ourselves the luxury of choosing.

The incident raised a critical issue for would-be public-interest journalists, what professional journalists call "objectivity". This widely accepted concept helps torpedo journalism's potential to promote positive societal change. Broadly speaking, it governs the basic reporting functions of recording eyewitness accounts of events, cross-checking the facts with alternative sources and attempting to balance parties' different viewpoints.

The problem is that journalists commonly misinterpret objectivity as meaning neutrality. They sterilise their stories with he-said-she-said accounts, leaving audiences plain bemused. In trying to be neutral, reporters omit the necessary context and background to allow people to make sense of an issue. They would do far better to aim for accuracy and fairness, declaring their subjectivity from the outset. No one should be ashamed of that – the news production process is inherently and inescapably subjective. Choosing which subject to cover, whom to interview, how to order the facts gathered, what prominence to give one story over another – all are subjective decisions. Throwing a cloak of supposed "objectivity" or balance over the top has the perverse effect of neutralising news, making it utterly spineless.

US media critic Ben Bagdikian demolished the idea of objectivity in *Media Monopoly*, even while sympathetically explaining how it arose. Its effects are to play up official, establishment sources and crowd out those things that undermine their authority and credibility. It hides the realities of private power, leaves unchallenged the public image power projects and weeds out vital interpretation and explanation in stories lest the writer be called biased.[154]

Had I been "objective" I would not have gone on the climate activists' civil disobedience march in Copenhagen. I would certainly not have joined arms with protesters in a human chain pushing towards police lines. I would have missed out on a vital sense of protesters' courage, their very, everyday normalness. No one would have given a second thought to questions of journalistic objectivity had I chosen to get accredited as a reporter. I could have schmoozed the conference corridors talking to business lobbyists and those national delegates busy trashing all chances of a deal. No problems of objectivity there. So a reporter spending time with people trying honestly to inject some urgency into a political process is biased and polemical, betraying the very codes of journalism. At the same event, interviewing the deal wreckers is just fine. Try explaining that logic to a polar bear.

That is not to say public-interest journalism should forget professional standards. It should operate according to openly declared ethics, standards and procedures. Those should come from exhaustive and transparent consultation, including with audiences. As far as ethics are concerned, these are certainly something for journalists and their publics to establish. While it is not for me to preach my personal leanings to anyone, I declare here my own position. I draw inspiration from the teachings of the monk and peace activist Thich Nhat Hanh, work he calls engaged Buddhism. His Five Mindfulness Trainings represent a non-sectarian vision for global spirituality and ethics. They examine ways to transform violence, fanaticism, and dogmatism and to reduce exploitation, social injustice, stealing, and oppression. Of particular relevance to journalists is the pledge not to spread news that is uncertain or to utter words that cause division or discord. It is no mean personal and professional challenge.[155]

As for goals, all public-interest journalists do well to define what they're about before even picking up a camera or opening a notebook. My aim is to produce truthful, fact-based reports that include accurate context and honest interpretation of events. The stories I choose to do, the way I prioritise them over others and order facts or interviews, are aimed at radically improving the public accountability of our governance. It is a personal code that will remain a perpetual work-in-progress, to be finessed in collaboration with similarly motivated others over time. The result might be a collated reporting handbook for public-interest journalism and maybe a code of practice.

There's plenty of existing material from which to beg, borrow and steal, in true journalistic tradition. *The NewStandard's* handbook provides an excellent start and still exists online despite its mother publication's demise. It lays out principles for reporting and editing, story style and choice, workplace functioning, income sources and worker payment. *Indymedia's* principles of unity are also valuable, setting the operational code for its global network of independent media centres (IMCs) and feeding into individual IMC rules and practices. The *Real News*, the global online video news network, translates its vision for alternative reporting into a series of priority themes for coverage. Even the *Reuters* handbook, if you ignore its cant about freedom from bias, gives solid advice on the basics of both reporting and writing. If that's not enough sources of inspiration, there's always the US State Department.[156]

The weekend video training workshop I arranged, for all its flaws, gave a few local activists a taste for what's possible. All were aged 50 or more and lacked the same easy familiarity with computers, videos and the Internet of the generation below them. They made up for it in political knowledge and experience, the equally vital second element of public-interest journalism. The only way to build up both political knowledge and practical experience is to learn and to do, separately or both together.

That was the purpose of the videos I have done to date, my first attempts at public-interest journalism. They comprise English and French-language reports published on commercial, ad-driven video upload sites such as *YouTube* and *Dailymotion*. Each one illustrates possibilities for public-interest journalism, in their style and content but also in the different layers of governance they address. Similar reports and treatments could be done from almost anywhere in the world, depending on reporters' personal safety questions.

One I did with fellow reporter and media activist Corentin Charpentier, on the trials of Monsanto maize protesters, was probably the most similar in style to a conventional news report. One big difference was that we paid to do it, spending €40 in fuel and road tolls and working for free. It took a combined 24 hours' reporting and travel time plus another 12 spent editing and publishing. We re-used old DV tape and already had or borrowed the equipment we needed to film. In conventional terms, we did a week or so's work for one person on standard hours, not that there are such things in reporting.[157]

The result was valuable training with a modest public result. Our main report was a 7-1/2-minute film that had logged all of 2,000 views four years or so later. A second, shorter film, featuring the full speech of the Malian political activist Aminata Traoré at a side event, drew more than 17,000 hits. Though I could have pushed both videos harder, put on English-language subtitles and pasted links around other sites and comment threads to boost their reach, that wasn't my objective.

Shooting no-edit video reports using modern smart phones, which cuts out a huge chunk of both work and cost, stretches the potential of this reporting approach while maintaining reasonable quality.

Framing: the unconscious hands directing our reason

What made the report different to conventional ones was that it got done at all. Outside of the build up to French presidential elections, which drew media towards the likely candidate José Bové, one of the accused, there would have been little interest beyond local or regional media. A second thing, more important, was that I chose to present the story through the lens of public accountability. That reflected my own personal "framing" of the story, or story angle.

Understanding frames and learning how to recognise them is critical to the effectiveness of public-interest journalism. This is not some obscure journalistic term but something deeper and more fundamental for reporters and their publics alike. Our brains use frames constantly, usually unconsciously, to understand and interpret events around us. They are the biological and cultural filters that help us perceive the world, mental stereotypes and pictures that help us sift rapidly through a mass of incoming signals to make sense of them. They're of huge benefit to humans from an evolutionary perspective, allowing our brains to develop the extraordinarily rich processing capacity that sets us apart from other species.[158]

Where frames become problematic, which is critically relevant for good governance advocates, is in their implications for human reasoning. Our brains' use of frames bypasses conscious reason. The way facts are presented directly influences the conclusions we draw from them, the same information presented differently prodding us towards different ones. Our reason's influence is dimmed without us even knowing. That presents a glorious opportunity to information presenters who do understand framing. They include the sophisticated communications advisers so beloved of modern politicians, business and finance.

So frames are no abstract concept for brain specialists but a growing part of our daily realities. Their skilful use explains how voters are persuaded to back candidates whose policies directly undermine their interests, for example persuading poor people to back tax cuts and other subsidies that help the rich.

That bombshell discovery is credited to Richard Wirthlin, chief strategist to Ronald Reagan during his first US presidential run in 1980. His breakthrough was to understand why voters who didn't agree with Reagan on political issues still voted for him. Reagan's strength was that he intuitively talked of values not issues, connecting to people and appearing authentic to them. That meant they felt they could trust him with their votes. The ex-Hollywood president was a picture of honest, trustworthy, simplicity. He spoke to people's mental frames of those desirable qualities, drowning out their reasoning about the practical effects of supporting him. Skilled manipulators of frames know how to make turkeys vote for Christmas, with us being the turkeys.[159]

The significance of frames is a recent discovery of cognitive science, quickly grasped by professional communicators. US Democrats were on the wrong end of them in the 2004 presidential victory won by George W Bush. Their pained analyses found how their opponents cleverly defined then occupied the campaigning space, using skills the Democrats neither knew nor understood. They have caught up since, as have politicians and corporations elsewhere, while we the people are generally still flailing behind.[160]

If we care about making our governance systems accountable we must do better, as audiences and would-be public-interest journalists. That means learning about frames, how to recognise them and how to counter their effects with alternative ones that promote the public accountability of our governance. If we don't, we leave our unconscious minds open to political manipulation. UK news audiences are lucky to have the *News Frame* blog by media critic Brian Dean. His near-daily updates untangle how frames not only characterize political issues but also influence how audiences assign blame, which influences the potential policy responses they might favour.[161]

Putting public accountability at the core of journalism creates a frame that challenges the ones put forward by politicians and business to achieve the exact opposite. It encourages us to reject slackly defined notions of "democracy" as automatically a good thing. It makes us ask why markets, "free" or otherwise, should determine our politics and to question how endless economic growth is somehow essential for our welfare. That opens the way to imagining another world is possible and working out how we might build it.

Ceci n'est pas une democratie

I wasn't aware of changing frames when I sought out Charlie Bauer during the French presidential elections of 2007, yet that is what I did. Rather than interviewing the sociologist about the different candidates, their policies or who might win, I asked instead about the democratic process itself. That frame change, from blind acceptance of existing structures to a scepticism motivated by concerns about public accountability, opened the way for a very different interview.

Public-interest reporters must recognise the importance of existing frames then replace them with alternatives based on accuracy, fairness, social equity and accountability. That means adopting different mental and practical approaches to those of conventional journalists. If reporters must talk to politicians or business people, they should ask about the legitimacy of their roles as arbiters of public policy and why we should heed them. Those aren't the usual questions they face.

People do watch frame-changing journalism. The Bauer interview, available in French only, logged 30,000 online hits with no promotional efforts. It shows the possibilities of journalism focused on national governance quality, elections particularly.[162]

Building a national network of journalists working on such questions would help build momentum for improvement and change. Network output could be aggregated on a single site using newsfeeds and keywords. The channel would feature those who have taken the time to venture beyond conventional politics. Stories could focus on ordinary people's thinking about public accountability and their everyday experiences of politics. It would present a huge change from journalism that dogs the heels of politicians. Reports might explore alternative governance structures, not necessarily formal political ones. They could feature interviews with participants explaining what works, what doesn't and how to seed such practices elsewhere. There are commune-level experiments in France that reject the conventional, formal hierarchies. They adopt more open and accountable decision-making processes involving a far wider base of the population. All offer opportunities for public-interest journalists to cover.

Building networks locally, nationally and globally

The best hope for network building is to start locally. Improved local political knowledge and journalism skills have the immediate potential to inspire significant, real-world changes in governance. Regular, free film screenings, free media trainings, communal equipment purchase and use are all good primers for success. Sharing training materials and running workshops in nearby areas can help seed the ideas elsewhere. Going from the local to the national requires still more relationship building. It can be done face to face or at a distance. Annual reporting festivals can showcase output and offer chances to exchange best practice with other public-interest journalists.

Things might stop there – developing local and national reporting levels in any country presents a major challenge that might take years to achieve. It won't be enough given that modern politics routinely stretches beyond national boundaries. Public-interest journalism must accommodate these overseas elements despite the attendant complications of getting the material. Local and national networks can draw on participants' shared languages, political cultures and backstories. That's not the case with continent-wide or global networks. Increased operational distances and political complexity adds another hurdle. For all that, the exact same guiding principle applies, which is a shared intent to do journalism in aid of radically improving our governance structures.

The practicalities of cross-border work are more complicated but not impossible, as shown by *Indymedia*. It demands the building of working relationships and trust, smoothed by appropriate knowledge, cultural sensitivity and awareness. All this as unconstrained, long-distance travel becomes increasingly unacceptable due to both climate change and peak oil. We should anticipate these problems by learning to work collaboratively from both ends of stories. Public-interest journalists who cut their teeth locally or nationally can use their work to attract collaborators in other countries. Together they can tackle cross-border stories on the practices of big-brand multinationals, or banks and traders in global financial markets.

Making contacts becomes easier as people become familiar with different social media. That might be via advocacy group introductions, through friends, and colleagues past or present. Relationships can flower between reporters in different countries simply by making contact through their websites, blogs, video upload accounts or Twitter. They can evolve over time, with or without face-to-face contact, blooming into fully collaborative projects. The best currency in a world of exchange will be honesty and integrity, timeless, universal qualities even if they might be open to abuse. Cross-border teams can align their priorities on particular issues so as to begin more conventional-style reporting work. The sharing of story planning, task allocation and execution will produce pooled text, audio and video materials. Editing these for audiences at either end would result in lower-cost journalism with global resonance and context, something we sorely need more of. Reporters can adapt material for reports aimed at their respective home audiences, cross-checking for factual errors or cultural misunderstandings. Some projects might produce a single film, others a series of reports edited for local use.

Such cross-border collaborations are already happening. One example, from 2007, involved Scottish filmmakers teaming up with ones from Brazil's Felixlandia province to make *Carbon Connections*. The two communities were connected by the ill effects of hosting projects involving the oil major BP. The Scottish end faced direct pollution from a refinery while the Brazilians suffered water scarcity problems due to plantations of fast-growing eucalyptus intended to offset BP carbon emissions. The challenge is to make such projects commonplace and easy while encouraging high quality reporting.[163]

A multi-layered global news network

Multiplying these alliances, and aggregating their output would start to look like a global grassroots reporting network. Different strands could focus on governance black holes such as the IMF, the UN Security Council, the WTO or World Bank. Others could dig into the various specialist bodies that are meant to regulate global banking and international financial markets, accountancy issues and tax.

Take the IMF as an example. Public-interest tie ups could illustrate the impacts of its policies on public health and on poor people's access to food, education, shelter. Reporters could highlight the IMF's "free"-market ideology, a dogma bolted into place by Washington's dominance over staffing and policy. As for specific stories, there are dozens. One could be to report on the IMF's impact on national HIV/AIDS policies in Africa. It could marry the policy knowledge of an IMF expert in Washington with evidence of real-life effects as recorded by one or more reporters in target countries. Reports could be compiled at either end for local audiences and also for global ones.

Reporters would share the guiding principles of public-interest journalism, delving into governance failures and exploring alternative approaches. Their work would make clear which parties and interests dominate decision-making and how that plays out in socially and politically inequitable outcomes. They would present a polar opposite to most conventional coverage, which accepts the legitimacy of these institutions and chronically overplays the arguments of their chief operators and beneficiaries.

Civil society embeds

Questions of how to improve public accountability would inform reporters' story choices, the angles they chose for stories and the hierarchy of facts and sources carried within them. That would mean more time and seriousness given to civil society and civil disobedience activists, even to the point of doing more first-person reports from within protests. If we are to have journalists embedded with military operations, something that usefully shows the horror of ordinary soldiers' lives, why not also have activist or civil society embeds?

The news production process for public-interest journalism would need flexibility and differentiated time and money spent by reporters and editors depending on their capacity and resources. Richer ones might have to give more time, equipment and even money to get things done. They might cross-subsidise their reporting with other, paid or better-paid work. Donations or subsidies should not promote a donor's authority or story agenda over the recipient's. They would have to be freely given, freely received and influence neutral.

A shining example of what's possible is the Chiapas Media Project. This bi-national partnership provides video equipment, computers and training to marginalized indigenous communities in Southern Mexico. At its heart are the Zapatistas, whose movement has featured in hundreds of videos, films, books and websites created by people looking in from the outside. CMP aims to give local people some control over the medium and the message, letting them tell stories from their own perspectives.[164]

Creating such projects elsewhere, building local expertise in media production, is a necessary first step to the creation of wider media networks. Rich-country activist media groups, while building their own bases, could also foster groups in poorer countries. They might tie in with development aid agencies that support media capacity building or link up with people emerging from journalism training programmes.

Global public-interest journalism could also aggregate different strands and cross-reference work on the different governance bodies, drawing out patterns of failed accountability. Reporters could coordinate their work with similarly motivated expert bloggers. The increasing numbers of former staff or public servants turned critics would be a rich source of recruits. People like ex-IMF chief economist Simon Johnson, now a doughty critic of bank mis-regulation.

A similar reporting network is needed for the EU's accountability void. Its output would link the policies from Brussels institutions to those of national capitals and regions in the EU's 27 member states. The unifier for reporters would not be their respective national interests but rather the question of EU political accountability as a whole. The Reuters of my time occasionally nodded towards national accountability questions, usually with an Anglo Saxon or market tilt and a tendency to favour bigger nations over smaller ones. Most conventional journalism accepts the legitimacy of EU institutions as a given, a few British ones being the exception. That ignores the glaring reality, not least what happened with the Lisbon treaty's highly controversial ratification.

European public-interest journalism would need reporters throughout the territory and beyond its borders to look into EU policy impacts. Their role would be to highlight the winners and losers from policies. Rules of operation and content moderating would need to guard against network output being peppered with the hate speech or anti-immigrant diatribes that often accompany EU critiques. Migration is certainly a valid EU issue, as it is in richer countries the world over. The role of public-interest journalism would be to address the topic in its full context, illustrating the push factors forcing people to move, their journeys and the realities for everyone at their arrival points. With that context in place, doing stories on communities affected by immigration would be richer and more representative of the issue.

Other story examples could focus on the EU-wide implications of a particular policy, something like a reworked version of the GMO story I did out of France. Together with others, I might have continued the story with interviews and investigations, sharing material with reporters in other countries. Equally, I might have worked with public-interest journalists elsewhere in the world to look at Monsanto's activities and political influence more generally. Establishing rolling lists of priority public-interest journalism stories, on wikis or other Internet platforms and perhaps with annual meetings of grassroots projects, could be a way to coordinate and focus people's energies.

Another network could cover the United States, adapted to reflect the balance of federal and state powers but still focused on accountability. Reporters would share the same remit as their equivalents elsewhere around the world, aiming to make policy makers more accountable to the mass of citizens while also looking at other governance models.

The ingredients are already there in the new media and technology geyser that is the United States. Its citizens pour forth alternative, grassroots media using all the latest available software and hardware. Social media innovations, free software movements and networks such as the emerging Hacks/Hackers network all illustrate the country's enduring energy and creativity.[165]

For all the buzz of new technologies marrying up with journalism, the point of it all remains trying to improve public accountability. That means cutting-edge technology allied to public-interest content, not flashy applications that look great but say nothing.

Examples of innovative activist journalism include Greater Philadelphia's Media Mobilizing Project and LA's Mobile Voices (VozMob). The Los Angeles one allows immigrants and low-wage workers to create stories about their lives and communities direct from their cell phones, a skill Britain's VisionOntv also teaches and promotes. Another is the Banyan Project, explicitly aimed at strengthening democracy. Its plan is to set up local US hubs producing original, Web-based journalism serving poorer people and engaging their civic energy. The plan is to have professional editors and reporters work with their audiences as collaborators and be accountable to them in cooperative partnerships. Banyan foresees revenue from selling ads, with all the risks that means for skewing content. Set against that, its advisory board includes members who seem aware both of the problems of journalism and the crisis of political accountability created by multi-national corporations.[166]

Despite these alternative media outlets, which include *Democracy Now!* and sites such as *TomDispatch.com*, they remain remote from the broader public. Nor are there nearly enough of them, alone or acting together in networks, for the global scale of the governance problems we face. That leaves space for networked public-interest journalism to flourish. Walking through the history of democracy as it applies to different places is a way to bring governance debates to a wider, less conventionally politicised audience. We need to highlight the mental trap presented by unqualified references to "democracy". Public-interest journalism should make it a rule of operation to use precise language to describe political realities. It needs to explain governance and public accountability to people in a way that doesn't insult or

202

preach to them. It's simple – people want more say in how they're governed. Our current systems and governors don't let us do that.

For powerful structures such as the United States and the EU, public-interest journalists would also need to consider policy fall-outs on people elsewhere – such as the African farmers forced out of business by subsidised farm imports. That would require more cooperative, cross-border relationships, the same as for global journalism strands.

The result of all these networks would start to look something like a global news operation wedded to popular governance. It might have hundreds, possibly thousands of nodes dotted throughout the world. Probably none would exactly resemble any of the others and any combination of them might work with others at one time or another. Any individual reporter or media organisation could contribute reports or share material focusing on different layers of governance, depending on their resources and expertise. The overall vision is for a global-level news network enmeshed with regional, national and local ones. Each part could act autonomously or in concert as required by stories and issues. That whole would be a broader, deeper version of what I'd originally, naively thought might be possible at Reuters.

I would hope the idea would appeal to existing alternative media such as *Indymedia* and its worldwide network of IMCs. Participation would of course depend on the wishes of each one's members. *Indymedia* took off during the Seattle WTO protests of late 1999, reporting stories from the disparate opponents to corporate-dominated global trade rules. Its activist media makers, web designers and computer experts hit on a model that quickly bloomed into more than 150 IMCs within a few years, primarily in North America and Europe. Its mantra that ordinary people "be the media" won wide appeal before its many manifestations hit inevitable snags.

A big problem, identified by media academic Victor Pickard, was constant tensions between *Indymedia's* decentralized, consensus-based structure and its goals of media democracy. In practical, journalistic terms, that could mean ponderous decision-making that hindered the production of stories in a timely fashion. He saw a deeper contradiction in its tortured relationship with neoliberalism, the global capitalist ideology its members want to fight. As much as *Indymedia* fought the system, it was also born by it and perpetuated some of its inequalities. "Like neoliberalism, *Indymedia* also depended upon the free labour of the relatively privileged, the knowledge of the predominantly white, male tech sector, and the technological infrastructures and industrial economies of the global North."[167]

This is not something activists have ignored, in fact they have spent many hours on many occasions and in many countries trying to fashion solutions. Their efforts are necessarily works in progress, not least because of the fundamentally radical nature of the project. Pickard spent several years volunteering for the Seattle IMC. He sees *Indymedia's* Principles of Unity as the glue binding the network together. Set against them is the trickiness of trying to balance democratic modes of working with efforts to overturn existing corporate media models. He quoted one activist's encapsulation of the issue in May 2003:

"It would be far more 'efficient' to just have a nice polite little totalitarian dictatorship, benevolent or not, and simply follow orders. We would 'get a lot more done.' But that would be ridiculous. Go work with any other media organization and you can do that."[168]

Having tired of the "polite little totalitarian dictatorship" that was Reuters, that's not something I'm about to try again. Yet I can't escape my roots in global news agency journalism, an immensely influential part of the media business even if it is not widely recognised as such. Some form of people-driven global news network, positioned between alternative media such as South Korea's *Ohmynews* and *Indymedia's* radically democratic-but-niche IMCs, still awaits its creators. Without it, wholesale news provision is left to the existing commercial news agencies, whose prodigious outputs flow to subsidiary media clients around the world. Google News, personal blogs, Twitter and Facebook may have nibbled at these news agencies' near-stranglehold on breaking news but they have yet to compete as reliable or consistent providers of basic, fact-based news over sustained periods.

Agencies' enduring hold is despite the explosion of information sloshing around the planet. A case in point was Osama bin Laden's assassination by US soldiers in May 2011. Within 12 hours of the news breaking, there had been around 40,000 news stories and blog posts and an estimated 2.2m tweets.[169]

That gush differs hugely from a recent past dominated by global news agencies like the one I joined in 1994. *FT* commentator John Gapper said despite the upsurge in material, only a tiny elite was smart enough to navigate such complex news flows, the vast majority still needed it pre-digested. His view displays all the classic arrogance of conventional journalism, a modern version of Woolf's disdain for the idea of mass popular wisdom. No one pretends all people have the ability, interest or available time to scour news flows. Somewhere between Gapper's tiny elite and most of humanity lies plenty of space for something very different from the conventional media process. Filtering the stream with public accountability and transparency in mind would produce a very different digest to what we get from those same conventional media. It would open the door to citizen-driven reporting that tackles governance issues from local to global levels.[170]

Such a network of networks won't spring up overnight. The technology challenges will probably be easier to crack than the governance ones. The process will require the building of many more local groups of politically engaged and informed public-interest journalists, and their linking through networks. Clearly, it is a project for the long haul, even if it has already begun. Its stories could examine and expose the case for political reforms – the changes necessary at each level of governance to produce something more akin to government by we the people.

This book's final chapter addressed the constitutional conversations going on in financial-crisis-blighted countries such as Iceland and Ireland. Any would-be governance champion should follow those debates. They have lessons for all of us, not least the euro-zone countries caught in the cross-hairs of global debt market speculators. The case for reform is relevant to anyone who thinks political power should lie with us and not with effective dictators hidden behind layers of mock democracy.

This agenda for democracy and journalism is radical by definition and necessity – the problems we face go to the roots of our political systems. It demands the questioning of global capitalism's most sacred cows, of economic growth without end, the sovereignty of financial markets, of reckless deregulation and privatisation. There are decades of work ahead. That it has already begun, most recently with various Occupy movements around the world, should be encouragement enough for more people to get stuck in.

The question of how we are governed is a multi-millennial one. It evolved from a process begun when most of our ancestors dropped hunter gathering for sedentary farming. That change spurred human specialisation and wealth concentration, tipping governance hierarchies from the horizontal to the vertical. To put power in the hands of people, using directly accountable governance systems, requires us to flatten out those hierarchies once again.[171]

Now that our sense of ourselves as a species has expanded to the global level, that process can begin. To do so, we must manage our inter-locking governance structures. Continuing to fail will leave the vast mass of us exposed to exploitation by the very few, the 99 percent under the heels of the one percent. At the same time, Western consumer culture is causing the Earth to be progressively despoiled, its resources depleted and many of its species driven to extinction. Far more than one percent of us are to blame for that.

The hopeful news is that many people, some journalists included, are already active in their resistance to the political status quo, each one generating pressure for reform. Those efforts are starting to take root, often chaotically, confusingly and in many different places and languages around the world. The advent of cheaper, faster information exchange gives those efforts a potentially game-changing turbo boost. That is not to say Twitter or Facebook can set us free, they most certainly won't given their core drivers are commercial. What they and others can do is to contribute to the wider, deeper, richer global exchange now taking place, one spanning the written, spoken and filmed word and image.

We shouldn't kid ourselves that the Internet is a one-way good news story for democracy and journalism. Cyberutopians' wilder fantasies are rightly put in their place by the likes of Belarus technology writer Evgeny Morozov in *The Net Delusion*. He lays out how governments themselves have used many of the same technologies to throttle dissent. What certainly is possible is to use the availability of cheap, mass publishing and communication technologies to build networks of public-interest journalism.[172]

Get going wherever and however you can

The question for all of us is how to join in the process, where to start, and what topics to tackle. My answer, not meant to be glib, is to do whatever fits your circumstances in terms of resources, energy, skills and available time. Then do a bit more. The billions of people around the world who struggle daily to find food, shelter and medical care, plenty of them in nominally rich countries, have enough on their hands with basic living. That doesn't stop some getting stuck in nonetheless. They include people such as the Palestinian cameraman Emad Bornat, whose fearless work I learnt of during a visit he made to France.[173]

Plenty of others, while they may have enough to sustain themselves, are busy holding down one or several jobs just to keep themselves from joining the first group. That leaves the rest of us to make best use of what US social media commentator Clay Shirky calls a growing cognitive surplus. It's a fancy term for the unallocated time we can choose to direct towards creation rather than consumption. Its collective potential is magnified by the mass coordination possibilities of the Internet. Channelling that towards a shared goal of tackling our public accountability deficits should overwhelm what Morozov dubs "slacktivism", the signing of a few online petitions and goofing around the Internet all day. We need to get outside our private bubbles, to meet and engage with real people in real-life projects. Keeping a skilful balance in that is critical but possible. People should avoid leaping off their sofas into the sort of time-pressured, personal-life disaster zone described by Saul Alinsky in his seminal *Rules for Radicals*.[174]

Our level of commitment quickly boils down to money, or time or both. For me, post-regular-salaried employment, I've had to mix my dreams of alternative journalism with personal re-education. Despite having swum for years in daily breaking news, my head full of current affairs facts, I struggled to grasp the intricate political realities of what I'd been writing about. Information overload has always been a hazard for news reporters. Today, it's common for everyone in our always-on societies, smart phones at the ready. By narrowing my focus to our governance systems, I turned down the noise and started seeing the underlying problems. This long-form editorial summary is the result.

I would recommend to anyone thinking of public-interest journalism that they define for themselves the "why" of their imagined work. It is far more powerful than simply swallowing someone else's. All the training, technical expertise and fancy equipment you can imagine can't magic up worthwhile editorial content without a political underlay. Developing a sense of our interlocking governance structures, how they work in practice, was an essential first step for me. Teaching and being taught helps hugely, both for the politics and the journalism.

Think outside the box on funding

As far as the money goes, my own model so far for public-interest journalism has been to do it for free. That cleared the time and headspace I needed to get down to the basics and to blow up some of my preconceived ideas. I am lucky for that luxury, a chance made possible by my age, country of birth and personal history, as well as persistent frustration with the realities of my chosen career. That model has worked since Reuters because I had some money already – from savings, the sale of what began as a heavily mortgaged London flat, sporadic freelance and consultancy work and the patience of a long-suffering, hardworking partner. These combined to allow me time to research and learn, to explore small-scale, alternative journalism and then summarise my findings. Mixing paid and unpaid work comes with all the potential for creating one more elitist worldview divorced from reality. I am conscious of that danger. The best guard against it is to seek and accept feedback. What I know for sure is my work since Reuters has been more stimulating, illuminating and personally rewarding than what I did there. It also offers far greater promise.

Regarding the specifics, my current funding approach tempers the problems highlighted by Herman and Chomsky's critique of mainstream media. The effects of media ownership and income are knocked back by virtue of me donating potential earning time to governance-focused journalism. I answer to no media owner, clients or advertisers when choosing stories, leaving me the challenge of not turning into a one-person news tyrant in my own right.[175]

I am lucky to have had those chances. Offering time and materials for free, and running training events, is part of my effort to pass some of it on. Public-interest journalism doesn't have to be done for free but great care must always be taken with its income sources, ownership and workplace governance. The British journalist George Monbiot suggests journalists should produce the sort of registry of personal interests required of politicians. It is an interesting idea I have not yet embraced myself. Monbiot also gives wise advice for anyone contemplating work in journalism.[176]

Alternative media projects are serially prone to failure, not least when they adopt avowedly public-focused agendas that rely on reader donations. Any buoyancy at the prospect of all the work must be tempered with the realities of previous examples, particularly those post-dating the Internet's wide availability. A notable one that tried to marry its politics and practices was the *The NewStandard,* a US-based online newspaper. Its creators saw the model and methods of profit-focused news as failing the public interest. Their alternative collapsed exhausted in 2007 after 3-1/2 years of life.

I kept in touch with one of its co-founders, Brian Dominick, after we met at the Z Media Institute course of 2005. We exchanged comments over his publication's corpse a couple of years later. He said how tough it had been to weave democratic critique into news stories in any consistent manner, something they'd tried to do from the start.

"Without tremendous resources — like the kind commercial media outfits have but squander — we found it extremely difficult to do our work the way we would have most preferred. We had to settle for just being much better than our corporate counterparts, instead of being perfect, which was often frustrating. We thought being much better would be good enough for bloggers and the like to take note and give us the boost we needed, but in the end, it was not," he said.[177]

Money is a critical problem – any project requires participants to be fed, housed and get access to the equipment, transport and communications infrastructure required to mount any sort of news operation. They also need to be trained, politically and journalistically, if they are to produce news that is credible, coherent and correct. *The NewStandard* ran out of both cash and staff energy, though its 100% reader-funded model, and refusal of money from either companies or foundations, allowed it to survive for a remarkable amount of time.

There are more optimistic alternative journalism stories, certainly on the individual level. One is that of former *Guardian* foreign desk editor Jonathan Cook. He left his newspaper in 2001 when it turned down a story about an unofficial shoot-to-kill policy used by Israeli police against non-violent Palestinian protesters. He said the rebuff drove home his sense that mainstream news coverage of the region routinely missed key aspects. Cook's out-of-the-ordinary response was to move to Nazareth to report on the lot of Palestinians living in Israel. The work eventually found him writing regularly for websites such as *Counterpunch* and *Electronic Intifada*.

"The Internet made people like me possible," Cook said in a 2011 interview with the news website *Mondoweiss*. "You can't live on it but it does mean you can be heard." He wrote solely for the Internet for nearly three years while supplementing his income by authoring three books on the region. He later re-established ties to conventional media, taking a reporting contract with *The National*, a wholly owned investment vehicle of the Government of Abu Dhabi.[178]

The key thing about Cook is not so much his mixed-income model but more his editorial focus. As one of the few freelancers regularly writing about the region he chooses what subjects he covers, freeing him from mainstream media's constant requirement for instant news and analysis. "I am also not tied to the mainstream agenda, which gives disproportionate coverage to the concerns of the powerful, in this case the Israeli and American positions," he says.[179]

If formerly conventional mainstream reporters can survive economically, the DIY model can clearly work. As their numbers grow, so does the potential for networks of journalists cooperating occasionally or regularly on broader reporting projects.

What of state-subsidised news?

The TNS model of 100% reader funding is probably the gold standard, giving reporters a full-time shot at doing their jobs. Mixed-income versions like Cook's are an alternative that are by no means easy either. Another model could be along the lines proposed by media critics on both sides of the Atlantic, involving some sort of publicly-mediated funding or subsidy for citizen-orientated journalism.

The case in the United States is made by Robert McChesney and John Nichols in their book *The Death and Life of American Journalism: The Media Revolution that Will Begin the World Again*. They say government support for journalism dates back to the country's birth, when newspaper and journal publishers enjoyed print and postal subsidies.

"Like all public goods, we need the resources to get it produced. This is the role of the state and public policy. It will require a subsidy and should be regarded as similar to the education system or the military in that regard," they argue.[180]

British ex-publisher Dan Hind reaches similar conclusions on subsidies, coupling his arguments with a more muscular assessment of the governance crises in Anglo-Saxon countries particularly. Creating the environment for people to think critically for themselves is the vital precursor to greater political accountability. The way towards people exercising sovereign control over their governance requires them to have regular, reliable information about the world and themselves, which is to say ourselves.

"Whatever else one wishes to change, a reformed system of information provides the only hope to securing that change by democratically legitimate means," Hind says. Those who control state and corporate institutions will act only once an informed public encourages or compels them to do so.

Hind suggests incremental steps, such as apportioning part of the annual licence fee Britons pay for the BBC to a system of public commissioning. He calculates that £80 million could fund the equivalent of 3,000 journalists and researchers to work full-time on matters of public interest or concern.[181]

The subsidy ideas are attractive but stand little chance of adoption any time soon, either in Britain or the United States. The political mood in both countries, for all its wrong-headedness, is for cutting back spending on societal goods, if not for subsidies to bankers, arms manufacturers and tax-dodging multinational corporations more generally. Gross invasions of privacy by journalists, not least by those of the more feral newspapers owned by Rupert Murdoch, make public sympathy for journalism subsidies highly unlikely. That suits the Murdochs of this world quite sweetly, of course, the real threat of media hounding and public humiliation for anyone tempted to take them on deters all but the doughtiest or most foolhardy. It is hard to see more than token government action resulting from the UK's Leveson inquiry into News International reporters' illegal hacking of mobile phones.

So what to do meantime? In the hope of funds gradually or eventually becoming available, we have to get on with the work as best we can. Practically speaking for me, that means practising more of the journalism I preach, giving rigorous attention to the state of our existing governance structures. With minimal editorial funds and no immediate prospects for any form of income from this work, the reporting will be necessarily local to where I live in rural southwest France. This is not the absurdly restricted domain that might be imagined. Potential subjects resonate around the world, ranging across food production, transport, housing, education, social exclusion and local political structures.

At the same time, monthly screenings continue, along with the accompanying debates. Training local journalist activists in video filming and editing workshops will build a supply of reports about the local area for local people, some of it with legs enough to travel elsewhere. The seeds have already been sown for work around the Transition Initiative ideas of local resilience in the face of climate change and peak oil. That will include using journalism to report on the efforts and sharing it with others.

Further ahead, the challenge is to create journalism networks campaigning for political reform at every level of governance – national, EU, global and our de facto governors in financial markets. All would generate public-interest journalism to both illustrate and demonstrate the possibilities and promise of real democracy, which is to say governance that is either by, or truly accountable to, the people.

The state of our Earth, measured variously by species extinctions, habitat destruction, resource exhaustion and pollution, has got dramatically worse in the two decades I have worked as a journalist. The state of our democracies, for all the promise of Arab springs and the Occupy movement, is hardly any better. The two are intimately entwined by virtue of our societies' deluded pursuit of endless economic growth on a finite planet.

It is easy to feel defeated in the face of such gloom, to succumb to the despairing picture presented in the earlier sections of Franklin López's *End:Civ Resist or Die*. It is possible, and much more uplifting, to take a determinedly optimistic view, the one explored in his film's second section. That means engaging in acts of political courage, compassion and altruism in an effort to effect fundamental change in our societies.[182]

The problems are so great that the dangers of attempting their solution are minimal. As one person among the world's billions, one lifetime in millennia of human history, why fret about failure?

[1] Stine Gry and fellow activist Tannie Nyboe were found guilty by the Copenhagen District Court a year later, receiving four months probation after what was a split decision by judges. They were jailed on appeal by the public prosecutor, having been found guilty of inciting violence by four of the six judges and sentenced to four months in prison, two of them suspended. See "Guilt by Association: Danish Court Punishes Climate Protesters" http://www.pacificfreepress.com/news/1/7445-guilt-by-association-danish-court-punishes-climate-protesters.html. See also http://www.guardian.co.uk/environment/2011/jun/02/activists-jailed-copenhagen-protest?INTCMP=SRCH, accessed on June 10, 2011.

[2] A few countries have one-off votes on national-level initiatives but no wholesale, regular governance structures that improve on representative democracy. Post-crisis Iceland did take things a step further for part of its constitutional reform process. See the Guardian's "Mob rule: Iceland crowdsources its next constitution", on http://www.guardian.co.uk/world/2011/jun/09/iceland-crowdsourcing-constitution-facebook, accessed on June 10, 2011

[3] See http://www.monbiot.com/career-advice/, accessed on October 13, 2011.

[4] Costs in the UK are nothing like as high as in the United States, with Columbia University Graduate School of Journalism tuition costing several tens of thousands of dollars to complete. See May 2010 Black Alumni Network
Newsletter /Our 30th year/ May 2010/ Vol. 30, No.5, downloadable via https://prdcms.journalism.columbia.edu/cs/BlobServer?blobcol=urldata&blobtable=MungoBlobs&blobheadervalue1=attachment%3B+filename%3DBA_Newsltr_May_2010.pdf&blobkey=id&blobheadername1=content-disposition&blobwhere=1212767814943&blobheader=application%2Fpdf, accessed on June 10, 2011

[5] The rules were relaxed in late 2010 when the Lord Chief Justice opened the way for the reporting of some court proceedings by journalists using Twitter, texting and email, though he placed some limits on the use of social media where they might influence juries. See the Guardian's "Lord chief justice approves use of Twitter for court reporting",

215

http://www.guardian.co.uk/technology/2010/dec/20/twitter-court-lord-chief-justice, accessed on June 10, 2011.

[6] See p51-53
http://webarchive.nationalarchives.gov.uk/20100419143351/http://www.aebc.gov.uk/aebc/reports/gm_nation_report_final.pdf, accessed on October 20, 2011.

[7] For a pdf document of the entire Laeken declaration of 2001, click on: http://www.europeannocampaign.org/uploads/media/laeken_en.pdf. The passsage in question comes from page 2, accessed on January 19, 2010.

[8] Financial Times, May 23, 2006. More such comments are summarised in the Open Europe document, "Who's afraid of a referendum? What do the public think?" downloadable from www.openeurope.org.uk

[9] See http://www.telegraph.co.uk/news/worldnews/1556175/New-treaty-is-just-constitution-in-disguise.html, accessed on January 14, 2010.

[10] Jens-Peter Bonde, in his free-to-download book "From EU Constitution to Lisbon Treaty" explains how national governments bypassed the referendum process the second time around. See
http://www.j.dk/images/bondes/From_EU_Constitution_to_Lisbon_Treaty_april_2008.pdf, accessed on January 14, 2010.

[11] See an explanation on EUABC.com, http://en.euabc.com/word/2176, accessed on January 13, 2010.

[12] http://www.eudemocrats.org/eud/news.php?uid=224, accessed on January 13, 2010. The alliance's former leader, the Danish ex-MEP Jens-Peter Bonde, wrote a free-to-download dissection of the process that took the EU constitution rejected by French and Dutch voters through to the final version. Though elements of his text are tackled in this chapter, the work bears reading in itself by anyone interested in finding out who dictates and drives the EU law-making process and how they do it.

[13] For the very readable full speech, see
http://brusselsblogger.blogactiv.eu/2009/02/24/speech-of-president-of-the-czech-republic-vaclav-klaus-in-the-european-parliament/, accessed on January 19, 2010.

[14] http://www.europeanvoice.com/article/2009/02/klaus-provokes-walk-out-in-the-parliament/64053.aspx, accessed on January 19, 2010

[15] See YouTube video of the speech on http://www.youtube.com/watch?v=tsVZ4VepQdg&NR=1, accessed on January 13, 2010

[16] See the Open Europe think piece http://euobserver.com/18/28743/?rk=1, accessed on January 25, 2010.

[17] Bonde's reader friendly version of the Lisbon Treaty explains in detail how much it has changed the EU system of government. Document downloadable from http://www.bonde.com/index.php/bonde_uk/article/reader_friendly_editio n_of_the_lisbon_treaty, accessed on January 20, 2010.

[18] See "From EU Constitution to Lisbon Treaty", op cit, p46.

[19] See "From EU Constitution to Lisbon Treaty", op cit, p42.

[20] See Friends of the Earth report "Too Close for Comfort" which charts the range and influence of biotechnology companies across the European Commission, http://www.foeeurope.org/corporates/pdf/too-close-for-comfort.pdf, accessed on February 17, 2010

[21] For a summary of the changes, see http://en.euabc.com/word/953, accessed on January 21, 2010.

[22] See Jens-Peter Bonde book "From EU Constitution to Lisbon Treaty", p74, op cit.

[23] See "Statewatch Viewpoint. Secret trilogues and the democratic deficit", by Tony Bunyan, September 2007, downloadable from http://www.statewatch.org/news/2007/sep/ep-co-decision-secret-trilogues.pdf, accessed January 26, 2010.

[24] For more information, see European Federation of Building and Woodworkers at http://www.efbww.org/default.asp?Issue=Posting+of+Workers&Language= EN, and, http://www.etui.org/en/Headline-issues/Viking-Laval-Rueffert-Luxembourg, accessed January 26, 2010.

[25] See http://europa.eu/institutions/inst/justice/index_en.htm, accessed on January 27, 2010.

²⁶ See http://www.europeanvoice.com/article/imported/mapping-out-cap/46169.aspx, and http://euobserver.com/9/8121, accessed on December 2, 2009

²⁷ For the figures see http://in.reuters.com/article/2011/10/12/eu-agriculture-idINL5E7LC1O020111012, and http://tgr.ph/ovuIZJ, both accessed on November 11, 2011.

²⁸ All figures from http://www.farmsubsidy.org/, accessed on December 2, 2009

²⁹ See http://www.telegraph.co.uk/news/worldnews/europe/eu/5852319/EU-farm-subsidies-paid-to-big-business.html, accessed on December 3, 2009

³⁰ See http://www.farmsubsidy.org/, and new reports such as http://www.nytimes.com/2009/07/17/business/global/17farms.html?_r=1, accessed on December 3, 2009

³¹ See http://farmsubsidy.org/news/features/ecj-reaction/ and http://farmsubsidy.org/news/features/who-runs-the-cap/, accessed on November 11, 2011.

³² See http://www.corporateeurope.org/global-europe/blog/pia/2009/08/05/no-apologies-serving-business, accessed on January 28, 2010. The Commission's summary of the event, which does not cite these quotes but refers to the exchange, is available from http://trade.ec.europa.eu/doclib/html/144511.htm.

³³ See http://www.corporateeurope.org/system/files/files/resource/Open+Doors+Report.pdf, accessed on January 28, 2010.

³⁴ For one alternative suggested by a coalition of civil trade groups, see http://www.s2bnetwork.org/s2bnetwork/download/DraftTowardsAltTradeMandate_090909.pdf?id=313, accessed on January 28, 2010.

³⁵ For a detailed account of the process, see the Statewatch publication "The Shape of Things to Come – EU Future Group", available for download at http://www.statewatch.org/analyses/the-shape-of-things-to-come.pdf, accessed on February 9, 2010.

36 See the 2009 statement by the European Civil Liberties Network, downloadable from

http://www.ecln.org/ECLN-statement-on-Stockholm-Programme-April-2009-eng.pdf. The Commission communication is available for download from http://eur-lex.europa.eu/LexUriServ/LexUriServ.do?uri=COM:2009:0262:FIN:EN:PDF, both accessed on February 17, 2010.

37 See an explanation of RFID on this U.S. campaigning website http://www.spychips.com/what-is-rfid.html, accessed on February 10, 2010.

38 See the European Data Protection Supervisor site's summary at http://www.edps.europa.eu/EDPSWEB/edps/Home/EDPS/Dataprotectio n/QA/QA2, accessed on February 17, 2010.

39 See Statewatch summary of the May 2007 meeting, available for download at http://www.statewatch.org/news/2008/jul/eu-futures-may-report-2007.pdf, accessed on February 10, 2010.

40 This section draws on two reports by Ben Hayes for Statewatch and the Transnational Institute: "Arming Big Brother", downloadable at http://www.statewatch.org/analyses/bigbrother.pdf, and "NeoConOpticon", downloadable at http://www.tni.org/sites/tniclone.test.koumbit.net/files/download/neocono pticon_0.pdf, both accessed on February 11, 2010.

41 It's not as if this hasn't happened before, with the EU's defence industry proper. The European Commission created the European Advisory Group on Aerospace in July 2001 to review EU policy and make recommendations. It comprised five European Commissioners, a couple of MEPs and seven aerospace industry chairmen, including those from Europe's four biggest arms companies. Its "Strategic Aerospace Review for the 21st century", or "STAR 21" report a year later recommended subsidising European industry, increased spending on aerospace R&D and more tax incentives. See "Arming Big Brother", op cit.

The EU's championing of biotechnology research and genetically modified organisms comes from a similar fusion of thinking by officialdom and industry, see "Too Close for Comfort", op cit.

42 See http://www.guardian.co.uk/technology/2010/feb/07/eu-computers-access-private-data/print, accessed on February 11, 2010.

43 See "Human Rights must be the cornerstone, not just a reference, of the Stockholm Programme" press release of October 7, 2009, issued by the European Association for the defence of Human Rights (AEDH), downloadable from http://www.aedh.eu/plugins/fckeditor/userfiles/file/Communiqu%C3%A9s/Press%20Release%20-%20Stockholm%20Programme%20-%20EN.pdf, accessed on February 11, 2010.

44 They're right, of course, though that doesn't mean the policy answer should be gold. This is an important and ever-current argument, beyond the immediate bounds of this book. It was ably and profitably expounded in August 1999 by the highly successful gold investor John Hathaway, a Senior Portfolio Manager at Tocqueville Asset Management L.P., portfolio manager of The Tocqueville Gold Fund. It is more briefly covered in the Daily Telegraph's "Flight to gold as investors lose faith in money". See, respectively, http://www.usagold.com/hathawaypyramid.html and http://www.telegraph.co.uk/finance/comment/ambroseevans_pritchard/2782078/Flight-to-gold-as-investors-lose-faith-in-money.html, accessed on February 14, 2011.

A better alternative to gold would be an updated version of the Bancor, a supranational currency, perhaps tied to a basket of commodities or currencies to replace the U.S. dollar. The idea, inspired by proposals made by the British economist John Maynard Keynes as part of a series of measures intended to revive the global economy after World War Two, was over-ruled at the time by U.S. negotiators. It has regained traction since the 2007 crisis, not least from Chinese central bankers and a committee of experts reporting to the United Nations General Assembly, see http://www.bis.org/review/r090402c.pdf, and http://www.bis.org/review/r090402c.pdf, respectively. None of these solutions tackles the fundamental problem created by what is called fractional-reserve banking, the practice by which private banks add new money to existing currency pools by writing loans worth several times their own assets in return for borrowers' promises to repay those loans plus interest over time. The practice creates an endless cycle of self-escalating debt that soon outgrows more conventional forms of wealth creation, leading to the characteristic and increasingly common blow outs we call "crises".

[45] See http://www.rightsaction.org/articles/mining_&_impunity_day_121010.html, accessed on January 24, 2011 and http://www.guardian.co.uk/business/2011/jan/31/wikileaks-bhp-billiton-peru-mining-communities, accessed on February 1, 2011. See http://www.guardian.co.uk/lifeandstyle/2011/feb/14/fairtrade-gold, accessed on February 14, 2011.

[46] See Market Manipulation? Applying the Propaganda Model to Financial Media Reporting, p79, by Peter A. Thompson http://www.wmin.ac.uk/mad/pdf/WPCC-Vol6-No2-Peter_A_Thompson.pdf, accessed on February 2, 2011.

[47] See Market Manipulation? p87, op cit.

[48] For the UK gold sales see the Daily Telegraph comment http://www.telegraph.co.uk/finance/comment/ambroseevans_pritchard/2801919/Monday-view-Counting-the-cost-of-the-Chancellors-big-gold-sell-off.html. For LTCM, see the English-language report by Le Monde Diplomatique, http://mondediplo.com/1998/11/05warde2, both accessed on February 4, 2011.

[49] See respectively http://www.telegraph.co.uk/finance/newsbysector/banksandfinance/5995810/IMF-puts-total-cost-of-crisis-at-7.1-trillion.html, http://www.reuters.com/article/2010/01/29/us-davos-banks-risk-idUSTRE60Q11S20100129,

http://fisher-in.com/index.php?option=com_content&view=article&id=292:bank-of-england-estimates-global-output-losses-from-financial-meltdown-at-up-to-200-trillion&catid=1:latest-news&Itemid=2,

all accessed on February 4, 2011. On the positive side, there is a minor one, authorities have recouped some of their money on the direct costs of the bailouts, see http://www.guardian.co.uk/business/2011/jan/26/citigroup-stake-sold-by-us-government?INTCMP=SRCH, accessed on February 7, 2011.

---

[50] See the Guardian's Lehman Brothers: Repo 105 and other accounting tricks, at http://www.guardian.co.uk/business/2010/mar/12/lehman-brothers-repo-105-enron?INTCMP=SRCH, accessed on February 7, 2011.

[51] See United States General Accounting Office report of February 23, 2000, http://www.gao.gov/archive/2000/gg00067r.pdf, accessed on February 4, 2011. For a blow-by-blow description of how moral hazard subsidises its beneficiaries, at the expense of taxpayers, their unprotected competitors and the financial system itself, see "13 Bankers" by Simon Johnson and James Kwak, Pantheon Books 2010, p203.

[52] See Business Wire announcement of Ashanti's launch on the NYSE on February 26, 1996, http://www.allbusiness.com/banking-finance/financial-markets-investing/7204773-1.html, accessed on February 9, 2011.

[53] See Financial Times story "All things to all men", of December 2, 1999, http://groups.yahoo.com/group/gata/message/299, accessed on February 9, 2011 and verified against original.

[54] For a succinct response to the idea of Chinese walls see "The Big Short" by Michael Lewis, Allen Lane 2010, footnote p205. It quotes Vincent Daniel of hedge fund FrontPoint Partners: "When I hear 'Chinese wall,' I think, You're a fucking liar."

[55] See Ashanti – the fully story, http://www.thefreelibrary.com/Ashanti+-+the+full+story-a058064815, accessed on February 9, 2011.

[56] See FT story, op cit.

[57] Ashanti shares were trading at $25 in London in early 1996, ahead of the company's listing on the New York stock exchange, with gold at around $400/oz, giving the company a market capitalisation of nearly $2.2 billion, by the author's calculation. AngloGold's final offer to Ashanti was made in mid October 2003, when gold was in the $370s. The respective values for Ashanti are not, of course, like for like comparisons and are given for purposes of a ball park illustration. More detailed valuations would assess the price AngloGold paid per prospective ounce of Ashanti gold, or per ounce of annual production less the average cost of production. See articles by AP, fin24 and historical gold price chart, http://news.google.com/newspapers?id=vhoiAAAAIBAJ&sjid=lqYFAAAAI

BAJ&pg=3942,2761644&dq=ashanti+goldfields+corporation+share+price+history&hl=en,

http://net-145-057.mweb.co.za/Companies/Board-recommends-AngloGold-20031015, and,
http://www.kitco.com/scripts/hist_charts/monthly_graphs.plx, all accessed on February 10, 2011.

[58] For full details of the class action, see downloadable files listed at
http://www.whafh.com/modules/case/index.php?action=view&id=74. For final settlement details, see "Notice of proposed settlement of class action etc.",
http://www.whafh.com/modules/case/docs/2948_cid_3_Ashanti%20Goldfields%20Settlement%20Notice%20.pdf

[59] See the New York Times explainer box on AIG,
http://topics.nytimes.com/top/news/business/companies/american_international_group/index.html?inline=nyt-org, accessed on February 11, 2011.

[60] See NYT explainer, op cit.

[61] For the squid quote see Taibbi's "The Great American Bubble Machine",
http://www.rollingstone.com/politics/news/the-great-american-bubble-machine-20100405?print=true, accessed on February 11, 2011. "Griftopia", Spiegel & Grau, New York 2010, which blames the recent mortgage collapse, commodities bubble and tech bubble on a relatively small number of bankers and traders acting without fear of sanction from a U.S. government that does not represent U.S. citizens. For Taibbi's professional career before hitting the big time with Rolling Stone, see http://exiledonline.com/feature-new-york-times-hack-eats-horse-sperm-pie/, and, for a critique of that career, see http://open.salon.com/blog/sarah_j/2010/03/01/misogyny_in_exile.

[62] See SEC complaint,
http://sec.gov/litigation/complaints/2010/comp21489.pdf, and New York Times "Goldman Settles With S.E.C. for $550 Million",
http://dealbook.nytimes.com/2010/07/15/goldman-to-settle-with-s-e-c-for-550-million/. Criminal investigations in the same case have yet to yield any charges, see "U.S. starts criminal probe into Goldman: source"
http://www.reuters.com/article/2010/04/30/us-goldman-probe-idUSTRE63S67T20100430. All articles accessed on February 14, 2011.

[63] See http://www.propublica.org/thetrade/item/why-the-sec-wont-hunt-big-dogs, and http://www.propublica.org/article/cheat-sheet-whats-happened-to-the-big-players-in-the-financial-crisis, accessed on October 27, 2011.

[64] See the Press Complaints Commission's finding on the case, http://complaints.pccwatch.co.uk/case/3580/, accessed on February 14, 2011.

[65] See the Guardian's "A tale of two City slickers", accessed on February 11, 2011.

[66] See SEC filing http://www.sec.gov/litigation/litreleases/lr19051.htm, accessed on February 14, 2011.

[67] See for the SEC settlement, see http://www.sec.gov/news/press/2003-56.htm, for the rehabilitated Blodget, see http://www.fool.com/investing/small-cap/2004/11/24/the-rehabilitation-of-henry-blodget.aspx, both accessed on February 14, 2011.

[68] April 2010 data from the Bank of International Settlements put daily average foreign exchange market turnover at $4 trillion, 20% higher than in 2007. The BIS attributed the growth to high-frequency traders, banks trading as clients of the biggest dealers, and online trading by retail investors. See http://www.bis.org/publ/qtrpdf/r_qt1012e.htm, accessed on February 15, 2011.

[69] For an account of the Florida shenanigans and President George W. Bush's election victory, see "The Best Democracy Money Can Buy", by Greg Palast. First Plume Printing February 2003.

[70] See Reporters without Borders 2002 index at http://en.rsf.org/press-freedom-index-2002,297.html, accessed on February 25, 2011.

[71] In early April 2004, I wrote a story about a boardroom tussle at Proton entitled "Proton CEO thwarts ouster effort – industry sources". It earned me and Reuters a damages claim for alleged libel. The legal ping-pong lasted long beyond my remaining time at the company, fizzling out finally in February 2008. Its conclusion featured a Reuters statement, in which I had no part, expressing the company's regret for any "distress, inconvenience or embarrassment" caused to one of the plaintiffs by the story. The affair provided first-hand experience of the absurdities of a widely discredited legal

weapon, Malaysia's version drawn directly from the British original. Not least is the expense it entails for all parties, those most likely to prosper being the ones who can afford to lose. I was grateful both for Reuters's skilful and supportive legal counsel, far more so than my editors on the case, as well as for the company's deep pockets.

UK-style defamation laws remain a massive barrier to good journalism, a legal shield that hugely favours richer parties over poorer ones.

[72] See former State Department employee William Blum, author of *Rogue State: A Guide to the World's Only Superpower* "Goodness has nothing to do with it", available at http://www.commoncouragepress.com/index.cfm?action=book&bookid=194. See also http://www.thirdworldtraveler.com/Blum/WBlum_Speech_Nov2007_VT.html, both accessed on October 31, 2011.

[73] See Human Rights Watch's Background: The ISA in Law and Practice, http://www.hrw.org/reports/2004/malaysia0504/2.htm#_ftnref20, accessed on March 1, 2011.

[74] See "Malaysia's Sarawak State Elections 2006, Understanding a Break in the BN Armor", p4, at http://www.ndi.org/files/2118_my_sarawak_090106.pdf, accessed on March 1, 2011.

[75] Ibid.

[76] See *The Daily Star* article "A sister steps out", http://thestar.com.my/lifestyle/story.asp?file=/2008/3/30/lifefocus/2076271O&sec=lifefocus, accessed on March 2, 2011.

[77] See Freedom House's survey results for the year 2010, p16, http://www.freedomhouse.org/images/File/fiw/FIW_2011_Booklet.pdf, accessed on April 7, 2011.

[78] Cuba's long-time president Fidel Castro handed titular power to his brother Raul in 2006, since when very little has changed with regard to the country's political freedoms. For the comparative statistics between Cuba and South Africa, see United Nations Development Programme Human Development Report statistics

http://hdrstats.undp.org/en/countries/country_fact_sheets/cty_fs_CUB.html, and

http://hdrstats.undp.org/en/countries/country_fact_sheets/cty_fs_ZAF.htm
l. The comparison of wealth comes from fact sheet data for the two countries'
Gross Domestic Product per capita, in purchasing power parity US$, which is
to say Cuba's average of 6,876 versus South Africa's 9,757. For a more general
overview comparison of the composite data by country, see
http://hdr.undp.org/en/statistics/. All pages accessed on June 7, 2010.

[79] The plan subsequently failed in the face of richer countries' refusal to give
ground on farm subsidies and allowing freer trade in agricultural goods, the
one market in which poorer countries had a decent chance of scrabbling some
commercial advantage.

[80] Quoted in "Globalisation and the New Realities" by Mahathir Mohamad,
Pelanduk Publications (M) Sdn Bhd, Malaysia, p15.

[81] See "Globalization and its Discontents", by Joseph E. Stiglitz, W W Norton
and Company, London and New York, p89.

[82] See http://taxjustice.blogspot.com/2008/04/six-hundred-billion-drained-
from-africa.html as well as the book "Capital Flight And Capital Controls In
Developing Countries, that the piece references, http://www.e-
elgar.co.uk/Bookentry_Main.lasso?id=3513ee , accessed on March 8, 2011.

[83] See IMF Article VI, Section 3,
http://www.imf.org/external/pubs/ft/aa/aa06.htm#3, accessed on March 8,
2011

[84] See http://taxjustice.blogspot.com/2008/04/six-hundred-billion-drained-
from-africa.html and http://www.imf.org/external/pubs/ft/aa/aa06.htm#3,
accessed on March 18, 2010. Later figures are even higher, such as those
quoted in "Tax Us If You Can. Why Africa Should Stand up for Tax Justice,"
http://www.taxjustice.net/cms/upload/pdf/tuiyc_africa_final.pdf, accessed
on March 8, 2011.

[85] See Financial Times opinion piece "Stop this timidity in ending tax haven
abuse" http://www.ft.com/cms/s/0/63cdb642-ea03-11dc-b3c9-
0000779fd2ac.html, accessed on March 18, 2010.

[86] See the Guardian's "Capital controls back in the IMF's toolkit",
http://www.guardian.co.uk/commentisfree/cifamerica/2010/mar/01/imf-
capital-controls, accessed on March 8, 2011. Whether such thinking will

survive the departure of the IMF chief Dominique Strauss-Khan, to face assorted charges including attempted rape, is another matter.

[87] See http://www.brettonwoodsproject.org/art-565325, accessed on March 23, 2010.

[88] "Privatization trends and recent developments", by Sunita Kikeri and Aishetu Fatima Kolo , World Bank, November 2005. See http://econ.worldbank.org/external/default/main?pagePK=64165259&theSitePK=469382&piPK=64165421&menuPK=64166093&entityID=000016406_20051108153425, accessed October 12, 2006

[89] "Latin America: The End of an Era", by Mark Weisbrot, International Journal of Health Services, Vol. 36, No. 4 (2006), http://www.cepr.net/index.php/publications/reports/latin-america-the-end-of-an-era/, accessed March 26, 2010.

[90] The impression comes from WTO negotiation procedures requiring "consensus". Walden Bello, senior analyst at the Philippines-based think-tank Focus on the Global South, says that translates into decisions being arrived at informally, via caucuses convoked in the corridors by the trade ministers of major trading powers. Formal plenary sessions, which in democracies are the central arena for decision-making, are reserved for speeches, he says, citing WTO ministerials in Singapore in 1996 and Geneva in 1998 as examples. The approach renders obscure a talks process where smaller, weaker countries are pressured to conform to the "consensus" forged among major trading powers, he says. See http://www.tni.org//archives/archives_bello_agenda, accessed on March 10, 2011.

[91] See "Whose Trade Organization?", a book Wallach co-authored, whose introduction is available at http://www.citizen.org/documents/IntroForWeb.pdf, accessed on April 2, 2010. The Wallach quotes in this passage are taken from the online introduction.

[92] See http://www.tni.org//archives/archives_bello_agenda, accessed on March 10, 2011.

[93] See http://www.iosco.org/about/, accessed on April 13, 2010.

[94] See for example the BIS proposals for improving banks' corporate governance, http://www.bis.org/publ/bcbs168.htm, and recommendations

for dealing with the risks posed by cross-border bank structures, http://dealbook.blogs.nytimes.com/2010/03/19/i-m-f-chief-suggests-fire-brigade-for-europes-banks/#more-196259, both accessed on April 8, 2010.

[95] See http://www.iaisweb.org/index.cfm?pageID=28, accessed on April 13, 2010.

[96] See http://www.iasb.org/NR/rdonlyres/F9EC8205-E883-4A53-9972-AD95BD28E0B5/0/WhoWeAreMarch2010.pdf. See also the evidence of regulatory capture and the dependence of such supposedly independent bodies on those activities that they are meant to regulate, as detailed in http://papers.ssrn.com/sol3/papers.cfm?abstract_id=1310290, both accessed on April 8, 2010.

[97] See "Weapons of Mass Deception. The uses of Propaganda in Bush's War on Iraq" by Sheldon Rampton and John Stauber, p91-98.

[98] For Z Media Institute's introduction and overview see http://www.zcommunications.org/zmi/zmi.htm, for a sample year lecture programme and faculty see http://www.zcommunications.org/zmi/zmicourses.htm, both accessed on March 16, 2011

[99] They lasted 3-1/2 years until April 27, 2007, producing nearly 3,000 original news stories over that time before insufficient reader revenues caused them to close. See http://newstandardnews.net/, accessed on September 7, 2011.

[100] For an exhaustive account see "The Best Democracy Money Can Buy", by Greg Palast, first published in 2002 by Pluto Press, London.

[101] See author's unsubtitled YouTube video report http://youtu.be/V9x8xIN0FXY, accessed on September 8, 2011.

[102] See http://youtu.be/6h4va-TaRE4, accessed on January 30, 2012.

[103] Interview with the author, December 2006

[104] According to Hansard, the British parliamentary record, the time between the start of the March 18 debate and the vote was around 10 hours. The Department for Environment, Food and Rural Affairs, says more than 240 hours of parliamentary time since Labour came to power in 1997 were spent debating hunting. See, respectively,

http://www.publications.parliament.uk/pa/cm200203/cmhansrd/vo030318/debtext/30318-06.htm#30318-06_head1 and http://www.defra.gov.uk/rural/hunting/hunting_qa_f.htm#8, accessed on January 19, 2007.

[105] See Hansard, op cit, for the full record of the March 18 debate and the vote.

[106] See the results of a survey conducted in August 2007 by Opinion Research Business, available at

http://www.opinion.co.uk/Newsroom_details.aspx?NewsId=120, accessed on March 17, 2011.

[107] See "'Old' and 'New' Europeans united: public attitudes towards the Iraq war and US foreign policy", Centre for European Reform intern John Springford. http://www.cer.org.uk/pdf/back_brief_springford_dec03.pdf, accessed on April 6, 2011

[108] See http://news.bbc.co.uk/2/hi/europe/2765215.stm, accessed January 19, 2007. See also http://observer.guardian.co.uk/iraq/story/0,12239,896511,00.html

[109] See "The Triumph of the Political Class", by Peter Oborne, Simon and Schuster UK Ltd, 2007, p287-291.

[110] See the House of Commons Public Administration Committee report of March 2004, http://www.publications.parliament.uk/pa/cm200304/cmselect/cmpubadm/422/42204.htm#a1

[111] Downloadable from http://www.makeitanissue.org.uk/think_/archive_/, accessed on February 1, 2007

[112] See http://www.economist.com/node/18895032, accessed on September 8, 2011.

[113] See French-language video http://www.youtube.com/watch?v=ly6QHxzVn4o, accessed on September 9, 2011

[114] See http://youtu.be/z9L5L1YQEuQ, accessed on February 24, 2012.

[115] The Official Report, House of Commons (5th Series), 11 November 1947, vol. 444, cc. 206–07, from http://en.wikiquote.org/wiki/Churchill, accessed on May 28, 2010

[116] "The Politics Companion", Matthew Stadlen and Harry Glass, p44.

[117] See Thomas R. Martin, with Neel Smith & Jennifer F.Stuart, "Democracy in the Politics of Aristotle ," in C.W. Blackwell, ed., Demos: Classical Athenian Democracy (A. Mahoney and R. Scaife, edd., The Stoa: a consortium for electronic publication in the humanities [www.stoa.org]), http://www.stoa.org/projects/demos/article_aristotle_democracy?page=7&greekEncoding=, accessed on June 3, 2010.

[118] See "British democracy? No thanks!", http://www.opendemocracy.net/node/361, accessed on April 5, 2011.

[119] Richard Kraut, http://www.philosophy.northwestern.edu/people/faculty/kraut.html, writing the introduction to a series of excerpts on Aristotle from

"Classics of Political and Moral Philosophy" by Steven M. Cahn, p181.

[120] See media commentator Jay Rosen's "Why Political Coverage is Broken", http://pressthink.org/2011/08/why-political-coverage-is-broken/, accessed on September 12, 2011.

[121] For a sweeping historical account of democracy's evolution as a term and as political practice, see "Setting the People Free" by John Dunn, Atlantic Books, London 2005, including p58, which describes the translation of *"demokratia"* into the Latin language by the Dominican Friar William of Moerbeke, from Aristotle's "Politics", in the 1260s. It was not until the French Revolution, in 1789, that the term began to be used again in any sort of positive context to describe a system of government or political philosophy.

[122] The United States trailed only China, Iran, North Korea and Yemen in the number of executions effected in 2010, though its relatively larger population means it would rank lower among the 23 countries when it comes to executions per head of population. See http://www.amnesty.org/en/library/asset/ACT50/001/2011/en/ea1b6b25-a62a-4074-927d-ba51e88df2e9/act500012011en.pdf.

[123] For Hamilton on representation, see The Federalist Papers No. 35, http://press-pubs.uchicago.edu/founders/documents/v1ch13s25.html. For Madison see No. 10, http://avalon.law.yale.edu/18th_century/fed10.asp and Notes of the Secret Debates of the Federal Convention of 1787, Taken by the Late Hon Robert Yates, Chief Justice of the State of New York, and One of the Delegates from That State to the Said Convention, http://avalon.law.yale.edu/18th_century/yates.asp, all accessed on June 9, 2010.

[124] Obama concessions for the Senate bill, come June 2010, included expanded offshore drilling, subsidies for nuclear power and carbon capture and storage in return for a modest carbon cap. See http://theclimatedesk.org/articles/obamas-rahm-climate-bill, accessed on June 11, 2010.

[125] For incumbency data see http://www.opensecrets.org/bigpicture/reelect.php. Campaign funding data comparisons were calculated by simple division of 2008 election figures from http://www.opensecrets.org/bigpicture/incumbs.php?cycle=2008, giving for the House $335,101/$1,356,510 = 0.25, and, for the Senate $1,152,146/ $8,741,224 = 0.13, pages accessed on June 22, 2010.

[126] See http://www.opensecrets.org/pres08/index.php?cycle=2008, accessed on June 22, 2010. For the Obama $1bln figure, see the Guardian's "Barack Obama eyes $1bn re-election bid as Republicans ponder challengers", http://www.guardian.co.uk/world/2011/apr/04/barack-obama-re-election-run, accessed on April 7, 2011.

[127] See "Vickers report: banks get until 2019 to ringfence high street operations" http://www.guardian.co.uk/business/2011/sep/12/vickers-report-banks-given-until-2019?intcmp=239, accessed on June 15, 2012.

[128] See Dunn's comparison of the US and French revolutions, op cit p130.

[129] For one of many descriptions of Athenian democracy, see "British Democracy? No thanks!" by Paul Cartledge, http://www.opendemocracy.net/node/361, accessed on June 2, 2010. See also Princeton/Stanford Working Papers in Classics, "What the Ancient Greeks Can Tell Us About Democracy".Version 1.0 September 2007. Josiah Ober, Stanford. From http://www.princeton.edu/~pswpc/pdfs/ober/090703.pdf, accessed on June

9, 2010.

[130] The term "third wave democracy", coined by the Harvard University political scientist Samuel Huntington, describes the process by which the world's democracies grew from about 40 in 1974, only a few of them outside the West, to 117 by 1995. The first and second waves occurred between 1828-1926 and 1943-1962, each time with reverse waves undoing some of the gains. Academics might classify 2011's events as a fourth wave or a continuation of the third. See "The Third Wave" http://books.google.fr/books?hl=en&lr=&id=6REC58gdt2sC&oi=fnd&pg=PR11&dq=huntington+third+wave&ots=S12SOmBxEZ&sig=bzFR9UK1JT d0PGGp-n1Vn-rNTTY#v=onepage&q&f=false, accessed on May 26, 2010.

[131] This point alone is worth several books. It is not pursued here. For a good first insight into the debate, albeit one that does not address the idea of representative versus deliberative government, see the work of Larry Sabato, particularly his book "A More Perfect Constitution", via http://www.amoreperfectconstitution.com/, accessed on June 7, 2010.

[132] For the EIU's 2010 report, see http://www.eiu.com/public/topical_report.aspx?campaignid=DemocracyInd ex2011 and http://en.wikipedia.org/wiki/Democracy_Index, accessed on February 25, 2012.

[133] For the State Department definition, see http://www.state.gov/r/pa/ei/bgn/2886.htm#political. On the question of Cuban democracy, unexpected as it may seem, the country does hold regular municipal, provincial and national elections. For an analysis of their quality as democratic exercises, see the academic Peter Roman's "The Lawmaking Process in Cuba: Debating the Bill on Agricultural Cooperatives", http://www.sdonline.org/38/2-roman.html, or fellow academic Steve Ludlum's piece on participatory democracy, http://www.cuba-solidarity.org/cubasi_article.asp?ArticleID=50, all three, accessed on July 26, 2010.

[134] See Nicholas Shaxson's *Treasure Islands*, the Bodley Head 2011, a detailed critique of the world's secrecy jurisdictions and the people who run and exploit them.

[135] Where to start? Here's one example, involving JP Morgan and Magnetar: http://www.propublica.org/article/after-sec-settlement-with-jpmorgan-will-other-banks-be-forced-to-pay-up-too, accessed on June 23, 2011.

[136] Beyond the Ballot – 57 democratic innovations from around the world, commissioned by the UK's Power Commission, details a series of innovations in democratic participation from around the world. See http://eprints.soton.ac.uk/34527/, accessed on February 20, 2012.

[137] For more details see blog entry "The fight for new democratic forms" by Demoex founder Per Norbäck, http://pernor.wordpress.com/2011/01/18/the-fight-for-new-democratic-forms/, accessed on April 11, 2011.

[138] For a sense of what Transition Town Totnes has already achieved in the small amount of time since its launch in 2005, see http://www.transitiontowntotnes.org/content/what-has-ttt-ever-done-us. For a global map of Transition Initiatives, see http://www.transitionnetwork.org/initiatives/map, both sites accessed on April 11, 2011.

[139] Questions of the tactics of engagement or confrontation as they relate to Transition Towns are explored in depth in "The rocky road to a real transition" by the Trapese Popular Education Collective and in the response by Transition Town Totnes co-founder Rob Hopkins and commenters on http://trapese.clearerchannel.org/resources/rocky-road-a5-web.pdf and http://transitionculture.org/2008/05/15/the-rocky-road-to-a-real-transition-by-paul-chatterton-and-alice-cutler-a-review/ respectively, accessed on April 12, 2011.

[140] Grassroots Political Parties in Sweden, by Ovid Pacific Boyd. Electronic Government Master's Program, Örebro University, Sweden. http://www.metamorphica.net/papers/Grassroots%20Political%20Parties%20in%20Sweden.pdf. http://senatoronline.org.au/sols-purpose, accessed on July 30, 2010

[141] For Iceland's official site on the constitutional reforms, see http://www.stjornlagathing.is/english/, for an idea of the National Forum's ideas, see http://www.thjodfundur2010.is/frettir/lesa/item32858/ and a local blogger's assessment of the process, http://icelandweatherreport.com/2010/10/gearing-up-for-a-constitutional-

review.html. For details of Ireland's Constitutional Convention, see Fine Gael and Labour's Statement of Common Purpose, http://www.redroom.com/blog/ajdunlea/fine-gael-and-labours-statement-common-purpose-ireland and an accompanying critique, http://politicalreform.ie/2011/03/30/deliberative-democracy-and-political-reform/. For We the Citizens, see http://wethecitizens.ie/about_us/faq/. All sites accessed on April 13, 2011.

[142] See the film money "Money as Debt" for an explanation of the basics, though its latter sections strays into less rigorously researched territory. View paid-for online at http://www.moneyasdebt.net/ or free via a web search.

[143] It is hard to get figures on exactly how much territory the Zapatistas control or how many people, the region continues to suffer ongoing, low-intensity conflict. Using a combination of sources, this PBS report http://www.pbs.org/frontlineworld/fellows/mexico0803/1.html and the corresponding Wikipedia entry for Maryland, http://en.wikipedia.org/wiki/Maryland, the estimated extent of territorial control is 32,133 sq km of the state's 73,887 sq km total, which is to say 43%. Both sites accessed on July 30, 2010.

[144] See "We Learn As We Go" – Zapatista Women Share Their Experiences, by Hilary Klein, at http://www.towardfreedom.com/women/1224-qwe-learn-as-we-goq-zapatista-women-share-their-experiences, accessed on July 30, 2010.

[145] Democratic Deficits, Critical Citizens Revisited, by Pippa Norris. See Table 6.1 in Chapter 6, http://www.hks.harvard.edu/fs/pnorris/Acrobat/CriticalCitizensRevisited/Chapter%206.pdf, accessed on July 30, 2010. Whilst Norris rejects wholesale claims of falling support for elected governments and a corresponding crisis in democracy across the globe, her work highlights the widespread persistent gap between people's aspirations for democracy and the reality.

[146] For the full speech, delivered to an audience that included the author, see http://www.350.org/nasheed, accessed on May 24, 2010.

[147] The arguments for and against human-induced climate change are beyond the scope of this book. The Maldives in no place gets higher than 2.3 metres. Scientists say sea levels have been rising 3mm annually since 1993 and could

be tens of centimetres higher than present levels by the end of the century. The complexity of climate science is such that no one can say with certainly exactly how much levels will rise or how the additional influences of storm surges will play out in low-lying territories such as the Maldives. See, for example, http://www.newscientist.com/article/dn16732-sea-level-rise-could-bust-ipcc-estimate.html, accessed on May 26, 2010.

[148] Nasheed resigned as president in February 2012 after having been forced to do so "at gunpoint" by police and army officers, the BBC reported him as saying. See http://www.bbc.co.uk/news/world-asia-16945764, accessed on February 25, 2012.

[149] See EIU 2010 democracy index, op cit.

[150] See http://youtu.be/Hvr5LTUf_XU, accessed on September 29, 2011

[151] For a fuller version of the Woolf quote along with political science findings from the United States and Britain showing such attitudes to be so much bunk, see "The Return of the Public", by Dan Hind, Verso 2010, p127-128.

[152] See the French-language website for La Fédération des Vidéos des Pays et des Quartiers see http://www.vdpq.org/pages/qui-sommes-nous, accessed on May 11, 2011.

[153] See http://www.universalsubtitles.org/en/about, accessed on November 22, 2011.

[154] See the relevant online excerpt at http://www.thirdworldtraveler.com/Media/DemoMedia_Bagdikian.html, accessed on September 24, 2011.

[155] See http://www.plumvillage.org/mindfulness-trainings/3-the-five-mindfulness-trainings.html, accessed on October 3, 2011

[156] For The NewStandard download, see http://roottruth.org/book/newstandard-contributors-handbook, for Indymedia https://docs.indymedia.org/Global/PrinciplesOfUnity, http://www.indymedia.org.uk/en/static/mission.html, and http://www.indymedia.org.uk/en/static/editorial.html, for the Real News essay, see

For Reuters, see http://handbook.reuters.com/index.php/Reporting_and_Writing_Basics, all accessed on September 26, 2011. For the State Department, well, look it up yourself.

[157] For the main report, see http://www.youtube.com/watch?v=ly6QHxzVn4o, for Traoré, see http://www.youtube.com/watch?v=46uqjxBwyJ4, for a related blog post on the journalistic practicalities of the day, see http://patrickchalmers.wordpress.com/2007/03/16/alternative-journalism-or-same-old-same-old/, viewing statistics from April 19, 2011, when all three sites were accessed.

[158] See "Framing: A Short Primer", on http://newsframes.wordpress.com/framing/, for examples of common frames, along with other pages on the same site, accessed on September 27, 2011.

[159] Framing is a counter-intuitive subject. A good place to start as is the free book *Thinking Points: Communication Our American Values and Vision*, published by George Lakoff and the Rockridge Institute. Available for download from http://www.cognitivepolicyworks.com/resource-center/thinking-points/, accessed on September 26, 2011.

[160] See The New York Times magazine piece "The Framing Wars", http://www.nytimes.com/2005/07/17/magazine/17DEMOCRATS.html?pagewanted=1&ei=5070&en=e3e686efd4fa97c5&ex=1183608000, accessed on September 29, 2011.

[161] See http://newsframes.wordpress.com/, accessed on September 27, 2011

[162] See http://youtu.be/z9L5L1YQEuQ, accessed on February 27, 2012.

[163] To watch Carbon Connections online, see http://www.carbontradewatch.org/multimedia/the-carbon-connection-video.html, accessed on April 29, 2011.

[164] See Chiapas Media Project http://www.chiapasmediaproject.org/cmp/about-englishespa%C3%B1ol, accessed on September 30, 2011.

[165] See Hacks and Hackers http://hackshackers.com/about/history/, accessed on November 22, 2011

[166] See http://banyanproject.com/index.php?title=Main_Page, accessed on September 29, 2011.

[167] See Pickard's paper "United Yet Autonomous" on http://www.victorpickard.com/upload/UnitedyetAutonomous.pdf and Robé's "Be the Media: The Current State of Activist Media and the Work of Franklin Lopez" on http://www.popmatters.com/pm/feature/129560-be-the-media-the-current-state-of-activist-media-and-the-work-of-fra/P1, both accessed on May 11, 2011.

[168] See Pickard's "United Yet Autonomous", op cit, and also the Indymedia Principles of Unity http://docs.indymedia.org/view/Global/PrinciplesOfUnity, accessed on May 12, 2011.

[169] Only the FT would push out the story "Bin Laden death sees Twitter traffic soar", a story comparing the Internet traffic generated by the Saudi's execution versus the recent British royal wedding and the 2010 Football World Cup in South Africa, but there you are. See the story's latter paragraphs for sourcing on the tweets, or look them up yourself directly via the tweeters' accounts, http://www.ft.com/cms/s/0/44a50716-757e-11e0-8492-00144feabdc0.html#axzz1M7hFPXxF, accessed on May 12, 2011.

[170] Gapper's analysis of changing trends in the journalism convention of confirming stories as true before publishing also glossed over the serially changing "facts" of the operation put out by the U.S. administration, but that's a separate point. See "Half-baked news from Abbottabad", http://www.ft.com/cms/s/56a22e1e-7680-11e0-b05b-00144feabdc0,dwp_uuid=c8e15fd6-3658-11da-bedc-00000e2511c8,print=yes.html, accessed on May 12, 2011.

[171] See http://jeffweintraub.blogspot.com/2005/09/jared-diamond-on-why-invention-of.html, accessed on April 19, 2011, which includes reference to "The Worst Mistake in the History of the Human Race" By Jared Diamond, University of California at Los Angeles Medical School, Discover Magazine, May 1987, Pages 64-66.

[172] For Slate's review of the Morozov book, see "Tangled Web.

Authoritarian regimes, alas, know how to exploit social media, too," http://www.slate.com/id/2281743/pagenum/all/#p2. For the rejoinder see

Clay Shirky's Cognitive Surplus, a review of which was carried by *Wired* magazine on http://www.wired.com/magazine/2010/05/ff_pink_shirky/, both accessed on April 29, 2011.

[173] See blog post "Big media screws small nobody?", http://patrickchalmers.wordpress.com/2007/12/26/big-media-screws-small-nobody/, accessed on May 4, 2011.

[174] See "Rules for Radicals" by Saul Alinsky, Vintage Books edition, October 1989, p64-65.

[175] There is of course an advertising subsidy involved by way of the "free" video upload services such as Google's YouTube and similar sites such as DailyMotion and Vimeo.

[176] See http://www.monbiot.com/registry-of-interests/ and http://www.monbiot.com/career-advice/, accessed on September 30, 2011.

[177] For a blog I wrote about the death of TNS, which includes an exchange of comments at the end, see http://patrickchalmers.wordpress.com/2007/04/24/new-standard-rip/, for a concluding self-assessment by the publication's own staff, see http://newstandardnews.net/about/?page=obituary, both sites accessed on May 13, 2011.

[178] See "Reporting from the perspective of 1948 – a profile of Jonathan Cook", http://mondoweiss.net/2011/05/reporting-from-the-perspective-of-1948-a-profile-of-jonathan-cook.html, accessed on May 13, 2011

[179] See http://www.jkcook.net/, accessed on September 30, 2011.

[180] For an extended interview with the authors on Democracy Now!, see http://www.democracynow.org/2010/2/4/robert_mcchesney_and_john_nichols_on, accessed on May 13, 2011.

[181] "The Return of the Public", by Dan Hind, Verso, London 2010, p154-165.

[182] To watch the whole documentary online, see http://endciv.com/, accessed on May 13, 2011.